P9-DNS-487

Further Praise for *The Seasons Alter*

"The issues raised in this fine study could hardly be more important—in fact, they are the most important ones that have arisen in human history. The appeal here for conversation on these matters at every level is nuanced, imaginative, deeply informed, and penetrating—and not least, lucid and appealing, a welcome guide for the thought and interchange that is an urgent necessity if there is to be a livable world."

—Noam Chomsky

"What a refreshingly unorthodox book! It transforms the multifaceted dilemma of global warming into an inspiration for tackling problems collectively by engaging in informed discussion. Holding high the Greek ideal of democracy as a passionate yet respectful dialogue, it serves to lift the fog of uncertainty blinding many to the problem of climate change."

—Gerd Gigerenzer, director, Max Planck Institute for Human Development

"At a moment when reason itself is under assault, it is hard to imagine a book more timely than Kitcher and Keller's *The Seasons Alter*. In six admirably clear and different chapters they provide models for reasonably discussing the most urgent issue we now face. At the 2016 Democratic Convention, Michelle Obama gave a memorable speech on the need to take the high road in the face of attacks that appeal to the lowest sensibilities. Those looking for ways to do so in the fight to keep climate change deniers from destroying the planet should read this book now."

—Susan Neiman, director, Einstein Forum

"In the wake of recent elections that have highlighted political polarization in democracies worldwide, Kitcher and Keller ask: Can we talk through our disagreements about climate change? *The Seasons Alter* models how respectful and responsible conversations on this issue could go, and shows where we might head if we take such conversations seriously. An important exploration of a deeply important issue of our time."

—Elizabeth Anderson, John Dewey Distinguished University Professor of Philosophy and Women's Studies, University of Michigan, Ann Arbor

"Philip Kitcher and Evelyn Fox Keller have reimagined the bitter, confusing debate over climate change as a series of clear-eyed, fair-minded dialogues between people who care about one another even when they disagree. Setting stereotypes and shouting aside, Kitcher and Keller set out the strongest, most nuanced versions of arguments on all sides. The science is lucidly explained; the politics is candidly confronted. This book models what a civil, civic conversation about the biggest issue facing the planet should look like."

—Lorraine Daston, director, Max Planck Institute for the History of Science, Berlin

"The public discourse over human-caused climate change risks becoming stale if we fail to continually find new and inventive narratives for communicating the science and its implications to the public. In that vein now comes *The Seasons Alter*, a brilliant treatment of the topic that employs conversation and real human emotions to convey its message of urgency and hope."

—Michael E. Mann, Distinguished Professor of Atmospheric Science, Penn State University, and coauthor of *The Madhouse Effect*

"Full of information and organized as a series of intense, but civil, conversations, this volume models the kinds of interactions we need to have across our disagreements about climate change and what we can or ought to do to avoid its worst consequences."

—Helen E. Longino, Clarence Irving Lewis Professor of Philosophy, Stanford University

"Climate change demands action, but denial, doubt, and delay stand in the way. Philip Kitcher and Evelyn Fox Keller aim to overcome these obstacles by offering examples of careful, constructive, and cordial conversations. *The Seasons Alter* shows not only how to think but also how to talk about climate action."

—Glenn Branch, deputy director, National Center for Science Education

THE SEASONS ALTER

THE SEASONS ALTER

How to Save Our Planet in Six Acts

Philip Kitcher and

Evelyn Fox Keller

LIVERIGHT PUBLISHING CORPORATION

A Division of W. W. Norton & Company
Independent Publishers Since 1923
New York / London

Printed in the United States of America
First Edition

Manufacturing by LSC Communications, Harrisonburg, VA
Book design by Ellen Cipriano
Production manager: Anna Oler

ISBN 978-1-63149-283-9

Liveright Publishing Corporation
500 Fifth Avenue, New York, N.Y. 10110
www.wwnorton.com

W. W. Norton & Company Ltd.
15 Carlisle Street, London W1D 3BS

1 2 3 4 5 6 7 8 9 0

For

Jorge William and Leo and Sully,

Cale and Chloe,

and all the other grandchildren

The seasons alter: hoary-headed frosts
Fall in the fresh lap of the crimson rose;
And on old Hiems' thin and icy crown,
An odorous chaplet of sweet summer buds
Is, as in mockery, set; the spring, the summer,
The childing autumn, angry winter change
Their wonted liveries; and the mazed world,
By their increase, now knows not which is which.
And this same progeny of evils comes
From our debate, from our dissension;
We are their parents and original.

WILLIAM SHAKESPEARE
A Midsummer Night's Dream

CONTENTS

PROLOGUE

The seasons alter. Or so it seems. People observe changes. They reflect on the human future. And they ask: What progeny of evils will these alterations breed?

Some things we know already. Around the world, droughts are occurring with increasing frequency. Desperate people divert old watercourses. Violent conflicts break out as neighbors struggle to protect their access to water. New deprivations intensify old hostilities. And changing temperatures bring animals into new relationships. Pathogens mutate. Some of them make their ways into human populations. Old diseases flare up. New diseases are born.

Will these trends continue? Will their effects devastate the lives of our grandchildren and those who come after them? Might the altering seasons even portend the extinction of our species? Or something close to it?

Perhaps such anxieties are the products of untrustworthy predictions and feverish imaginations. Perhaps they should be dismissed by sober common sense and cool reason. Or perhaps not. Just how serious are the threats that face us? Imagine a future in which people will assemble to hear speeches like this one.

Climate Day Address (2159)

We come together today, on Climate Day, to remember and to mourn. For decades now, this day has been an occasion for us to reflect on the disasters of the last century and on the afflictions they visited on so many. We commemorate the billions whose lives were full of grinding hardship and who died prematurely and unnecessarily. However many times we mark this day, however many words are uttered in recalling the past, our remembrances will always fall short. We shall never exhaust the deep well of suffering.

All of you know the tragic historical record. You recall the folly, the selfishness, the negligence, and the irresponsibility that dominated world politics in the late twentieth and early twenty-first centuries. The failure to take action to limit climate change put the future of our species at high risk. So, as we remember and mourn, we must also reprove. No moral words are too stern to indict the world leaders, and the citizens they represented, who refused to listen to what they were told—repeatedly and insistently—by their scientific advisors.

We, the survivors, have been extraordinarily fortunate. Humbly, and with sincere compassion for the vast majority who were wiped out, we express thanks for the continued existence of our species. For it could so easily have been otherwise. By one of history's great ironies, what allowed humanity to live on was the kind of catastrophe foreseen by the scientists and climate activists who campaigned so valiantly—and with so little success—during the Decades of Denial.

After the failure to meet the entirely inadequate targets on which the world's nations had temporarily agreed, the Water Wars of the 2060s and 2070s broke out almost simultaneously in several regions. They erupted in the area formerly known as the Middle East, in what used to be called "Mexico," and, surprisingly, on the previously peaceful continent we still call "Australia." With rivers and lakes running dry, neighboring groups competed for—and then fought over—the few remaining sources of water. The warring factions were connected by ties of kinship or friendship to people in many other countries. Before long the conflict had spread around the globe, and, by 2072, battle raged on all the continents.

It was only a matter of time before one of the combatants, confronting imminent defeat, made the desperate decision to use nuclear weapons. A sequence of nuclear exchanges occurred, beginning in 2079, in Asia. Because almost all the warheads deployed were the relatively primitive missiles developed by the former "North Korea" and the former "Pakistan," the devastation was by no means as great as it would have been if that appalling decision had repeatedly tapped the arsenals of the superpowers.

Yet it was enough to bring the world to its senses. The Peace of Cairo, ratified early in 2080, drew up plans for resettling people in new homelands. The human population was to be divided into groups of allies, with each group assigned a distinct territory, widely separated from its most bitter adversaries. By that time, of course, much of Africa was already uninhabitable—as were large parts of Asia and tropical South America. In 2081, the Major

Migration began, as the designated groups assembled, and then set off for their newly assigned territories (all of them, of course, in regions near the poles).

We do not have a clear picture of what happened next. Our doctors have not been able to identify the precise source of the Great Pandemic. Very probably, the new disease emerged in one of the populations of birds still reared for human consumption. Despite repeated warnings from medical authorities, the habit of breeding fowl and eating them persisted in many regions of the world. The transfer of viruses from birds to human beings, which is known to have occurred earlier on a smaller scale, is the most likely cause of the pandemic that almost eliminated our species.

Quite possibly, this monstrous dying was not the result of a single disease. Perhaps there were independent genetic changes, mutations in different avian populations, even in different bird species, enabling viruses previously confined to birds to make the jump to human hosts. Yet we can be certain of this: one or more infection spread very rapidly through almost all the groups of migrants.

The years of warfare had taken their toll. Many of those now traveling to the new homelands were already weakened, and ripe for infection. Food, water, and shelter had been in short supply for a long time in some parts of the world. The few surviving diaries testify to an almost complete breakdown of hygiene. We also know that many of the routes the migrants took led across land blighted by nuclear explosions. Our doctors think it probable that many new mutant viruses had emerged in the wake of those explosions, and that one of these—or some of these—infected the wanderers as they scavenged for food in the devastated areas.

The Great Pandemic almost extinguished humanity. Considerably less than one half a percent of the people then living survived. We are not sure how those who did—including our own ancestors—were able to resist the disease. Perhaps they came from the few regions where food and water were still reliably available. Better nourished than the other migrants, they may have been able to throw off the infection. Or, more probably, the assigned routes separated the two surviving groups from the other travelers very early in their journeys. After the new disease emerged, the lucky ones never met anyone from an infected population. So they were able to make the journey to our homeland, here, in what used to be called "Northern Canada." A few others, as you know, followed a different route. Today, the Laplanders, descendants of the only other group of survivors, are also holding a ceremony of remembrance.

We, the two human populations of our century, look back on this catastrophic history with a mixture of sadness, anger, and humble thankfulness. Surely we must mourn the billions who died in the Great Pandemic. Surely we must condemn the people who argued while the planet burned—the people whose blithe indifference created the conditions under which almost all human beings died. But we must also acknowledge a tragic truth. Without that dreadful disease, without its appalling reduction of humanity, our species would certainly have become extinct by now. For the peace declared in Cairo would inevitably have broken down. As the populations grew within the new homelands, competition for resources, particularly for water, would have provoked new hostilities. Eventually, there would have been another episode of nuclear warfare, one powerful enough to wipe out the entire human population. The future of humanity depended on there being far fewer of us. We needed to flirt with extinction in order to survive.

The survivors learned hard lessons—lessons they have transmitted to us across the generations. Because of the carelessness of those who lived in the Decades of Denial, just two large areas of the globe were left available for human habitation. Those who made their way here were few enough in number to thrive in their new home. Knowing what had happened, they resolved never to increase beyond the limits of the territory to which they had come. They made the vow our children repeat every morning as their school day begins: we are stewards of this land, guardians of it for those who will come after us.

That tragic winnowing, the Great Pandemic, wreaked incomprehensible destruction—but it also brought much-needed instruction. Our lives are simpler, and in some ways more limited, than those of the people who gambled with the human future on our planet. No doubt we have lost many things from that older human world. In the shadow of its enormous suffering, we have also learned an important lesson: to preserve all that is most important, most valuable, in human life, even if, to do so, we must give up lesser things. That understanding is the key to our survival.

And now let us bow our heads for a few minutes, and remember the billions whose deaths, whose unwitting and undeserved sacrifices, have made it possible for humanity to live on.

Dystopian fantasy or timely cautionary tale? It's a hard question, for sure, but one that can no longer be avoided.

PREFACE

Clearly, we need to talk.

For three decades, climate scientists have been warning us about threats to the human future on our planet. Here's a short version of what they say. "Since the industrial revolution swung into high gear, the Earth has been getting warmer. Our practices of using fossil fuels and emitting greenhouse gases are responsible. Unless we want our descendants to inhabit a dangerous world, we must change our ways."

The experts urge us to act. But before we can act, respond *collectively* to the predicted threats, we ought to talk. To decide on a plan, and figure out how to carry it out.

First, of course, we need to decide if the danger is real, and if it's as large as the scientists say it is. Even if they're wrong, even if they exaggerate, these questions need to be settled. Waiting around and leaving them unresolved is effectively ignoring what we've been told. Delaying is equivalent to denial. And we shouldn't deny without considering the questions seriously—without talking them through.

Of course, there have been conversations. Many of them have been loud. Ill-informed. Polarizing. And the result has been to marginalize the topic. To leave it off the political agenda. Elections come and go, and the candidates mostly avoid the subject—almost always they fail to address the *large* questions involved.

That's not for lack of trying on the part of outstanding authors. There are plenty of excellent books to which anyone interested can turn. Often they provide detailed information about some aspect of the climate change problem—valuable insights for the political advisors who might help craft policy. Yet they have failed to start an informed democratic discussion—one that not only sparks a demand for taking the problem with the seriousness it deserves, but also encourages politicians to listen to their advisors when they plead for climate action. What's urgently needed is something that makes it impossible to evade the subject.

And that's what we hope to provide. This book is for just about anyone. It aims to encourage conversation. We want to stimulate discussions in all sorts of ordinary places. In churches, synagogues, mosques, and temples. In community centers and workplace cafeterias. In bars and restaurants. In schools and universities. In family living rooms and around the dinner table.

We hope to give readers tools for more productive conversations about six complex issues. Conversations that are constructive, careful, and amicable. Because we recognize how ambitious our goal is, we've tried to *show* what we have in mind. As a result, most of what follows consists of dialogues. All but one of our dialogues involve just two characters: Jo (female) and Joe (male). They are different people, found in different situations, and they come in different ages. They discuss the six important questions we think need to be answered. Although they disagree, they tend to like—even love—one another.

It may seem surprising—or confusing—that different characters have the same names. In our dialogues, sharing a name means sharing a point of view. Jo is always the voice of climate action. Joe consistently resists. He holds back in all the ways thoughtful people do. Later versions of Jo tend to build on what earlier Jos have said. Later Joes effectively concede some points that previous Jos have made—they offer a new line of resistance.

Joe isn't a demon or a callous monster. In fact, he's as good a person as Jo is. He's reasonable and (we hope) sympathetic. The points he makes are important. He shows how it's possible to oppose calls for climate action in various ways and at various stages. His objections need to be heard and discussed.

But we have to be upfront. Joe isn't our voice. Jo conforms more closely to what we believe. If you read these dialogues, you may end up convinced by her—and thus agreeing with us.

That isn't our major purpose in writing. We'll be perfectly happy if you identify with some version of Joe. If you believe we've sold him short. If you think you could make his case better than he does. Any reasonably sized dialogue on a complex subject inevitably stops too soon. You may well feel that crucial arguments or significant facts have been neglected. And even if we'd written at far greater length, you could surely still make complaints of that kind. Our aim isn't to *finish* the conversation but to *start* it. What's important to us is to prompt *you* to talk. To exchange ideas with those around you, with those who agree with you, and especially those who don't. To have conversations in all those ordinary places. Conversations like the ones Jo and Joe engage in. Constructive, careful, and amicable.

Democracy depends on fruitful discussions of important issues. It has sometimes worked well in the past—in exchanges about the Vietnam War, or about how to respond to AIDS, or whether there are dangers from research using recombinant DNA. We've tried to capture the spirit of those successful exchanges, and to provide some blueprints for improving discussion about the major question of our times.

Still, we hope you'll go beyond the dialogues we've provided, and do *better* than our characters did. The sources listed in the notes are intended to help you get started. With luck, with *lots* of luck and public determination galore, better conversations might develop into a political movement—one that could eventually lead to a global policy addressing the predicted dangers posed by climate change.

But first—we need to talk.*

---

*This book was completed before the presidential election of 2016, which now threatens American withdrawal from the 2015 Paris accord along with the breakdown of any international commitment to reducing emissions of greenhouse gases. Our emphasis throughout the book on the need to talk and on the importance of a grassroots political movement issues from our belief that even *more* extensive actions are needed than those agreed upon in Paris. We might well argue that recent political developments are the result of the absence of constructive dialogue. Certainly, they suggest that the need for discussion, engagement, and political pressure from below is now even more urgent than it already was.

THE SEASONS ALTER

ONE

IS IT REAL?

Morning Joe

It is 9 a.m. on the morning of December 13, 2015. A sunlit kitchen. Jo, a woman in her early fifties sits at a wooden table. A bowl containing the remains of some cereal has been pushed aside. A mug of coffee stands next to her hand. She is reading on an iPad.

The door opens. Joe, a man of similar age, comes in. He is slightly disheveled, and looks sleepy.

Jo looks up. Smiles.

Jo: (*Excitedly.*) They finally did it!
Joe: (*Bemused.*) Who? What?
Jo: Paris. The climate talks. They reached an agreement. (*Pause.*)
Joe: Oh . . . that stuff again . . .
Jo: Don't be grumpy, Joe. (*Pause.*) It's an important moment. A real breakthrough.
Joe: Uh huh. (*Pause.*)

(*She turns glumly back to the iPad. He brings from the counter the bowl of cereal she has prepared for him, and pours himself a cup of coffee. He sits down opposite her.*)

Joe: (*More upbeat.*) So. A day off. For both of us. Are you ready for some fun?

Jo: Yes. I've been looking forward to it. (*She looks up.*) But before we go out—and I know you're going to think this is silly—could we . . . talk about the climate news? I know last time we tried to discuss this stuff, it didn't go well . . . our biggest fight in years . . . but I'd like to try again—properly. After all, we have time, right?

Joe: (*Thoughtfully.*) Yes . . . yes . . . we do have time. But we also have plans. All week, I've been looking forward to today. I don't want to spoil it with a big argument, and then spend our time together wishing we hadn't said what we did. (*He takes a swig of coffee.*) Or not bring it up. Then have it hanging between us. (*They look at one another.*) OK. But let's be . . .

Jo: . . . careful. Gentle with one another. (*She smiles at him.*) Thanks, Joe. And I promise. Once properly. Then if we can't agree . . .

Joe: . . . we'll agree to disagree, and drop it. Good. But do let's try to avoid what's happened before when we've talked about this. (*Pause.*) So where do you want to start?

Jo: Well, I know you think it's all junk. Bullshit. Hype. So let's think together about the basics. All these countries have now agreed on some minimal claims. Climate change is real. We cause it and it's going to continue. You think all that's wrong.

Joe: *Wrong*? *Maybe* they're right. But I don't think anyone knows. The jury's out.

Jo: While I think the evidence is enough. Compelling, even.

Joe: You're not a scientist!

Jo: True. But I trust the experts. Just like you. We listen to doctors about our health. Why shouldn't we listen to climate scientists about the health of the planet?

Joe: Because others disagree. How do we know who to trust? Plenty of scientists think this climate stuff isn't well supported.

Jo: No. *No.* Virtually nobody trained in climate science thinks that. The naysayers come from other fields. Meteorologists, physicists, engineers. And, as you know, sometimes their scientific work is funded by people with vested interests. Fossil fuel companies. Right-wing foundations. The Koch brothers. (*Pause.*)

But we're getting ahead of ourselves. Let's think about the evidence.

Joe: Fine with me. Supposedly the Earth is warming in some abnormal way, right? I've seen the graphs. A gentle slope downwards for centuries. Then a sharp turn upwards. It *does* look like a hockey stick. But how does anyone know these diagrams are accurate? I know you don't think our planet came equipped with little thermometers set up around the globe, all conveniently hooked up to printers churning out useful records of the temperatures through the ages. So where do the figures come from?

Jo: Well, we have records for the past century or so. Those show how quickly the Earth's temperature has gone up . . .

Joe: Sure. But who knows if that's abnormal? Maybe it's occurred lots of times in the past thousand or so years. Maybe it's nothing to worry about.

Jo: We're going too fast. We need to step back a bit. Let's think about what we're trying to measure. It's the average planetary temperature—the global mean temperature, as the experts call it—the gmt, for short. You're right. That's really hard to measure. You'd have to calculate it by collecting all the imaginary values delivered by those imaginary thermometers. And you'd need a representative sample of places. So you have to make choices. You first have to decide how to weigh contributions from sea and land. From urban areas and the country, different altitudes, and so on. Lots of possibilities.

Joe: Right! So maybe there's no such thing as the gmt, considering that people can calculate it in different ways and get different results. The climate people have made arbitrary choices, and so they get their graphs, and others . . .

Jo: No, Joe. That's not right. True, there are lots of ways to compute the gmt. But we're interested in how it changes over time. If it turns out that all the reasonable ways of making the calculation give graphs with roughly the same shape, you're entitled to conclude that that's what's been going on.

Joe: Reasonable? Who decides what's "reasonable"?

Jo: There are standards. It's not something arbitrary. You need an unbiased sample. You wouldn't get anything you could call an average temperature if you focused on places that were unusually hot or unusually cold. Or if you made some truly weird collection mixing sea temperatures with those on mountaintops. Climate scientists have to divide up the Earth's surface into a grid. Then, for each time they consider, they must figure out the temperature at some place representing each little square of the grid. Finally, they calculate the average. Of course they look hard at one another's choices. They have lengthy discussions about what's really representative, and what statistics you use to do the averaging—lots of technical stuff that's really hard to understand. But I think you can see what's gone on. A whole bunch of people around the world have argued about how to measure the gmt. They've come up with a number of alternatives they think of as pretty reasonable—although, of course, people have their favorites!—and all of them give the same answer about the trend over time. It's always the hockey stick.

Joe: OK. But how do they actually get reliable data? They don't have those little thermometers with printers. So how do they do it? (*He leans back in mock preparation for being sold a bill of goods.*) I'm braced. Tell me about the corals and the tree rings.

Jo: I'm not going to. (*Smiles.*) You're let off. Neither of us knows enough science to work through the details. You're always vulnerable to being conned by people who tell you about "mistakes" in the tree-ring data—and I'm equally susceptible to being taken for a ride by folk who want to gloss over errors. We just don't have the background to guard against deception. But we can recognize the *structure* of the reasoning.

Joe: The *structure* . . . ?

Jo: Yes. Non-experts—people like us—can't follow all the details. My eyes glaze over when I try to work through the statistics. But I can get an idea about how the reasoning is supposed to go. How connections are made.

Joe: How does that help? You're admitting we can't figure out for ourselves whether the science is sound . . .

Jo: Wait and see!

Joe: I'm skeptical.

Jo: (*Grins.*) I know. (*Pause.*) But let me try to explain. What I'm going to say comes in two bits. First there's a logic-and-science bit. Then there's a social bit.

Joe: Fine. I'll play along.

Jo: OK. (*She taps her iPad; Figure 1.1 appears on the screen.*) Here's one of the standard graphs showing the gmt over the last few centuries.

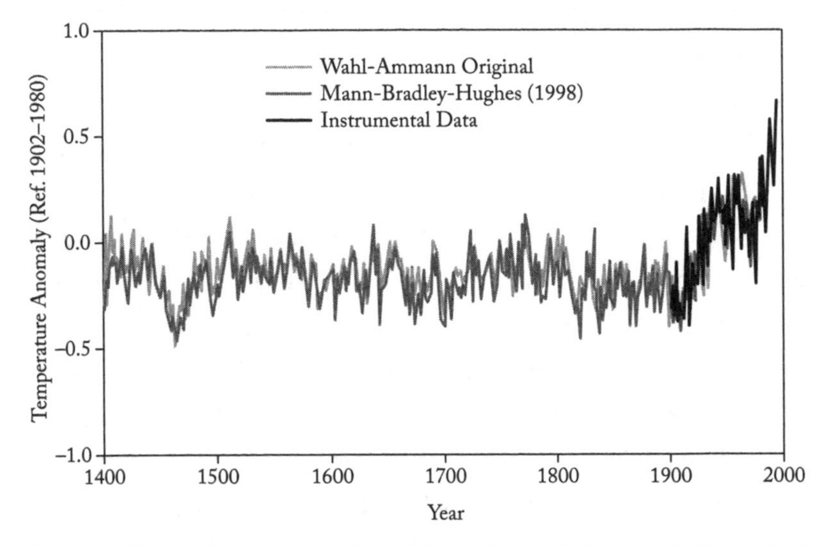

Figure 1.1 The original reconstruction of the gmt from 1400 to 2000 (the work of Michael Mann, Raymond Bradley, and Malcolm Hughes) together with the later, confirmatory, analysis of Eugene Wahl and Caspar Ammann.

Joe: Guesswork!

Jo: Hey, you said you'd play along! (*Pause.*) OK? (*Pause.*) OK. So how did the people who drew the graphs get all the points they needed? The recent part isn't so hard. We have reliable temperature measurements in some parts of the world for about a hundred and fifty years. But even that isn't entirely straightforward. There aren't records for all the places and all the times we need. So researchers have to use statistics to fill in the gaps. Stuff I'm not going to try to get into.

It gets worse when we try to go further back . . .

Joe: I knew it. Tree rings and corals.

Jo: Well those are some of the things they measure. But don't get bogged down in the specifics. Go back to your quip about thermometers with printers. Of course, the Earth didn't come equipped with thermometers exactly like the ones people use to measure temperatures today. Or with printers exactly like the one in your office. But there *were* parts of the installation package that were just as good.

Joe: Trees and coral reefs.

Jo: Precisely. Remember our trip to see the redwoods. All those signs saying that this tree was 450 years old and that one 675. Do you think that was just guesswork?

Joe: No. If I remember rightly, scientists can date a few trees by independent checks. Something whose age we can estimate gets embedded in the tree at some point. Wasn't there an arrow found in one of the trunks?

Jo: Right. That sort of thing helps. But even more important is the fact that we can observe tree growth in the present. People can study how the growth rings vary as the trees age. How the size of the rings depends on the temperature during any given year. You and I don't know the wrinkles. How experts assign ages to trees that are centuries old. But we can grasp the general idea. You use a process you can observe in the present to measure how things were in the past.

Joe: And, according to you, that's the way climate scientists can tell what the temperatures were in the places where the trees grow. They can calibrate. If the average temperature was such-and-such, the size of the ring would be so-and-so. But aren't there other factors affecting how trees grow?

Jo: Yes. So you have to explore all those wrinkles we don't know about. Setting up the "thermometer" so it measures accurately is quite complicated . . .

Joe: How are you so sure it's been done properly? You admit we can't follow the complications. But without going into them, we don't know what to think. Maybe they did a sloppy job, left something out they should have considered . . .

Jo: Be patient! I promise to come back to that. For now, let's focus on the general method. Scientists observe processes in the present. They show how, here and now, something they can measure indicates the average yearly temperature. Then they measure that variable for periods in the past, and calculate the average yearly temperatures for particular places. They do this lots and lots of times, using *different* ways of measuring—sometimes it's tree rings, sometimes corals, sometimes other things. When their various "thermometers" tell the same story, they feel confident about the reliability of the data. Finally, they average over a reasonable sample of places to figure out the gmt. *That's* the structure of the reasoning. I think of it as *building on what you know.* Seems a pretty good method to me.

Joe: So long as it's done properly. (*Holds up his hands in mock apology.*) But I'll be good. I'll wait.

Jo: You *are* being good. I appreciate it. (*She grins.*) OK. Next step. (*She taps on the iPad, bringing up Figure 1.2.*) Here's the temperature graph again, along with a graph showing the concentration of carbon dioxide in the atmosphere over the same time period.

As you can see, the correlation is pretty clear. And it would be even more striking if we had figures for the concentration of CO_2e . . .

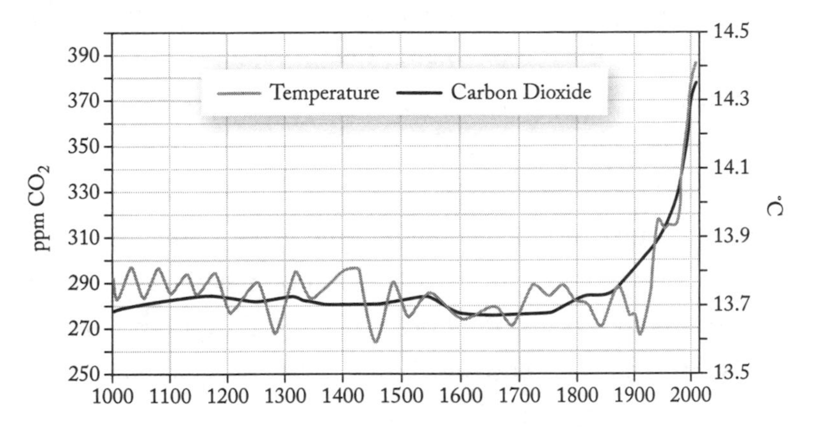

Figure 1.2 The correlation between the gmt and the concentration of carbon dioxide in the atmosphere.

Joe: CO_2e? Sorry. You'll have to explain. I know what CO_2 is—carbon dioxide, right? But what's CO_2e?

Jo: Climate jargon. But not hard to understand. As you know, everyone talks about carbon dioxide in connection with climate change. But there are other greenhouse gases. Methane, for example. They have different impacts. Methane has a more intense greenhouse effect than carbon dioxide. But it hangs around in the atmosphere for a shorter time—"only" a decade or so, rather than centuries. Because the impacts are different, scientists need some way of representing the effect of having a mixture of gases in the atmosphere. So they treat the methane (and other gases like nitrous oxide) as if it were the amount of carbon dioxide that would give the same effect. The same oomph. Everything is measured in terms of equivalents of carbon dioxide. CO_2e.

Joe: I see. So what's behind *this* graph?

Jo: Same story. Scientists have been measuring the concentration of CO_2 in the atmosphere for the last fifty years. There's a station on the top of Mauna Loa in Hawaii. You measure the past by finding air trapped in ice. Of course, you have to know the time at which the ice formed. But you can figure that out by using all the various ways in which geologists assign dates to strata. More building on what you know.

Joe: I don't think it's as simple as that. From what I've read, you don't find obvious boundaries when you drill down into ice. Figuring out just how old a particular level is depends on making assumptions.

Jo: You're right. Dating does involve assumptions. Sometimes you can use information about when a volcano erupted to help construct the time scale. Or you can use the concentrations of radioactive elements. The important thing is that you get the *same* picture from *different* ways of calculating the dates.

Joe: OK. I'll keep playing along. So, you've shown me a correlation between the concentration of CO_2 in the atmosphere, measured in parts per million, and the average temperature of the planet. You want to say that the graphs showing the correlation have been constructed by using a sensible method—and I agree it's a reasonable way to do things. Provided, of course, it's done properly. And we've agreed to postpone the issue of why I should believe that. But, even if I were convinced so far, all you've shown is a *correlation*. Sure, the concentration and the temperature both go shooting up since the Industrial Revolution—two blades of two hockey sticks. By itself, the correlation doesn't prove we're responsible. Correlations happen all the time. That can happen even if neither factor causes the other. Our old barometer is pretty good at telling us when a storm is coming. But storms don't cause the barometer to fall—before they arrive! Nor does our barometer have some special power to produce storms just after it falls.

Jo: Yes, you're exactly right about causes and correlations. (*Pause.*) But I have to admit feeling tempted by the idea of being the weather goddess. Tripping out to the hall and tapping the old barometer. Causing the sun to smile when our friends are having a party, and raining on the parades of all the neighborhood pains. Pity it's only a fantasy. (*Pause.*) But back to work. My next job has to be to show why we are the culprits in the Case of the Warming Planet.

Joe: You sound like Sherlock Holmes—or better, Dr. Watson.

Jo: My child, you speak more wisely than you know. This *is* going to be a detective story. But first, you have to know a bit of the backstory. As I understand it—and here I think everyone agrees—the greenhouse effect was recognized over a hundred years ago. People calculated the amount of solar energy coming in to the Earth, and the amount radiated back again. They first thought the difference would tell them the gmt. But it didn't. The figure was about 30° Celsius too low. Then scientists realized that some of the radiation reflected back is trapped by the atmosphere and sent back to the Earth's surface. Radiation of particular wavelengths. And the trapping depends on the concentrations of gases in the atmosphere. Some Swedish guy figured this out, I think. He found out the importance of carbon dioxide.

Joe: OK. So what?

Jo: Well, it shows that as you get more CO_2 in the atmosphere, that causes the gmt to go up. So there is a causal connection between burning coal and oil and gas, releasing lots of CO_2, and heating up the planet.

Joe: But that doesn't prove that we "committed the crime." Suppose we go out for dinner. I eat and drink too much—unlikely, I know! Later that night I'm really, *really*, sick. You might not be so sympathetic—again, unlikely!—telling me I should have been more careful. Of course, you'd be right to think my overindulgence *could* have been responsible. But maybe it wasn't. Maybe all that food and wine would have made me a little queasy, but no more than that. Maybe the real culprit was the spoiled fish I ate.

Something similar could be going on with climate change. There are *lots* of things that can cause variations in the average temperature. Our distance from the sun varies, sunspot activity varies, volcanic activity varies. In what I've read, they say that all these things could be what affects global warming. Maybe the greenhouse effect is like my imaginary overindulgence. One of these other factors is the spoiled fish.

Jo: Fair point. But those other ideas don't stand up when you look hard at the data. They can't explain the correlation in the graph. Of course, you need *something* to explain it. Nobody thinks you can just chalk it up to coincidence. Remember when the boys were in their teens. Every time they hung out with that shady kid who lived round the corner, they came back smelling of cigarette smoke. You didn't suppose for a moment it was just chance. But compared to the evidence we had about that, these graphs are correlation on steroids.

Joe: I wasn't suggesting there was *no* explanation for why the hockey sticks are so similar. My point was that there are *alternative* explanations. Different from the ones the scientists you like favor. *Maybe*, one of these other explanations is the right one. Because there are other possibilities, the jury's still out.

Jo: But it's not. You're assuming that all these supposed rival explanations haven't been considered. They have. Climate scientists have looked. According to them, distance from the sun, sunspot activity, volcanic eruptions, all those supposed possibilities, just don't fit the observed trends.

Joe: Now we're back with their say-so. I bet you haven't looked closely at how sunspot activity varies over time. I bet you can't even produce a complete list of all the possible alternatives. So why are you so confident that the climate guys have done all the things they should have done?

Jo: You're right. As we've agreed, we aren't experts. This is another place where we don't have the competence to judge the details for ourselves. But the strategy climate scientists say they've used is a sensible one. I'll call it *considering alternatives*. It's really the method of Sherlock Holmes. You remember the line: "When you have eliminated the impossible, what remains, however improbable, must be the truth." You can think of the scientists as rounding up all the suspects, and showing that only one—the greenhouse effect—could have done the dirty deed. Actually, in this case, the explanation that remains after all the others have been eliminated isn't particularly *improbable*. But it's surely *unwelcome*, at least in some quarters. That doesn't affect Holmes's maxim. Surely you'd be happy to sign on, if he'd said, "When you have eliminated the impossible, what remains, however unwelcome, must be the truth." Wouldn't you?

Joe: I guess so. Now I see where you're going. You think there are two strategies of good science that stand behind the so-called climate consensus. One is *building on what you know*; the other is *considering alternatives*. I'm quite happy to think they're reliable strategies. But the big issue is whether they've actually been applied—thoroughly, responsibly—by the climate people. You admit that you and I can't follow the details. So how can we be sure they've done their job properly? Especially when there are others who deny that. I don't see how you've made any real progress.

Jo: Good. We agree on where we are and what the crucial issue is. I said earlier there would be a logic-and-science bit and a social bit. We're done with the logic-and-science bit. Now comes the social stuff.

You know, when you think about it, just about everything you and I believe, is dependent—maybe directly, maybe indirectly—on what we've learned from others. Modern life would be hopeless if we had to figure everything out by ourselves. So part of learning is learning who to trust about what. As I said, you trust our doctor to tell you about your health. You trust the plumber to tell us what's wrong when the sink is blocked. So why should we question the judgment of a group of scientists specializing in a particular area?

Joe: Easy. Because they don't speak with a single voice. Of course, some of them *say* they all agree. Newspapers say they all agree. But there are dissenters and doubters. And when the experts are divided, it's only prudent not to leap to conclusions. Especially when accepting those conclusions would have serious consequences. We shouldn't be asked to make big changes in how we live when the question remains open.

Jo: I agree with a lot of that. The consequences of recognizing that we are heating up the planet are serious. If the experts were really divided, we ought to ask them to iron out their differences. Give us a firm verdict. But they're not divided.

Who are these dissenters? You can find out by googling them. A truly tiny number have credentials as climate scientists. A few more are meteorologists. Most come from more distant parts of science. In many cases, you can also learn who funds their research. Wanna guess?

Joe: Vested interests?

Jo: Exactly. So, when people (like President Obama) say that 97 percent of climate scientists accept the minimal claims, that's correct. In fact, probably a conservative estimate.

Joe: Sorry. Flashing that figure doesn't cut much ice with me. You seem to be buying into an old myth. Aren't you viewing scientists as pure—a kind of "secular priesthood," dedicated to finding the truth? These guys may have all sorts of motives for raising alarms about a warming planet. You're very quick to recognize the shadow of Big Oil behind the dissenters' research, but you don't ask questions about the people you like. You seem to see them as saints in lab coats, disinterestedly warning us of the perils to come.

Jo: I plead not guilty. Of course I know scientists are people, with human impulses and human motives. They aren't driven by any pure "search for truth." But they're not the Sopranos either. And like most of us, they're helped in doing things properly and not cutting corners by the fact that they work with others. People who look at what they're doing, and sometimes criticize.

I remember a conversation I once had with a scientist. A really eminent biologist. We were in a parking lot, and he was about to drive home. As he got into his car, he said: "Like most people, you think scientists want the truth. They don't want the truth. They want to be right." That really puzzled me. For a long time, I couldn't see the difference. Finally, I got it. Scientists don't just want it to happen that the truth emerges from some activity in which they participate. They want to be the ones who find out the truth. Actually, they probably want to be the ones who find it out and are recognized for doing so. They want their ideas to triumph—but not because the ideas are wrong, and they somehow pull the wool over everyone's eyes. They want their peers, and maybe a broader public, to see that their ideas are true. They want credit.

And that sort of motivation makes a huge difference to how people act. How do you get a lot of credit? By doing something big and splashy. What better way to do it than by exposing the flaws in some important conclusion that all the rest of your community accepts?

Joe: No, it's too risky. Not toeing the party line would get you thrown out. If you really want credit, you shouldn't rock the boat.

Jo: I think that's dead wrong! First off, the leading climate scientists aren't Mafia bosses. They aren't that unscrupulous, and they don't have that power. And there's a whole big world waiting to welcome anyone who could expose errors in the orthodox reasoning.

Remember where our logic-and-science bit left us. Climate scientists have used two sensible strategies. You worried—reasonably—about whether they'd been thorough in pursuing them. What I'm now suggesting is that, if they hadn't, some of their ambitious colleagues would have been *very* eager to show them up. If the data behind the graphs were insufficient or if the statistics had been fudged or badly done, that would provide a great opportunity for some young researcher. Make your name by exposing the mistakes. Or showing how some viable alternative explanation of the correlation had been left out. Scientists are *really* fond of asking their peers whether they have considered some rival approach.

Joe: But maybe there's some mistake nobody is able to see? Or maybe there's some community-wide interest in getting lots of money for climate research?

Jo: Are they fools, or are they knaves? Of course, it's possible there's some deep flaw in our current understanding of the atmosphere and the climate, something future science may someday correct. That's possible in *any* field of science. We can always wonder if what we believe about the basic structure of matter is right, if there are hidden flaws in our biochemistry, or whatever. Even the best established science isn't graven in stone. We never achieve complete certainty.

But when engineers try to build nanomachines, when medical researchers investigate new drugs, when doctors advise their patients, they have to work with the science of the day. The same goes for climate change. As a former defense secretary might say, you have to design your climate policy with the science you have.

So if you want to think climate scientists are fools, you're adopting a *really* skeptical attitude. One you wouldn't take on in other areas of science. Might everything we believe about molecular biology be tainted by some deep mistake? You don't take the possibility seriously.

Joe: No. But maybe you've made the wrong comparison. Climate science isn't like molecular biology. It's more like one of the social sciences that are still feeling their way. Educational psychology, say. There are common assumptions, things all the practitioners use to "build on what they know" or in "considering alternatives," but these assumptions are fundamentally flawed. Outsiders from more advanced fields can see that. They make legitimate criticisms. But nobody within the field gets it. They're all within the grip of a mistaken point of view.

Jo: I agree that some sciences are better developed than others. So their predictions are more secure. But climate science has lots of completely uncontroversial successes. It tells us plenty of things everyone applauds as reliable and worth knowing. Just like molecular biology. The criticism of climate science is quite selective. Focused on this one domain.

So I don't think your diagnosis is right—some fundamental flaw that only outsiders—clever physicists!—can see. Climate scientists aren't fools. But if you think they're knaves, you have to assume some kind of global conspiracy. All over the world, climatologists are engaging in some pretense, presumably to gouge funding out of their local agencies. And nobody blows the whistle? Even though the kudos for spilling the beans would be enormous? Surely it doesn't pass the laugh test . . .

Joe: OK. OK. Now I see how your argument works. First you get me to admit that there are good scientific ways of constructing the graphs, and explaining the strong correlation. Then you point out how odd it would be for there to be sloppiness in following these strategies or some kind of grand deception. Because, as you put it, "scientists want to be right," there would be huge incentives to be the great whistle-blower. And that hasn't happened within the expert community . . .

Jo: (*Excitedly.*) No it hasn't. But over the years, you *have* seen just what my story about scientific motivations would lead you to expect. The reconstructions of past temperatures have been probed and debated. And because of the public clamor all those "rival stories" get checked and rechecked—scientists show in detail why you can't explain the observed data in terms of variations in solar activity and things like that. And you can imagine how gratefully any exposé would be received in certain quarters . . . (*She pauses.*) But you look pensive.

Joe: I am. I'm thinking.

Jo: But you're not convinced . . .

(*Pause.*)

Joe: Too soon to say. Let me ponder what you've said. No promises, though.

(*Pause. Jo gets up and goes round the table. She stands behind Joe, placing her hands on his shoulders.*)

Jo: Thanks, Joe. Thanks for listening. (*Pause. She bends forward and brushes his cheek with hers.*)

And now the rest of the day is ours. Let's go and enjoy ourselves.

Understanding Joe

Many scientists and public commentators are fond of declaring that such-and-such is "now known." Plenty of the things they characterize in this way are *not* known—at least not broadly known—for the very simple reason that a lot of people don't believe them. Joe is one of those people. He doesn't know what is "now known" about climate change.

Joe is a reasonable man. He is far from stupid. Indeed, he is thoughtful and well-intentioned. For years, he has been clear about Jo's commitment to tackling climate change. He has made serious efforts to inform himself. But, until this morning at least, he has not succeeded.

How is that possible? What has gone wrong? These are important questions. We need to understand Joe, and the large number of actual people who resemble him. For many of the harder questions about climate change, questions beyond the scope of this breakfast conversation, ordinary citizens need to decide which group of self-described experts to believe. Unless we get clear about the sources of Joe's resistance to a consensus among natural scientists, members of a profession usually accorded high credibility, there will be little chance of making progress in areas where the evidence is more tangled and confused.

Joe recognizes fundamental features of the situation. Neither he nor Jo can work through the technical details for themselves. And what public debate takes place is loud and rancorous. Different groups presenting themselves as experts offer rival hypotheses about what is happening to our planet. Joe doesn't know whom to trust. He concludes that, for outsiders, non-experts like Jo and himself, "the jury is out." There is no basis for supporting immediate action, or for celebrating the Paris Agreement.

He also sees that the question is too important to be decided by taking a leap in the dark. To be sure, if Jo's "minimal claims" about the climate are correct and if nothing is done to limit the emission of greenhouse gases, bad consequences may follow. But, equally, if those claims are wrong and if people are still required to make radical changes in their lives, their sacrifices—possibly very large sacrifices—will be entirely unnecessary.

Ordinary folk are often prepared to change their ways when they can see terrible effects of continuing on the present course. Discovery of the dangers of taking particular medicines sometimes produces an immediate wave of renunciation—think of the reaction to the tragic news about the effects of thalidomide. Less immediately pertinent scientific conclusions are often happily absorbed, not because the evidence (or even the new result) is well understood (consider contemporary particle physics), but simply because the science is perceived as bringing no great threat. By contrast, when a scientific finding would have enormous impact on the ways people live, on human wants and aspirations, resistance is natural. Indeed, it is perfectly *reasonable.* Imagine how you would react to a report announcing "scientific conclusions" that human beings in a group to which you belong—people like you—lack the capacity for performing various kinds of socially valued tasks. (If you belong to a group that has historically been stigmatized, this will not be hard to imagine.)

The minimal claims Jo argues for are naturally heard as issuing an order: "Reduce the use of fossil fuels!" For many people, obeying the command would be difficult; they cannot find alternative ways to keep their dwellings warm or to travel to their places of work. Their troubles would be intensified by any governmental policy of lessening national dependence on coal, oil, and natural gas. Costs of transportation and heating would go up, with a broad impact on the costs of the necessities of life. Those who already struggle to make ends meet understandably fear a grimmer future in which the "scientific" imperative will rule.

So they ask: "Are you sure?" It's a question that *should* be posed. The scientific community *should* then make special efforts to explain what has convinced them that the Earth is warming and that our emissions of greenhouse gases are responsible. Climate scientists have addressed the legitimate demand. Admirably. Their sustained efforts have fully discharged their responsibility to inform and yet, even now, the message has barely sunk in. If a similar delay were to attend each of the later stages of acting to contain climate change, any hopes for averting the predicted threats to the human future would be dashed.

Why, given the strenuous efforts of climate scientists, has their message not been heard? The glacial pace of public uptake reflects how common Joe's situation is. All over the affluent world, and particularly in Anglophone countries, a significant percentage of citizens would agree with Joe. They hear public figures offering divergent opinions, and they know they cannot resolve the technical questions for themselves. They also recognize that a decision would have consequences for their daily lives.

Many of them probably share Joe's reluctance to talk—or think—about the topic. They see the question as thoroughly politicized. Believing that the current evidence doesn't settle the issue ("the jury's out"), they suspect people of taking sides based on *political* convictions. Those who favor certain kinds of social change will welcome the idea of a warming planet, seeing the supposed "threats" as demanding the policies they have long favored. Those who oppose the changes react by dismissing climate change as a hoax. The reluctant onlookers want to avoid taking a stand until the controversy is settled—resolved by scientific findings, not by political predilections. And the kind of resolution they expect is one that silences all disagreement.

Unfortunately, there's no safe fence for these agnostics to sit on. Their standard for a final resolution is unrealistic—a situation in which the opposition melts away is unlikely to occur, at least in the near future. Anyone who tries to dodge the issue of identifying which side is trustworthy is in for a long wait. So, in effect, the agnostics make a choice. In deferring decision, they opt not to act. Joe and his kin are thus likely to oppose political leaders who follow the scientific consensus and urge immediate steps to limit climate change. Instead, they tend to vote for those who promise not to do anything precipitous—either for representatives who think more evidence is required or for the more forthright ones who denounce "junk science." Yet many of the voters, perhaps a very large majority, are deeply committed to the welfare of future generations that may include their children and grandchildren. By not trusting the climate science consensus, they risk sabotaging some of their most important goals. Their electoral choices may well work against what they most want to achieve. Indeed, the representatives who adamantly oppose any climate action may share this fate—they too may actively promote what they most wish to avoid.

As Plato—no friend of democracy—saw long ago, champions of democratic government defend it on the grounds that it advances human freedom. By expressing your views in a policy-making forum or in voting for candidates who will act on behalf of your society, you have the chance to achieve the goals that really matter to you. Plato saw this alleged freedom as illusory. In his view, the masses are too stupid to know what would be best for them. If decisions are left in their hands, the society will blunder into catastrophe after catastrophe. Such elitist ideas about the distribution of native intelligence are thoroughly mistaken, but the same disastrous ends can come about if sensible, intelligent, voters—people like Joe—are badly misinformed. Not knowing what is "now known" proves as perilous as native stupidity.

Whether or not knowledge is power, ignorance can be impotence. The societies we call democracies often provide the appearance of self-determination. Their citizens troop to the polls and express their choices. But when their opinions on an important topic are false—or even when they are unsure of something that is "now known"— the fundamental value of democracy, its promotion of freedom, is decisively undermined. If democracy is to live up to its billing, there must be channels through which information can flow to the citizens so they can appreciate where their interests lie. Otherwise, by a perverse irony, the action supposed to advance their goals—marking their choice on the ballot—may undermine what they most want.

Of course, there is supposed to be an already available solution to the potential problem of citizens' not being able to discern what is good for them. Democracies celebrate free and open discussion. Through such discussion, the electorate is supposed to become well-informed. If Joe attends carefully, he should end up with the ability to vote for candidates whose policies will accord with his interests. But the actual public debate surrounding climate change has done exactly the reverse. Instead of informing Joe, it has left him full of doubts. The source of Joe's difficulty in deciding what to think about climate change—in figuring out whom to trust—is the character of the public conversation he hears around him.

How has a democratic institution—free speech—intended to help inform the citizens in their political decisions, turned out instead to breed doubt and confusion on important issues? The actual marketplace of ideas is strikingly different from the ideal defended by its most eloquent champions. The classic, stirring, defenses of "free debate" usually concentrate on questions about which ordinary people might eventually decide for themselves.

When the issues turn on scientific technicalities, matters are very different. In these cases, a decision about which people to trust becomes necessary. Hence, so long as dissenting voices can keep talking, so long as they can pose as having as much authority as their opponents, thoughtful listeners will find it difficult, even impossible, to make up their minds.

And the "free debate" can be carefully managed. Those who speak, or speak the loudest, may not be held to any standards of accuracy. They may repeat the same falsehoods again and again, without suffering any convincing refutation. Some constituencies may be able to pay for extra time at the microphone. Perhaps money can be supplied to support further reiteration of the funders' favorite claims. So a worthy ideal fails to correspond to the way we live now.

Joe has attempted to form a justified opinion about an important topic. He has seen and heard speakers disagreeing, he has visited rival websites, and has attended as one party impugns the competence or the sincerity of its rival. He lacks any ability to identify directly which of the two is mistaken. His resultant uncertainty translates directly into inaction—he distrusts the international agreement that so excites Jo.

We need to improve this situation, and the change must come quickly. Trying to make our actual public discussions completely consonant with the splendid ideal of "free debate" is surely too ambitious a task. But it is necessary to find channels for creating a more informed public. How can that be done?

One—blunt—answer would make a partial concession to Plato's critique of democracy. Allow that citizens have the right and the responsibility to make up their own minds about all sorts of issues but insist on telling them, very clearly and firmly, what the designated experts have agreed on. Different communities of experts are to advise, and their deliverances are to be faithfully reported without further debate, so that citizens may understand how their interests might best be promoted. This proposal has probably been approximated in some societies during the past decades.

But its defects are evident, especially to those democrats who recall the historical battles against censorship and established "indices of permitted opinions." Although the particular deliverances of scientific inquiry should not be subject to popular vote, the practices through which authoritative knowledge emerges should undergo the scrutiny of the broader society. Citizens should be able to convince themselves that the research communities have arrived at reliable information that might usefully advance the public good. How, then, can we find a middle way between a simple governmental declaration (almost certainly counterproductive) that the expert opinion is to be accepted without further question, and the current distortion of the ideal of free and open discussion, that diminishes citizens' chances of forming well-grounded opinions?

Perhaps by establishing public committees, by analogy with juries, who would "hear" issues about disputed scientific claims. Or perhaps by introducing more demanding standards for scientific reporting, and recruiting to journalism people with a strong enough scientific background to advance public understanding on the most important issues. One thing is clear, however. Any attempt to reform the current—dysfunctional—marketplace of ideas will have to meet skeptical challenges. New institutions for improving the flow of information cannot simply announce the return of the virtues of the old BBC or claim to have resurrected Walter Cronkite. Critics will be quick to see through any ceremonial laying on of hands, and will regard the newcomer as the rebirth of *Pravda*.

In any event, to rely on these kinds of reforms would be to wait too long. We can't afford further delay. Hence (as explained in the preface) this book follows a different strategy. The thought of a single public discussion gives way to multiple sites of conversation. In community centers and in workplace cafeterias, in churches, mosques, and synagogues, in schools and in homes, we hope people will come together for serious discussion, trying to resolve the many questions about climate policy. Because our official public conversation has degenerated into confusing clamor, many of these people will be misinformed. Yet, perhaps, they may work through the issues—patiently—as Jo and Joe do. If they are aided by willing helpers, people with some knowledge of climate science and the other research areas affecting climate policy, perhaps the barriers to clear understanding may be overcome.

In the end, though, trust will be an essential component of the conversations. As Jo and Joe both see, they cannot scrutinize the technicalities—the tree-ring data, the statistical analyses—for themselves. So we recommend the strategy Jo deploys. It is too dangerous simply to respond to the public cacophony by concluding that "the experts" disagree, and waiting for the decisive finding to end the clamor. But even for outsiders, nonspecialists like Joe and Jo, there are avenues to a sensible decision. They can try to understand the general form of the reasoning underlying the rival pronouncements, and then seek explanations of how the protagonists come to their contrary verdicts. If the position of one party can be shown to rest on what appear to be reliable methods, and if some misapplication of those methods would be highly unlikely—because any honest mistake would have been spotted, and any alleged conspiracy would be incredible—there's a basis for trusting the advocates of that position. Moreover, confidence should be deepened if the opposing objections are readily explained in terms of the political or economic motives of those who raise them.

The issues ahead are difficult. Often they are technical. Sometimes the experts are divided. Coping with the disagreements may sometimes require attending to the logic of the reasoning, and sometimes trying to explain the contrary contentions in psychological, social, or political terms. Attempts at forming an adequate assessment of the climate challenge and an adequate response to it may still go awry. But in a warming world and with a confusing public debate, sitting down together and exchanging ideas and arguments is the best we can do. With luck—and perhaps, since the American election of 2016, an enormous amount of luck is now needed—it will be good enough.

TWO

SO WHAT?

Long-Distance Call

Evening. A sparsely furnished office, without windows, lit by neon lighting. Jo, a woman in her mid-twenties sits at a desk. Two telephones occupy a clear space to her right. Several piles of folders and loose papers take up most of the remaining desktop.

Jo looks around wearily. She yawns. One of the phones rings.

Jo: (*Answering the phone.*) Hello. Climate Action Hotline.

Joe: (*The male caller; he sounds hesitant, tired, unsure.*) Good evening. It is evening where you are, isn't it?

Jo: That's right. I'm in Berlin. (*Pause.*) Are you calling to volunteer?

Joe: No. No. That's not it . . . What I wanted . . . (*his voice trails off*).

Jo: So how can I help?

Joe: Well . . . I was looking for information . . . about climate change . . . what's likely to happen . . . how bad the threat . . .

Jo: Information? That's not really what we do. My job is to help recruit people. Coordinate political action. Things like that.

Joe: I'm sorry. (*Pause.*) I was hoping . . . (*Pause.*) A good friend suggested . . . He gave me this number . . . but maybe it's the wrong one . . .

Jo: You're calling internationally aren't you?

Joe: That's right. I'm not in Germany. My friend recommended that I talk to you. I was hoping . . .

(*Pause. She listens for him to continue. The phone is silent.*)

Jo: Are you still there?

Joe: Yes. You see I'm trying . . . to work out . . . what to do . . .

(*Pause. She listens. He remains silent. Then she hears a sigh.*)

Jo: Are you OK? (*Pause. She listens.*) Is something wrong? You sound . . . troubled.

Joe: (*Pause.*) A bit. More than a bit . . .

(*Pause.*)

Jo: Well, it's easy to get gloomy when it comes to climate change.

Joe: No. (*Pause.*) No, that's not it.

(*Silence. She listens.*)

Jo: I'm not sure I understand why you're calling. Can I help in any way?

Joe: Maybe it's best to explain the whole thing. I've found it so hard to talk to people I know. Most of them, anyway. It might be easier with a stranger. A voice on the end of a phone line. (*He pauses.*)

Jo: I'm happy to listen. I'll try to help.

Joe: The thing is . . . I've had some bad news. A few weeks ago. A diagnosis, actually. I don't have long . . . to live. Much less time than I thought. I'm not that old.

So I wanted to set my affairs in order. I have a bit of money. Not a huge amount. But enough to do some good. First, it seemed obvious. Give it to cancer research. After all, that's what's going to get me.

But I have this friend. A really good friend. Actually, the best support I have right now. I was telling him about my plan. He was kind, but he disagreed. "Cancer's important," he said, "but the best use you could make of your money is to give it to fight climate change." He suggested your group. (*Pause.*) Thought you'd be a good source of information. As well as being an organization I might support. Maybe there's another number?

Jo: No, no. This is our public line. When people call, we assume they already understand how serious the climate threat is—that's why they want to get involved. When a call comes in it's usually from someone who wants to volunteer.

Joe: That's not me. (*Pause.*) Actually, I've always thought the climate business was overblown. Not that I deny that it's happening. Just its importance. (*Pause.*) There are so many big problems in the world today. So many good causes. Why pick this one? People live in ignorance—die from ignorance. I could give money for education. Or to help with poverty. There's so much of it. So many people malnourished, no medical care. No jobs. Living in squalid conditions. Dying.

The threats from global warming seem . . . nebulous . . . by comparison. Poverty, ignorance, squalor—these things are obvious. So clear. Shouldn't I leave what I have to tackle them? Make what little difference I can?

But my friend is very persuasive. And he's also been wonderful these past few weeks. So I promised I'd call. Listen to what you had to say. About why this particular threat is so terrible.

Jo: I see. You'd like me to answer that question. I can try. I can tell you what's moved me. (*Pause.*) Climate change is going to cause *far more* suffering than the things you mention. It'll make all the problems you've talked about far, far worse—and create many more besides. There's nothing *nebulous* about it. What's coming is real suffering and on a vast scale. Large cities flooded. Huge numbers of people displaced. Major regions blasted by heatwaves. Prolonged droughts. Water sources drying up. Crops failing. Famine. Dehydration. Breakdown of hygiene. Diseases—probably plagues. Wars among neighbors desperate for water. And at the bottom of it all—death. Deaths by the millions—no, surely by the hundreds of millions. Or billions, even. Human lives blighted everywhere.

I could go on and on. (*Pause.*) But do you think a telephone call is the right way for you to learn about all this? Or that this is the right time for you?

Joe: Yes. I promised my friend I'd call. I need to make a decision about what I'll do with my money. And, frankly, I do better when I can concentrate on something else. (*Pause.*) You seem intelligent and well-informed. I'd like to hear more. Some details.

When I called, I didn't really know how to explain what I wanted—and I realize I've done it rather badly. You're right. "Nebulous" is the wrong word. I was confused when I asked my question. When I think about climate change . . . about leaving my money to help do something about it . . . I wonder about two things. How large, how terrible, are the potential consequences? And how likely is it that the dreadful things are going to happen? Sometimes I think the real catastrophes aren't that likely, and the likely effects aren't that bad. So the climate problem seems less worrying . . . more "nebulous" . . . than the other forms of suffering I might try to do something about.

You've said something about one of my questions. You've told me about the scale at which a lot of terrible consequences are predicted. And I want to hear more about that. But I'm also bothered by the other question. A lot of these predictions seem pretty soft to me. People talk about all sorts of dreadful possibilities for the future. As you did. But how likely are they to happen?

Jo: OK. I'm beginning to see why you think you might do more good in some other way. Why the climate threat appears . . . "nebulous." And I don't think you're unusual in the way you see things. *If* it's a confusion, it's not something unique to you. Some people believe the consequences won't be that dire or just not as bad as many aspects of the world we see around us right now. Others think they *might* be truly dreadful . . . *possibly* a lot worse than life is now . . . but they're not very *probable*. My guess is that many would put it the way you did, and say that the things we're sure will happen aren't so bad, and the really bad things aren't so likely to occur.

I'll try to answer both your questions and give you more detail about the consequences I already mentioned. I'll also try to address your worry that it's all speculative, starting with the uncertainty of the predictions. (*Pause.*) But it may take a little time. It's complicated. And I'm not very experienced in doing this. I can only tell you about what inspired me to get involved.

Before we begin, it would be good to know a bit about you. Could you tell me your name, and where you're calling from?

Joe: Joe—but I'd rather . . .

Jo: That's funny. I'm Jo, too.

Joe: Coincidence. (*Pause.*) But I'd rather not say where I live. It may sound odd, but I want the global perspective. I don't want you to give me a pitch aimed at showing why people *here* should be *particularly* worried. If I'm going to give money to fight climate change, I want to do it for the world as a whole, not just for one small part of it.

Jo: That's a fine thought. I wish I could say my attitude was as selfless as yours. As you've probably guessed from my accent, I come from India originally. Hyderabad. My family is still there. I got involved in climate action when I learned about the likely effects on that part of the world.

Joe: Well, of course I care about what happens close to home. But not only that. For a decision like this, I want to think on a larger scale. Human life everywhere on the planet.

Jo: OK. So let's start with the Earth's temperature.

Joe: Yes. If we continue as we have done, it's going to increase. Right?

Jo: Right. In fact, given what we've been doing, the planet is bound to get hotter, even if we change our ways. But unless we change, it's going to get a *lot* hotter.

Joe: How much? If we change, and if we don't.

Jo: This is where it gets really hard. Scientists can't say for sure. They can't even give us precise estimates of the chances.

Joe: I know. That's what's concerned me. Why I've thought it might be better to support efforts to tackle other human problems. All this uncertainty.

Jo: But it's not *completely* uncertain! Let's take it slowly. First, the baseline. Usually people talk about increases above preindustrial temperatures—the sorts of temperatures experienced around 1900. Then they ask how likely it is that you'll get a rise of so-and-so many degrees—measured on the Celsius scale—if the concentration of greenhouse gases gets to a particular level. So what's the chance of a 5 degree rise by 2100 if the CO_2e level is held below 450 ppm? (*Catching herself.*) Oh, I've gone too fast. Lots of jargon. Should I explain?

Joe: No, no. I get it. Greenhouse gases contribute differently, so you normalize the effect to the equivalent amount of carbon dioxide. And you measure in terms of parts per million.

Jo: I'm impressed. You've been reading.

Joe: Well, as I said, my friend is very worried. He's given me stuff to look at.

Jo: OK. There's considerable scientific agreement on some things. Here's one. If we continue emitting greenhouse gases as we have done—using coal and oil and gas—the temperature in 2100 will lie somewhere between 3°C and 7°C above the baseline. A few people think it could go even higher. But let's ignore them. After all, you're concerned that the threat is exaggerated. So we should stick with more conservative estimates.

Joe: Right. I listen to all these Cassandras prophesying doom . . .

Jo: Funny you should put it that way. Lots of people do, of course. But Cassandra's curse was to be given the power to predict the future—with a condition. Nobody would ever believe her. So if they really are Cassandras . . .

Joe: . . . we ought to worry. I get it. But are these dire predictions, even the ones made by the people you see as "conservative," correct? Should we believe them? When they tell us about how bad human life is going to be.

This is where I start to have doubts. Why won't there be some bad stuff and some good stuff? Surely some of the colder parts of the world will get warmer. People can move—shift their farming to Siberia, make wine in Scotland and grow pomegranates in Canada.

Jo: Fantasy! But it will take time to explain why. We need to go in stages.

Joe: OK. Let's go on from where you began. Just how will continuing as we have been—doing business as usual—affect the planetary temperature? Then I want to know what physical effects higher temperatures will have. On all the various regions of the world. All that leads up to the big question. What are the consequences for human life?

Jo: That's just the approach I had in mind! Here's the short version. If we don't change our ways, the gmt—the global mean temperature—will surely go up a bit. By 3 degrees or more. It might go up quite a lot more. Larger rises in temperature would cause more drastic physical effects. With *lots* of dangerous consequences for our descendants. So—more emissions, higher temperatures, greater physical changes, worse threats to human life. We can't *all* head off to Siberia. Lots of people won't be able to escape.

Joe: Right. So I'd really like to know the range of possible temperature increases, with the chances that they'll happen. Then for each region of the world, the physical effects of each of those increases. Finally, how that translates into what people's lives will be like.

Jo: I see. What you want is a kind of "ideal table." Laid out in four columns. In each row, the first column gives a figure for the CO_2e concentration when we finally give up emitting. The next column gives the rise in gmt at the moment when the full effect of that concentration is felt. The third identifies some particular part of the world, and the fourth specifies the chances of the dangerous things that could happen there. So in one row you might have—and I *am* making this up, you know!—550 ppm; 4.6°C; Northern Argentina; chances of floods 10%, chances of crop failure 12%, chances of bubonic plague less than 0.1%, and so on.

Joe: Yes, that's the sort of thing I want. But maybe the table should have a fifth column? One to register the consequences as people feel them. The bottom line. Estimates of the amount of suffering . . . and death.

Jo: That would depend on lots of things we can't know. What kinds of steps people take in the interim. How prepared various nations will be for what's to come. (*Pause.*) Maybe we should include the fifth column, and leave it blank? As a reminder of what's really important—and what we can't measure.

(*Pause.*)

I can't give you the ideal table, even in the original four-column version. I wish I could. But I can't. Nobody can.

Joe: That's what I expected. It's what makes me think the talk about climate problems is speculative. *Highly* speculative. Other threats we can be sure about. Terrorism. Poverty, all over the place.

Jo: There *is* lots of uncertainty. But it isn't *all* uncertain. You see, although I can't give you the ideal table, predicting what's likely to happen isn't complete guesswork. It may look like that. But it isn't.

Climate scientists often agree—at least roughly—on the chances that, if we practice business as usual, the gmt will go up by such-and-such an amount. One respected group of scientists thinks, if we don't engage in climate action, there's a greater than 50 percent chance of the gmt climbing by over 5°C by 2100. Others would be a bit more cautious, estimating a more than 50 percent chance of exceeding a 4°C rise. Do you know what those kinds of changes mean in physical terms?

Joe: Tell me.

Jo: Well, the last time the Earth's temperature was that hot—5°C above preindustrial levels—there was no ice anywhere on the planet. And there were crocodiles and alligators close to the poles!

Joe: Sure, 5 degrees sounds like a dramatic shift. But maybe it'll only be 4, or even 3.

Jo: By 2100. But there's nothing magical about 2100. If we keep going as we are—keep going *indefinitely*—we'll get there sooner or later. The sky's the limit—in both senses. Does it matter if it's by 2100, or by 2123, or by 2158? And sooner or later human life would become impossible. With a 10 degree rise, people in many places would collapse from heatstroke if they tried to work. Should we be content if that comes in 2216 or 2274 or 2301?

Joe: I see your point. When I've been thinking about business as usual, I've really been thinking about business as usual *up to a particular point in time*. Obviously, you're right. At some level, the planet would become too hot for us to live on it. Or, at least, to live in the ways we've come to enjoy. Some of us, anyway. So, sooner or later, we have to change. But why sooner?

Jo: That's just the right question! I can't really answer it without talking about lots of kinds of physical effects. And I can't discuss those without exploring the ways in which *local* climates change.

Let me give a silly example. The gmt is an average. You can get that average by having any number of distributions of temperature around the globe. So imagine the gmt goes up a lot, but in all the places where there's plenty of ice—the big ice sheets in Greenland and the Antarctic, all those mountaintops with glaciers—the local temperature either stays the same or goes down. All the ice would stay. No great meltdown. So, you see, it's important to figure out how the changing climate works locally.

And that's really, *really*, hard to predict. We do better when we're trying to forecast what's going to happen on average in a fairly large region. But if we try to predict on smaller scales there are important factors we don't know. Like what kinds of clouds will form, or just how the air will circulate. And that makes a difference.

Joe: Yes, I've heard that some types of clouds have a warming effect, while others tend to cool things down.

Jo: That's right. And it's not something most people realize. Do you have some background in science?

Joe: Some. A little, anyway.

Jo: Good. So let's think about predicting local climates. It's difficult, as I said, because small differences in some places can make a big difference to what happens elsewhere. So if we can't be precise about some crucial things our forecasts might go wildly astray.

Joe: Yes. That's what bothers me. Don't the predictions depend on coping with a huge number of variables? As I understand it nobody knows how to measure all the values. So climate models have to simplify. And what do the modelers do when they need values for things they can't measure?

Jo: Well . . . they can guess . . .

Joe: "Guess"? You seem to be confirming my skepticism about the whole business.

Jo: But they can try to tell in advance how good the guesses are.

Joe: Isn't there lots of disagreement?

Jo: About some things. Not about all. The mathematical equations governing the important atmospheric processes are well understood.

Joe: But that's not going to help if you don't have values to plug into the equations . . .

Jo: True . . . but let me explain a bit about how modeling works.

I'll start with basics. A very simple picture of the Earth tells us about the greenhouse effect. We think of the sun as radiating energy. Some of it gets absorbed, the rest is re-emitted. But part of what's re-emitted gets sent back by a kind of atmospheric blanket. And how much gets returned to the Earth's surface depends on what's in the atmosphere. Increase the concentration of carbon dioxide (or its equivalent) and more comes back. So the gmt goes up.

Joe: Yes, yes. I know that. I'm not doubting the basic facts. The planet's warming, and we're causing it. As I understand it, disagreement really sets in when scientists try to be more precise. To answer the kinds of questions I want answered.

Jo: You're right. But I was trying to use the elementary stuff—the simple greenhouse model—to make a point. You see, even with that a *vast* number of factors get left out. The thing is—*it doesn't matter.* Adding them back in wouldn't significantly change anything.

Joe: I'm not seeing how that helps you. From what I've read and heard, if we want to forecast how particular regions will be affected, it doesn't work that way. You *can't* neglect all those other factors. And—as I think you admitted—there are too many to include them all in any manageable model of the climate. So how do you get *any* firm conclusions?

Jo: You're right. Climate scientists have to decide which things they should include. But I haven't yet finished this bit of the story. Of course, once they've decided on the important factors, they have to assign values to lots of variables. And most of those they can't measure. So what do they do? Sometimes they make informed guesses. Sometimes they just guess. I know, you're going to say that's exactly your point, exactly what's made you skeptical. But . . . and this is the important thing . . . they can then use their guesses to try to simulate bits of the *climate history* of the regions in which they're interested. Suppose they want to see how central Africa is likely to be affected by climate change. They "tune" their model by seeing if it can deliver the data they have for central Africa in the past. Then they run the model forward into the future, and make a prediction.

Well, actually, that's not quite the way it works. They wouldn't be confident about any individual result. But often you have a number of scientists—or teams of scientists—working on a specific region. They make different choices about what factors to include. Different guesses about the values of things they can't measure. All of them run the models on their computers. Maybe many times. And, in some cases, they get agreement on a particular aspect of the climate in central Africa. Or whatever the region that's being studied.

Joe: OK. I see now. Sounds like a sensible approach. They consider alternative ways of doing things. When they all agree on something, they accept it as likely.

Jo: Yes. The ideal cases are those where there's complete agreement. Then they feel confident. So long as they're convinced enough alternatives have been considered. Sometimes, even when they can't agree on what will happen, they can estimate the chances of its happening. They can predict the probability. But there are lots of gradations here. That's why you find them saying things like "This is very likely; that's likely but not highly probable; this is more likely than not." And then there are cases in which the results are all over the place. When that happens they talk about possibilities. Scenarios.

Joe: So, your message is that there *is* plenty of uncertainty about many details, but that we can be fairly confident that some effects will result from allowing concentrations of greenhouse gases to reach a particular level. And occasionally *very* confident. Have I got it right?

Jo: Exactly. So let me start telling you about some of the changes we can predict. You mentioned earlier how some unpleasantly cold places are going to get warmer. That's right. But it's not always a blessing. Take Siberia, for example. Maybe you were thinking that lots of people might start to move there. Plenty of space. Big profits for the landowners. The trouble is the permafrost. Not that it'll still be there to interfere with farming. But that it won't. You see, if the permafrost melts, a whole lot of methane will be released into the atmosphere, giving a big jolt to the climate. That could cause a very sudden increase in the greenhouse effect.

The warming that's *already* occurred in the past century or so has made a difference. People have seen signs of permafrost melting. A further 1 or 2 degree rise would trigger melting on a *far* broader scale. And our climate models agree in predicting a value for how much the average Siberian temperature will go up, if we continue business as usual. Guess how much?

Joe: I haven't a clue. But I suspect more than 1 or 2 degrees.

Jo: Right. More than 4 degrees.

Joe: But hang on a minute. I started by inviting you to offer dire consequences for the human future. Things you could predict with something close to certainty. Now the very first thing you tell me about the future is that Siberia will get much hotter and global warming will accelerate as a result. I wanted to know what global warming will *mean* for us. How future people are going to suffer from it. Telling me that global warming is going to cause more global warming doesn't help. I need the bottom line. The human bottom line.

Jo: You're right. The Siberian example is useful in one way. It shows the agreement you worry we can't get. But it doesn't translate directly into dire trouble for people. So let me switch examples. You probably know about coastal flooding?

Joe: Yes. Sea levels are going to rise. Even in the next few decades. That's going to cause—already is causing—real problems for people who live on some islands. The Maldives, for instance, are literally going under. The people living there will have to move. I've heard about all this. I know there's scientific agreement about it. It's sad, of course. But as big a cause of human suffering as malnutrition? Lack of education? Unemployment? No medical care? I don't think so.

So I'm still waiting for a convincing case. Scientific agreement. Firm predictions. Grave human consequences.

Jo: You're underestimating the impact! It's not just a few small islands whose inhabitants will have to find new homes elsewhere. Rising seas will affect areas of the world in which lots of people, poor people, live. The Bay of Bengal, the North African coast. At the moment, about 60 million people worldwide live within one meter of the average sea level. About 13 million of them are in Europe—in the Netherlands, in England, in Germany, in Italy. The sea-level rise by the end of this century is expected to be at least half a meter. And, as I said, there's nothing magical about 2100. Once the Greenland ice sheet melts completely—and it isn't "if" but "when"—the average sea level around the world will rise by 5 to 7 meters. That would affect 200 million people if it happened today, and twice as many if it happened in 2100. Of course, that whole effect isn't going to happen overnight. It takes a while for that amount of ice to melt. But I hope you see the size of the potential impacts. From just this one factor alone.

Joe: OK. So lots of people have to move. Still not on a par with other human troubles. Suffering that goes on every day.

Jo: Don't be so sure of that. It's not going to go as smoothly as you seem to think. And rising sea levels are only one form of trouble. There'll also be heat waves. Temperatures in sub-Saharan Africa, the Near East, in parts of Central Asia—and in South Asia, where I'm originally from—are going to go up a lot. Sooner or later, unless we start to do things differently, it'll be impossible to live in these places. People's bodies just won't be able to cope with the heat and humidity. They certainly won't be able to work outside—grow crops, build houses, things like that.

Joe: You've come closer to addressing my questions. But I don't think you're there yet. What's the extent of the suffering? How terrible are the human consequences? As I keep saying, there are all these other problems. Obvious problems. Disfiguring people's lives. In the here and now.

Isolated examples don't do it for me. I need to know how bad it's likely to be in various regions of the world. And how sure we are about these terrible effects. Take me on a world tour. As we visit each region, tell me what the main threats are. Dreadful things we can be very sure are going to happen.

Jo: That's a good idea and I *will* do it in a minute. But first, there's something important I ought to explain. I think it'll help you see how you've been too optimistic. How you've thought of terrible consequences as tolerable. You see, when people hear about climate change, they tend to underestimate the dangers. That's because they think about it in a very particular way. As you just did when we talked about sea-level rise. It's really common. People focus on *constant effects* and neglect *episodic effects*.

The constant effects in a region are the ones that endure. Once a constant effect has happened, that's the way things are there from then on. If sea levels rise enough, some islands disappear permanently. Episodic effects aren't like that. A rise in sea level can leave you happily high and dry—most of the time. But then a big storm comes along with high tides and really strong winds and you get flooded. That didn't use to happen. Now, because of the higher average sea level, it does.

Joe: I get it. It's not just the average that matters. It's the variations around the average. Of course, if you increase the average, then if today's value is such-and-such an amount larger than the average, it's bigger absolutely than a deviation by that amount used to be. Assuming the distribution doesn't change.

Let's see if I understand it. I'll try a different example. Take one of your hot spots—India, say. In the old days, a really hot spell would be one in which the temperature climbed to 45°C (113°F) day after day. But now, after climate change has taken effect, the average is higher. Because of that the highs are higher. Maybe 49° (120°F) used to be really rare. Now it happens more frequently. The temperature never used to reach 53°C (127°F). Now it does. It's the new "really rare." Have I got it right?

Jo: Absolutely. I rather suspect you have more than "a little" background in science. (*Pause.*) In fact, the problem is even worse than that. You assumed—quite reasonably!—that the way fluctuations occur around the average would remain the same—and that does lead to the old extremes happening more frequently and to more extreme extremes you never used to see. Of course, there would be even more problems if the deviations changed in a particular way. Suppose climate change caused a greater tendency for temperatures to vary on the high side [Figure 2.1(b)]. So, to take your example, it's not just that 49° (120°) becomes more common, but that it becomes *much* more common. And the "rare" region doesn't just stop at 53° (127°) but allows some small chance of the temperature climbing to 55° (131°).

We've all grown used to thinking in terms of normal distributions. Those familiar bell-shaped curves. Climate may not work like that. In a warmer world, maybe the graph showing the distribution of something—temperature, storms, drought conditions, say—gets distorted. One end of the distribution—the bad end—gets fatter. A so-called "fat tail." That means there's *more* chance of the high extremes.

I know. This is really hard to follow. If I could draw a

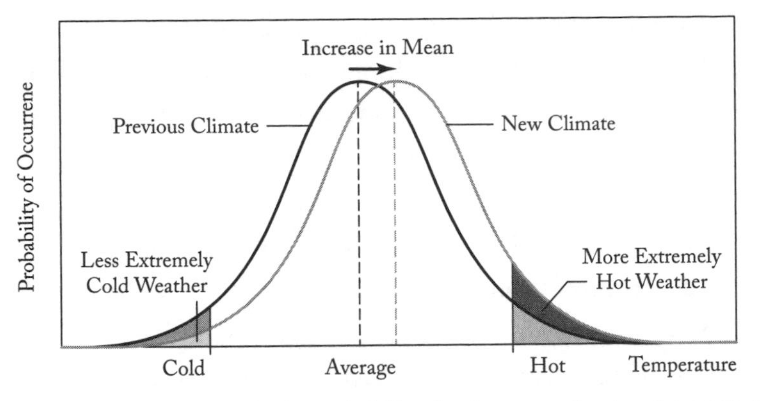

Figure 2.1(a) The change in the probability of extreme events when the mean shifts but the variation around the mean remains the same. This is the change Joe imagines.

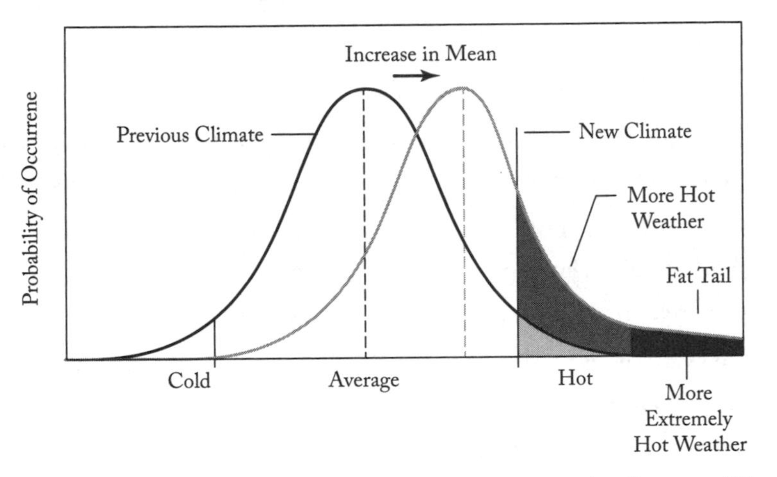

Figure 2.1(b) The change in the probability of extreme events when the mean shifts and the variation is skewed to give a "fat tail" at the "bad" end. This is the graph Jo would like Joe to see. (The change is exaggerated to show the effect.)

picture for you, it would be much clearer. Can you see at all what I'm getting at?

Joe: I think so. But is there any reason to think climate works that way?

Jo: Climate scientists think there is. Take storms, for instance. A warmer atmosphere can absorb more water vapor. So there's a theoretical reason for predicting that storms will be more intense in a warmer world. Higher winds. More rainfall. That's borne out by the extreme events we've been seeing during the past decades. Lots of very severe storms coming more frequently. More frequently than we'd have expected if the distributions were normal.

Joe: Can we go back a bit? You were talking about constant effects and episodic effects. You said we—I—tend to focus on the constant effects and neglect the episodic ones. If the average summer high temperature in a region goes up a little—say from 25°C (77°F) to 28°C (82°F)—we fixate on those values. The change doesn't seem too bad. Perhaps even welcome. But we ought to consider variation. If the average is 28, maybe each summer there are a few days—or more than a few—when the thermometer climbs to 33°C (91°F) and stays there. And people aren't accustomed to coping with that.

Jo: Exactly. In many places around the world, it's the episodic effects that pose the big threats. We've been talking about just a couple of examples. The two most obvious ones: higher temperatures and rising sea levels. Higher temperature has constant effects. Places can be warmer on average during the year. As you just pointed out, for lots of places that can seem no big deal. But higher temperatures produce episodic effects. The heat waves that come along. Even when people would be happy with a warmer average, those heat waves might prove really dangerous. Same story for sea levels. Constant effect—the water creeps a little higher on average. But it's what happens at high tide that matters. Especially when a storm hits and the tide is unusually high. Plenty of places are, on average, safely above the sea, and will still be, even as the planet warms. But what might seem like a safe haven becomes ever more vulnerable to large storms, especially if the warming increases the violence of the storms and the rate at which they come. Episodic effects again.

And these are just two sources of trouble. There are others. Mountainous regions may get less snow in the winter. Bad for the ski trade, of course, but that's not the main problem. A smaller snowpack melts faster in the spring. The result: floods in the valleys below—and then a period of serious drought. Another constant effect—many parts of the world will become a lot more arid. Sources of freshwater will dry up.

Joe: From what I read, it's happening already.

Jo: Right. And yet another thing. The oceans are becoming more acidic. That spells trouble for shellfish. They'll be smaller and there will be fewer of them. Result—lots of hungry fish. Fewer cod, fewer herring around. And one more. As the planet warms, plants start to grow in different places. Insects and other animals migrate. So there are new patterns of interaction among animals. Between animals and human populations. New possibilities for the spread of diseases.

Joe: OK. Lots of constant effects. Now, I suppose, you'll tell me about different types of episodic effects. Let me guess. Besides heat waves and storms we ought to worry about droughts, failures of crops, local floods, wildfires, and epidemics.

Jo: Good guess! It's not hard to see how our descendants might have to cope with lack of freshwater, with crop failures and food shortages, with flooded sewage systems, with the destruction of their homes, with no access to medical care, with diseases that "jump" from animals to us, with newly evolved viruses or bacteria, with parasitic infestations . . .

Joe: Hold on! You're doing what people always do in this sort of conversation. You're talking about "possibilities," things that "might" happen. "Scenarios" as you called them. I wanted to know what's *likely* to occur. *Really* likely. Surely you don't think we can predict the coming plague? Nobody can tell how germs are likely to evolve.

Jo: You're right. You and I are making a list of scenarios. Types of scenarios—droughts, fires, pandemics, and so on. We *need* that list. People so often forget about some of the important items on it. Especially about the possibilities of new diseases.

Of course you're right. We can't forecast whether a new disease is likely to emerge. (*Pause.*) I do want to tell you about the "very likely" stuff. But I feel it's wrong to leave out all the ways disaster might come. Even though we can't say how likely they are. Let me try to sort it out as we go.

Joe: Fine. So how about the world tour?

Jo: I'm ready. I know I seemed to go off track a bit. But I wanted you to see how different types of effects are relevant for different regions. Where should we start?

Joe: With the places that'll be most affected. That are *sure* to suffer a lot.

Jo: Africa and Asia—including my homeland. That's where most of the human population lives. Lots of places vulnerable to many different kinds of threats. High summer temperatures will make large parts of Africa and Asia uninhabitable. The North African coast and the Bay of Bengal—where millions of people live—will be periodically inundated. Severe droughts in lots of places—in Iran, the Sudan, and Somalia—those are just a few examples. Throughout South Asia and Southeast Asia, the wet seasons are going to be even wetter. Fields will be flooded. Sometimes crops will fail because there isn't enough water, and other times because there's too much that arrives too quickly. Within the next decades, every year will disrupt the food supply of some very large population. Millions of people—the ones living in the unlucky places—will suffer famine. We can be very confident about all that.

Joe: That's more the sort of thing I wanted to hear. (*Realizes what he has said.*) I don't mean that . . . sorry . . . I misspoke . . . what I meant was . . .

Jo: . . . that I've gotten back on track. Started to talk about predictions we can make with high confidence.

Joe: Yes. Of course, nobody wants these things to happen. Anywhere. And it's where you're from . . .

Jo: No need to apologize. Talking about these things is tricky. When I'm concentrating on something complicated, I don't always find the best words. As you've discovered. (*Pause.*) Let's go next to the least affected region.

Joe: North America?

Jo: No. Europe. Some people worry that large parts of the Mediterranean countries will experience severe droughts. Italy turns into a desert, say. From what I've read, that's a serious possibility but not something we can say is really probable. The major dangers will likely be episodic effects—floods and heat waves. Increasingly frequent, increasingly intense storms. Even worse floods than the ones of recent years. Along the

Danube. In Northern England. Intense heat waves. Worse than the one that struck France in 2003 and killed around 15,000 people.

It's interesting, though. Even though Europeans will get off relatively lightly, some European countries have been most active in trying to cope with climate change. That's why I'm here. In Berlin.

(*Pause.*)

Their attitude seems more like yours. Thinking more globally. About human beings everywhere. Maybe you're from Europe? Germany, even?

Joe: (*Remains silent. Long pause.*) Let's go on with the tour.

Jo: OK. (*Pause.*) I shouldn't have raised the question.

(*The other phone rings. Jo picks it up.*)

Jo: (*To Joe.*) Just a minute. I have to answer. I'll be right back. (*Into the second phone.*) Jo here. (*Listens.*) Yes, that's right. Tomorrow at 5. (*Listens.*) No. I can't talk. I'm on the other line. (*Listens.*) OK. See you then.

(*She replaces the second phone. Resumes her conversation with Joe.*)

Jo: I'm back.

Joe: I'm sorry. I'm taking up too much of your time.

Jo: No, no. It's not a busy night. I want to go on. Where were we?

Joe: Europe. Least affected, most concerned.

Jo: Right. Next up, Australia. Obvious threats. Heat waves, droughts, wildfires. It's already happening. Higher temperatures, drier conditions, bigger blazes than there used to be. It's only going to get worse during the rest of the century. Even higher temperatures, longer dry spells, ferocious fires. A lot of the bush is like a tinderbox. Just waiting for the spark. Will a fire destroy one of the major cities before 2100? You wouldn't want to bet against it.

Next: Central and South America. A bit of a mixture. Droughts in some places—much of Mexico and parts of Chile, for instance. The recent drought in Mexico—and there'll be far worse ones to come—affected two and a half million people. Other areas will have floods. Like parts of Brazil and Northern Argentina. Lots of recurrent heat waves. Much worse than Europe. Not as bad as Africa, though. And there's another clear prediction. The spread of insects that carry diseases into higher elevations. In some cities deliberately built "above the bugline" people are already getting bitten. That's only going to increase.

Joe: So here we *can* predict higher rates of disease?

Jo: Yes. The scientists aren't talking about new diseases. The problems are old friends. Or foes. Malaria, for instance.

I've left North America for last. Americans sometimes seem to think they can look on unperturbed. The bad stuff isn't going to affect them.

If they do think that, they're wrong. Canadians will be mostly OK. Unless, of course, their way of life depends on catching fish. Or they live near forests where wildfires could easily break out. But the continental United States is in for trouble. Not as much as Africa and Asia, or parts of Central and South America. But more than Europe and maybe—it's hard to say—more than Australia.

Lots of the threats are really obvious. American newspapers and television stations love to talk about the "storm of the century." Well, they're going to have a lot of candidates in the next decades. Every year or so, some new one is going to slam into the East Coast or the Gulf of Mexico. Plenty of low-lying cities and towns will get hit and be partially demolished. Those areas will be cut off, without power or medical supplies. Thanks to overflowing sewers, they won't have clean water. Past "disasters" will look like picnics.

That's not the only worry. Large chunks of the country will have periodic droughts. Especially in the Southwest. Not enough water to irrigate crops. (*Ever more excitedly.*) Imagine what would happen if California's Central Valley dried up completely—or if a flash flood turned it into a salt marsh. Imagine . . .

Joe: You're doing it again. More scenarios.

Jo: You're right. I got carried away. (*Pause.*) But the droughts *are* predictable. What they lead to depends on how people prepare in advance. The kinds of protections they put in place. It'll surely take a lot to cope with them. Maybe some dry periods will defy *any* advance preparation. We can't say.

Also, as in Europe, there'll be incredible floods along major American waterways—like the Mississippi. In the Pacific Northwest, as well. But the towns and cities in the East will face the biggest problems. By the end of this century, "unusual" high tides will force people to abandon some towns along the Eastern Seaboard, probably including at least one big city. Miami is only the most obvious candidate.

Joe: OK. Thanks for the tour. You've given me a sense of what we can confidently predict. Now I have to think. Are the global dangers you've described so grave as to outrank the human suffering caused by terrorism? Or malnutrition? (*Pause.*) Or cancer.

(*Pause.*)

Anyway, thanks so much for talking. I realize I called with an odd request. As you said, not really your job. But you did pretty . . .

Jo: (*Breaking in.*) Wait! Please don't hang up just yet. (*Pause.*) I don't want to leave it there. I don't think I've done justice to the full threat.

Joe: I was about to congratulate you. On doing a pretty good job.

Jo: But I haven't. You see, there was a reason why I kept slipping off track. Talking about scenarios, when you wanted firm predictions. Of course, the firm predictions *are* important. But they aren't *all* that's important. We can't just list them and say "That's it. The whole range of what to worry about." I know we can't assess the chances of many other things, but we shouldn't ignore them. After all, they *might* happen.

Joe: "Might" again?

Jo: I know. You want certainty. Or something close to it. High probability. But sometimes, when some course of events would be really catastrophic, you have to take it into account. Even when you don't know how likely it is to happen.

Joe: We disagree about that. I know a lot of people think the way you do. If there's a chance of some complete disaster, even if we can't specify it, even though the chance might be really tiny . . . infinitesimal . . . we ought to try to prevent it. I don't think that way. (*Pause.*) Especially now.

After all, disaster can come in so many forms. The Earth

might be hit by an asteroid. The airplane I fly on might crash. My friends might be infected with some undetectable disease. Should we change our ways because these things are possible? Prepare a defense against asteroids, give up flying, stop getting together with other people? (*Pause.*)

What I'm trying to say is this. There are too many large threats. We can't possibly act to ward off all of them. So we have to go for the major ones. The ones with a real chance of happening.

Jo: I agree. But the scenarios I kept wanting to present to you are still important. There are so many of them. So many terrible ones, and that matters.

(*Pause.*)

It's hard to put into words what's bothering me. But I'd like to try.

Joe: OK. Go on.

Jo: There's a single source: climate change. From it come lots of truly catastrophic prospects for the human future. And we can't tell if any of the terrible scenarios has a serious chance of happening. Maybe in all cases, the probabilities are really tiny. But there are so many cases. If we took any one of them, and focused on it, your attitude would be the right one. You can't spend your life bothering about things like that.

Joe: Or, in my case, what's left of my life.

Jo: Oh, I do hope you have more time—much more time—than you think! Predictions about an illness can go wrong, too. Maybe . . .

(*Pause; Joe remains silent.*)

Anyway, here's roughly what I feel. We'd be silly to fixate

on any of the scenarios. But equally silly to think we can avoid all of them. All the possible ways the future could turn out very badly. There *is* a serious chance that *one*—or more—of the dire possibilities will get us. Unless we do something, that is.

I know. That's too vague. Too abstract. Maybe I can make it clearer. Let's go back to something you said near the beginning of our conversation. You were imagining people moving into the parts of the planet that remain habitable. They discover they can no longer live where they have been living. So they pick up and move. All very serene and graceful.

But it won't be like that. When the wells dry up, when the big storms keep hitting, when the floods recur, when crops can't be grown any longer, the people will *already* be weakened. The migrants of the future won't be setting out in air-conditioned cars, with their precious possessions in tow. They won't be heading off for places where clean water flows and the food supply is assured. They'll be dirty and malnourished and they won't have had clean water in a while. They'll have to move with the few things they can carry. They'll be going into areas already inhabited by other people—people who are also struggling to survive. Many of the migrants will be sick. And the others, to whose lands they come will resist their settling. There will be fights, even wars. And that will cause more devastation.

These scenarios aren't isolated incidents. They're lots of bad effects in recurrent patterns. Chains of events spiraling into disasters.

Here's an analogy. One that's influenced me, because it's a

situation we know about, and one in which people suffer . . . suffer dreadfully today.

Imagine yourself in a city ravaged by a many-sided civil war. If you're to survive, you must venture out, day after day, and assemble the things you need. Maybe water and food will be available. Maybe they won't be. Perhaps you can scrounge medical supplies from a place where they've been dumped. On each of your journeys there are dangers of all sorts. They can arise at any number of points along your route. There may be bombs, or mines, or snipers, or street battles, or gangs of marauding looters. There are lots of factions, and danger could come from any direction. For each particular stage of your journey, the chance of some specific threat is very low. It's not very probable that the commando unit of the hostile purple faction is lurking around the next corner. The trouble lies in the vast number of potential dangers. That means the chance you'll make your way unscathed, day after day, week after week, is tiny. Even infinitesimal. Each day, you'll curse yourself for not having heeded the warnings and left for safety while you could.

That's how we should think about the future, if we don't act to limit climate change. So many bad scenarios, piling up on top of one another. Is it reasonable to think we can escape all of them?

(*Pause.*)

Joe: (*Reflectively.*) Yes. I see. You think it's a bit like playing Russian roulette. The gun has a really large number of chambers. So, each time you pull the trigger, you're overwhelmingly likely to survive. But if you keep playing . . . and keep playing . . . sooner or later it's going to end badly.

(*Pause.*)

Thanks. That's helpful. You've given me lots to think about.

Jo: But I haven't convinced you . . . have I?

Joe: That's not something to expect from a single conversation. But I *shall* think about what you've said. I promise you that. (*Pause.*) And you've helped. (*Pause.*) At a difficult time. (*Pause.*) I'm grateful.

Jo: (*Almost tenderly.*) I'm glad we talked. (*Pause.*) Good luck.

(*She hears a click as Joe hangs up.*)

Living with Uncertainty

We cannot tell if the scenarios Jo constantly mentions (or the one presented in the prologue) are likely to occur—or if they are such remote possibilities that we should dismiss them from serious consideration. Whether the human consequences are as dire as they are imagined to be depends on too many factors we don't know—including how people act, or fail to act, in the decades ahead. As Joe laments, so many details are uncertain. His response to the uncertainty is to focus on what can definitely be predicted. Jo is not content to be limited in this way. From her perspective, leaving out possibilities whose chances we can't specify underestimates the dangers.

Sober analysts might fault both of them for the vagueness of their exchange. Wouldn't it be far better to use cost–benefit analysis? Our conversationalists should have begun by *comparing* two—or more—possible courses of action. Showing that one line of conduct has bad results isn't enough to justify striking out in some different direction. For the rival options might be worse. Alternatives should have been on the table from the beginning. They also should have been formulated more exactly. And the discussants ought to have weighed the costs and benefits of each. So Joe and Jo go astray in two ways. They ought to have pursued a comparative analysis (considering the costs and benefits of trying to do something about climate change), and they should have proceeded much more precisely than they do.

The attractions of precision are easy to understand. A person, a community, a firm, or a nation must make a decision about how to act. The possibilities are canvassed. For each of the options there are potential gains and losses. Analysts start by assigning numerical values to the benefits, to the costs, and to the probabilities of all of the outcomes. Then they calculate the *expected value* of each course of action. That provides the appropriate measure of how well each one will do on average. So, in the end, they will be able to pick one with the highest expected value. The choice will be completely clear—there will be nothing "nebulous" about it.

Consider an everyday example. You contemplate an investment, learning that the chance of a 20% gain is 9 in 10, but that there's a 1 in 10 chance of losing 30%; alternatively, you could play it safe, and gain 10% for sure. What should you do? The expected value of each option is calculated by multiplying the probability of each outcome you might reach by choosing that option by the cost or benefit obtained from the outcome; then you add all the numbers you've just computed. Suppose you have $100 to invest. If you choose the riskier approach, you have a chance of 0.9 of gaining $20 (0.9 x 20 = 18) and a chance of 0.1 of losing $30 (0.1 x [-30] = -3). Your expected gain is $18 - $3—i.e., $15. That's more than the $10 you would receive if you played it safe. So you should prefer the (mildly) risky investment.

"But suppose having a particular amount of money was really important to you. If you ended up with less than $110, you wouldn't be able to reach a significant goal (paying off a debt, say, or securing your child a place in some valuable after-school activity). Doesn't cost–benefit analysis give the wrong answer?" No. Although the objection is perfectly natural, it is misdirected. Under the envisaged circumstances, the costs and benefits have been wrongly assessed. The true value of the money, in this context, depends on particular things you want to do with it. Effectively, any loss is as bad as losing everything, while small monetary gains are insignificant in comparison with the value of reaching your goal. So the value of $110 to you is much greater than anything less, and having $120 is only slightly better than having $110. When the scale is set up in the proper human terms (reflecting what matters to you), the cost–benefit calculation confirms the conclusion that you should play it safe.

This rudimentary sketch of cost–benefit analysis yields three morals. First, the approach depends on being able to supply numerical values for probabilities and for the gains and losses. (Sometimes, single values are not required; it suffices to know that the values lie in a particular range.) Second, monetary assessments do not always represent the correct scale of values. The fundamental currency is in terms of the impact on human lives and human welfare. Third, the straightforward (if misdirected) objection suggests that constructing the appropriate scale of values may depend on a prior *qualitative* approach to decision-making. The difficulties with taking gains and losses at their monetary value were exposed by recognizing that, when a loss would compromise your ability to achieve an important goal, the risky investment would be a disastrous decision.

Economists (or other fans of cost–benefit analysis) might try to avoid any retreat to qualitative thinking. They tend to think it's always possible to measure the exact strength of your preferences. That's done by asking how much money you would demand in compensation for failure to achieve your goal. But judging the risky investment to be a terrible decision in no way depends on giving an answer to this question, or even on there *being* an answer to the question. With respect to some human aspirations, many people are inclined to reject the idea that *any* monetary sum makes up for failure. How much money compensates for the loss of a loved one? Or the collapse of some enterprise to which you have dedicated your adult life? The most basic scale of values is determined by the quality of human lives, not by the monetary units economically minded policymakers so often offer as a surrogate. And the quality of a life doesn't always allow for precise measurement.

Many of our most important decisions are made on the basis of careful, but qualitative, reflection. Indeed, some of them revert to the qualitative framework after failed efforts at cost–benefit analysis. When Charles Darwin considered whether or not to propose to his cousin, Emma Wedgwood, he divided a clean sheet of paper into two columns. In one he listed the potential benefits of marriage—"delight of female society," "the regularity of domestic life"; in the other he recorded the costs—"loss of freedom to attend meetings of scientific colleagues," "time wasted in frivolous family pursuits." But that was as far as the cost–benefit analysis went. No numbers were assigned to measure costs and benefits or to estimate the probabilities. There was no calculation. Instead, in a far less careful and restrained hand, Darwin scribbled at the bottom of the page "Marry! Marry! Marry!"

Did one of the greatest scientists of all time fall sadly short in his decision-making? Surely not. Compiling the lists was helpful, prompting Darwin to reflect—to imagine vividly various aspects of his future life under each option. At that point, however, he had to react, allowing his overall sense of the better and the worse to guide him. That sense is not infallible. Qualitative judgment can easily lead us astray—as it does when people overrate the dangers of flying and underrate those of driving to the airport. When statistics are available to ground estimates of probability it is good to let them inform our choices; there is a place for cost–benefit analysis.

Much of the time—including with respect to our most important decisions—reliable statistics are *not* available. On these occasions, careful qualitative reflection is the best we can do. *Reflection* does play an important role here. It's important to ask whether the envisaged outcomes—the scenarios—are worth taking seriously or whether they are preposterous. People have to make *judgments* about what might occur, and what it might mean, and good judgment involves considering things from as many angles as you can. Fans of cost–benefit analysis probably distrust judgment because it is so hard to explain how to judge well. But sometimes there is no alternative. Precise measurements aren't there to guide us. When that happens, instead of conjuring numbers out of thin air, people do better to emulate Darwin.

As Joe and Jo do, and as most of us do much of the time. Many major life decisions, ranging from resolving to spend the rest of our lives with a particular person through choosing a home or a job to planning for children's education and for retirement, are based on qualitative assessments, made in clear knowledge of factors pro and con, for which we can't give numerical assessments of strength. People recognize a sea of uncertainties that undercut any assignments of probabilities. Often, when we appreciate the many ways in which a course of action could turn out badly, we back away. Even though we cannot say whether the chances of the bad scenarios are truly tiny, the sheer number of unpleasant possibilities leads us to pursue some alternative option. That point lies behind Jo's story of the many-sided civil war, and Joe's example of Russian roulette.

So our conversationalists are partially exonerated. They use the qualitative framework we rightly employ in our most crucial life decisions. They care about the lives of future generations. On this shared basis, Jo tries to show that the dangers of business as usual are real.

But her case falls short of a call for climate action. To seek an alternative course is not to find one. More specifically, it is not to find one whose perils, qualitatively assessed, are less than those we anticipate from continuing our current practices. The qualitative approach must absorb one feature of cost–benefit analysis, that of comparing available alternatives. Darwin rightly divided the virgin page into two columns.

Moreover, Jo's argument assumes that Joe cares about the lives of the world to come. This Joe does. But perhaps he is unusual in his concern or in the extent of it. Hence, the case for climate action depends on answering two further questions: How much should we care about the future? What are the likely effects of trying to limit climate change?

Some ways of saying "So what?" remain.

THREE

WHY CARE?

Jo's Boys

Late evening. An apartment, modestly but tastefully furnished. Joe, a man of about thirty, sits in an easy chair. A glass of wine is on the coffee table in front of him. He has picked up a framed photograph from the table. It shows two small boys, happily playing in the sand. Joe looks at it. Smiles.

A door opens. Jo, a woman of roughly the same age, enters. She is carrying a half-full wineglass. She sits down on the sofa, facing Joe.

He replaces the photograph.

Joe: Everything OK?

Jo: Fast asleep. Both of them. Looking angelic.

Joe: They look like great kids. (*He gestures towards the photograph.*) Happy. Healthy.

Jo: *I* think so. They've done well. Even in the difficult times.

Joe: The break-up, you mean?

Jo: And what came before. The quarrels. All his anger. (*She looks* *away briefly.*) But that's over now. They're settled, and they like it here. They don't even mind too much if I go out. Like this evening. (*Pause.*) Of course, it helps that they have fun with Sophia. She's smart, and really good with them. She lives just next door, too. If she ever has a question, she can ask her mother.

Joe: That gives you some freedom.

Jo: Yes. (*Pause.*) But this evening was a first. I don't normally go out to dinner.

Joe: Well, I'm really glad you agreed to come. I enjoyed it.

Jo: Me too. It was a bit of a change for me, though. Eating out is so costly—it's not something I do much anymore. With all the trouble I had finding work, I've become a bit of a Scrooge. I tend to count the pennies—and save for the boys.

Joe: Yes. I can understand the urge to save, to prepare for the bad times. As you know, it was hard for me too. I had to scramble a lot before I landed this job. Especially after the divorce. Two years of couch-surfing. Strained friendships. All that taught me to be careful. To try always to have something to fall back on.

Jo: And you never know . . . I don't want to be gloomy. But I can't help wondering—How long will it last? Do you?

Joe: Of course. It's hard not to worry. (*Pause.*) Funny, isn't it? The two of us. Such similar stories. Early marriages. Then the job crunch. Both of us spending so long finding work. Rejection after rejection. All the pressure. Each of us going through divorce. (*He looks directly at Jo.*) Probably harder for you, though. With the kids.

Jo: In some ways maybe. It certainly wasn't easy—three of us crammed into my childhood bedroom. My parents were kind, though. Sympathetic. But *so* disappointed. (*Looking directly at Joe.*) How worried are you? About whether the job will last.

Joe: Well, it seems a decent outfit. You probably know more than I do. You've been there longer.

Jo: Only a month. It seems solid—but these days, you never know—things change so fast. Most of the supervisors are nice enough . . . except for O'Brien . . . I've heard she likes to act tough . . . to curry favor with the higher-ups. (*Pause.*) How have you found it so far?

Joe: Not too bad. I think we have similar impressions. I'm not actively worried. But after the past few years I'm not taking anything for granted. (*Pause.*) I don't want to go through that again.

Jo: Neither do I.

(*Silence.*)

Joe: (*Tentatively.*) One thing I don't understand, though. You were talking about the baby-sitter—Sophia, right?—as if she'd sat for you quite a bit. But then you said you don't go out . . . Sorry, I don't mean to be nosey.

Jo: No, that's all right. I don't eat out as a rule. But I do sometimes go off in the evening. After the kids are tucked up in bed. Volunteering. Since I landed the job, I've taken it up again. I'd been doing it, off and on, for years, at the climate action center. It's been my great cause.

(*Pause.*)

Actually, that was one of the things—one of many things—that made trouble with Mark. He always resented it when I went out. Even though the boys were asleep. He couldn't understand why I did it.

(*She looks at Joe.*)

(*Very tentatively.*) Do you?

Joe: Well . . . I do understand having a cause. Wanting to do something. But . . . climate action wouldn't be my choice. (*He hesitates.*) Aren't there more urgent things to fight for?

Jo: I don't think so. (*Pause.*) I know many people think as you do. (*She looks directly at Joe.*) But I don't.

Joe: This is tricky. We don't know each other that well. (*Pause.*) At least, not yet . . . (*Pause.*) And I don't want us to misunderstand one another and get off on the wrong foot. (*Looking at her.*) Can I try to explain?

Jo: OK. (*She takes a sip of wine.*)

Joe: I don't know where you stand on political issues, and I don't suppose it really matters. All over the political spectrum, there are plenty of good causes and places to act to make things better. I'm all in favor of that. Before I was laid off, I did some volunteering myself.

And I'm not one of those people who deny that we're changing the climate. As far as I'm concerned, the science is settled. And I know there'll be consequences down the road. By the end of the century, people will have to cope with the mess we've made. (*He pauses. Takes a sip of wine.*)

One thing the past few years have taught me, though, is how hard life is for a lot of folk. People living here and now. The sort of people who could work steadily, do reasonably well, and be confident their kids would do better. Or people who came here because of the opportunities this country offered. (*He looks at her.*)

All that . . . gone. I felt that in the bad years. Not much hope for the sort of life I'd expected to have. Now maybe . . . a little . . . But I don't have the same faith I had as a kid. It seems so . . . precarious . . . (*He takes another sip of wine.*)

So if . . . *when* . . . I pick up again, get politically active . . . I'll want to try to help with these . . . pressing . . . problems.

I'm not a selfish person. At least, I hope I'm not—I try not to be. But why should the troubles of faraway people, people in distant places, people who'll live decades from now, why should those problems weigh more with me than those I see all around me?

(*He leans forward in the chair.*) And, though we know there'll be challenges in the decades ahead, we don't . . . can't . . . know much about what they'll be or where they'll strike. All full of uncertainty. Why not wait? Shouldn't we help solve the problems we can see clearly? Restore the opportunities we've lost. Make our economy strong again. Restore what we've lost. Wouldn't that be the best gift we could offer the future? (*He leans back, as if to show that he is finished.*)

Jo: (*Pause.*) That's a lot. (*Pause.*) Thanks. (*Pause.*) Not quite the conversation I'd expected. Not that I'd expected anything in particular. (*Pause.*) But good . . . in a strange way. I'm glad you explained. (*She looks directly at him.*) Don't worry. Mark would never have talked like that . . .

Of course, I don't agree. (*Pause.*) Do you want to talk it out? (*She glances at her watch.*) It's late. Perhaps . . .

Joe: No, no. I'm happy to pursue it. Even though we don't want to be late in the morning. These questions are important for you. I sense that. (*Pause.*) So tell me why you disagree.

Jo: For starters—your idea of building the economy for the future. Sounds plausible at first. But I don't think it is.

From what I've read, economists think the growth of the past century or so is *really* unusual. Something that's never happened before. Of course, as you point out, it hasn't affected all people equally, even in wealthy countries like ours. (*Pause.*) We both know that . . . all too well. (*Pause.*) Well, some of the experts think this growth will continue. People living at the end of the century will be a lot richer than we are. Other economists disagree. They see us as having hit a new plateau. The age of rapid growth is over.

And the debate among the experts doesn't take climate change into account. It ignores the shocks of coming decades—the floods, the droughts, the famines, the wildfires, maybe even plagues or wars over water. As you say, a lot of that is uncertain. But just *because* it's uncertain, we can't be confident that the economy will grow. Because of our inaction, it may decline. Catastrophically.

Just imagine the costs of responding to all the disasters. Or of preparing to meet them. Building desalination plants, to fill new reservoirs with fresh water. Constructing barriers against floods and fires. Rescuing people who are starving, who have no water and no shelter. Assembling armies of emergency workers.

Or are we just going to neglect those people? Let them die? Hundreds of millions of them. Possibly more than a billion. (*She takes a sip of her wine.*)

Surely it's better to act to reduce the rate at which these shocks occur! As my mother says, "An ounce of prevention . . ." It's so much harder to react once damage has been done.

You know . . . I encourage the boys to eat right and to be active. I don't say "Eat whatever you want. Sit on the couch and play video games. Sure, you'll get fat. And obesity is unhealthy. But don't worry. Medicine gets better all the time. When you start to have problems, doctors will be able to fix them."

Why should I take a different approach to the health of the environment? In which my boys are going to have to live.

For unselfish people like you—yes, you are unselfish, at least in what I've seen of you—the idea of massive future prosperity, enough wealth to meet the challenges of climate change, seems like a "convenient truth." But when you look closely, it isn't. The invitation to postpone action is fiction. A *dangerous* fiction. (*Pause.*) Sorry. That was a bit strong.

Joe: No. You were eloquent. It's a lot to reply to. (*Pause.*) Of course, you haven't told me your plan of action and how it would affect the economy. I could ask whether acting will make the economic future worse. The cure could be worse than the disease. But I won't. That would be another conversation—and a long one at that. Not for this evening.

Jo: I agree.

Joe: But another time . . . I hope. (*They smile at one another.*)* You've answered one of my points. My idea that ignoring the

---

*That future conversation might proceed along the lines of *Greek Idyll* (Chapter 4).

climate threat and building the economy might be the best way to help our descendants. Not as plausible as it initially sounds. You're right there. (*Pause.*) What about the other one? Don't we have greater responsibilities to fix problems we can see right now? Affecting people around us—and in all those other dying communities.

Jo: No. Of course, we *do* have a responsibility to help them. Just as we ought to prevent disasters for people who come after us. Both groups count. I don't think we can say one group counts *more*. It would be wrong to do everything for one and nothing for the other.

Joe: Are you saying that all people, no matter where or when they live, have a claim on us? An equal claim?

Jo: Yes . . . and no. Yes to the first bit, no to the second. It's hard to explain.

Joe: Give it a try.

Jo: Well, everybody who is in trouble has a claim on our help. But we're limited in what we can do. The challenge is to find a way to balance all the claims. A fair way. One using whatever resources we have to meet as many of the most urgent demands as we can. Not slighting any group.

(*Pause.*) When I volunteer, I leave the boys for three hours or so. I could stay home. Save the money I give Sophia. Add it to the account I keep for them. Maybe I'd also be less tired, less irritable in the morning. So, by working on behalf of future people, I take away from things I could do for the boys. I'm less of a good parent. But when I think about it—as carefully as I can—I don't see myself as neglecting them. I'm pretty sure the balance I make isn't perfect. Probably there's *no* perfect balance. But the one I strike seems reasonable. I think I could defend it to the boys—and to the future people. If they were here. Which, of course, they're not.

Joe: I get your point about the environment in which your kids will live when they grow up. You care about the future because you care about them. So you want to make sure things aren't too terrible in the next seventy, eighty, years. But, as I understand the predictions, dreadful things aren't going to happen—at least not here—during your kids' lifetimes. Maybe in distant parts of the world. Nothing to affect them, though.

Jo: We could argue about that. Can what happens to this country be separated from what goes on in the rest of the world? And what about the heat waves, storms, droughts, and floods that will directly affect us? But that's not really the point. Even if our nation serenely rides out the storms of the boys' lifetimes, even if the terrible effects of global warming come a century from now—and they will come eventually if people don't act!—we have a responsibility to try to prevent them. (*Pause.*)

My boys give me a stake in the future. Even in the distant future.

Joe: That's what I don't understand. Maybe I'm being obtuse, but I can't see how the people who will live in 2200 (say) matter so much to you. What are you to them, or they to you? All around you there are people, people you know or you bump into on the street, friends and neighbors, who have real, clear, urgent problems. You've been there, in the years of struggling for a job. Not just being without money. But the drumbeat of rejections. You come to see yourself differently . . . because others see you differently. I've been there. Seen the expressions on my friends' faces . . . as you probably did with your parents. You lose your self-respect . . . and any hope . . . (*Pause.*)

And it's not just the job situation. So many other big problems. There are lots of kids who go to awful schools and who'll have to struggle even more than we have. Homeless people. People who don't have the medical care they need. And their families. Their children.

Lots of things are falling apart all around us. There's so much to fix. Why be so focused on the distant future?

Jo: You're right. We ought to attend to all the problems you've brought up—and more. I feel that just as you do . . . especially when I remember the years of wondering if I'd ever regain my independence . . . if I could hope to offer the boys the opportunities I wanted for them . . . (*Pause.*) But we also have to protect future generations . . . from similar things . . . or much worse. Even people who will live centuries from now. (*Pause.*)

Being a parent has been so important for me. It's transformed my life in ways I could never have imagined. I hope one day my boys will understand that, and feel the same joy I've felt . . . it hasn't all been anxiety . . . when they have kids of their own. I also hope I'll be part of their kids' lives and be able to watch *them* grow up. So I'll have a further stake in the future. I'll worry about the world *they'll* inherit.

Does that make any sense?

Joe: Yes. I think I see it. Not that I've had that experience. Not yet, at least. (*Pause.*) But I don't think it takes you very far. Maybe into the middle of next century. Certainly not to the more distant future.

Jo: I think it does. You see, my worries about the future for any grandchildren I might have—and who knows whether that will happen?—the boys are only little—don't just come from the relationship I would have with them. There's another source of concern. My hopes for the lives the boys will lead. I imagine them caring about *their* kids in the way I care about *them*. So they'd be unhappy—too weak a word!—if they thought their children's lives would be difficult, would be blighted even. Since I want their happiness, I have an independent reason for wanting the ones they care about not to suffer.

And, in a strange way—I can't say it very clearly, but it's something I feel—that extends. I expect the grandchildren—and it's weird to talk about them so definitely—to worry about any kids *they* might have. I expect my boys to be concerned about *their* grandchildren. So my interest in the future goes one generation further. And beyond that. It's like a long chain, continuing indefinitely.

But you probably think I'm talking nonsense . . .

Joe: No. Not *nonsense*. Not at all. (*Pause.*) Listening to you, watching you as you talk about the boys, it's obvious how deeply you feel. It makes me sense a lack in myself, that I don't have such strong feelings.

(*Pause.*)

But I wonder. Don't these worries diminish? Start to fade away, the further you go into the future? Aren't you *more* concerned about the boys than about any kids they might have? And so on down the chain?

And maybe there comes a point at which the anxieties die out entirely? Perhaps around the middle of the next century?

Jo: I think you're right. At least partly. I *am* less worried about the more distant future than I am about what happens in the next few decades.

But I don't think my worries fade away as quickly as you suppose. Not by the middle of next century. Maybe by a thousand years from now. It's hard to fix a definite point. (*Pause.*)

Some years ago, I read an interesting book. By the British mystery writer, P. D. James. *The Children of Men.* This one isn't a mystery, though. Have you read it?

Joe: No.

Jo: OK, well, the central idea is that human beings become sterile. They're unable to have any more kids. So the characters in the book can foresee a future in which humanity becomes extinct. When I read the book I imagined being in that situation. Vividly—it's very well written. I found it horrific. If something like that happened, I'd feel my whole life was diminished. Suddenly senseless.

I'm not a conventionally religious person, but I do want to see my existence as having some point. And if it didn't connect with the lives of others, I couldn't do that. People who would outlive me. Linked to further people. For a long while.

Joe: But it couldn't be forever . . . Whatever we do, there's bound to be a time when the planet will become uninhabitable for human beings. A time when our species goes extinct.

Jo: Yes. You're right of course. But it matters to me that it isn't tomorrow. Or next century. Or even the century after that.

I guess I'm agreeing completely with the point you made earlier. My concern for the future does fade. If human beings go extinct in a million years, that doesn't seem anywhere near so dreadful. On the other hand, it doesn't die away as rapidly as you imagine. It remains really strong for a long time. For the period in which human lives will be affected by what we do—or don't do—to limit climate change.

(*Pause.*)

I'm not satisfied with what I've said. It doesn't really express everything I feel.

Joe: In what way?

Jo: Well, it was right to start with the boys. At least, I think it was. They're the focus of my concerns for the future. (*Pause.*) But it doesn't stop with them. There's more.

You talked about neighbors, friends, acquaintances, fellow citizens. How lots of them are struggling. You're quite right to think something should be done to help them . . . to lift them out of the binds they're in . . . give them real hope again. But also to protect the people like them who'll live here in the decades, the centuries, to come. It shouldn't be all for one generation, and nothing for the others, or all for today at great cost to what happens tomorrow.

And I feel the same need for balance when I think about people in other countries. In many parts of the world, people suffer terribly—lots of them facing far greater difficulties than those you and I experienced. Don't we have a responsibility to them? And to prevent their descendants from suffering even more from the effects of climate change?

As I said before, I don't think we can neglect any group completely. We have to do something to fix the problems around us, here and now. We ought to protect the future citizens of our country. But we also shouldn't neglect the world's poor. And we should try to forestall conditions that would make global poverty even worse. (*Pause.*)

And there's even more. The flip side to all the things that haven't been fixed. Our society—and other societies too—have achieved important things. Inventions that have made people's lives easier, and discoveries that have saved lives. Political institutions that have increased freedom. Rich cultures from which we can sample. We can't let that decay and lose all the things people value in their lives.

So we have a duty not just to preserve the natural environment, but to conserve our human heritage. (*Pause.*) Sorry. I'm rambling . . .

Joe: I don't think so. What you've said fits together. It's a coherent perspective on things. (*Pause.*) It's also very ambitious and demanding. How could we possibly do everything you ask?

Jo: We can't, of course. Not completely and certainly not immediately. Probably not even in the coming centuries. (*Pause.*) But we can do some things, and attend to the most urgent problems. At the very least, we can give hope to those who suffer from them.

Joe: Doesn't that bring us back to where I began? How can the unknown difficulties of the future be more urgent than those we see in the world today? Either those arising here, or the even more terrible sufferings of the world's poor.

Jo: Because dreadful as present conditions are, in many respects, climate change is going to make them far, far worse. Many more people affected and feeling more intense misery.

I also think we may be able to do more than you suppose. We should ask ourselves what really matters. What are the things that make the difference in people's lives? What can we give up without sacrificing anything important? You know, in a tiny way—a *really* tiny way—I see some of the trade-offs I make like that. The money I save for the boys is better spent on them than having a meal out. Dedicating an evening to volunteering does something more important than anything I might do by staying home. The "sacrifices" are worth it.

Maybe we could do a better job of helping people—present *and* future people—if we thought about what really matters in life and what's dispensable. The frills.

Joe: It's a very demanding moral perspective. Are you asking people to give up everything they enjoy? To lead Spartan lives? No room for . . . this (*he picks up his wineglass and drinks the small amount of wine remaining in it*). If you'd sent the money you paid for the wine to the right charity you could have helped starving children in Africa.

Jo: I know. I've heard questions like that before. And they're serious. I'm torn.

(*Slowly, carefully.*) We shouldn't ask people to abandon what's most important in their lives. A world in which everyone gave up too much, sacrificing what they really care about, would be really bleak. When this conversation began, I started with what was most important to me. My boys and their future. That seemed natural.

But was it right? As I went on, I wasn't completely satisfied with what I was saying. There was this other voice. In my ear. Nagging at me. (*Pause.*) Well, actually, it was your voice, reminding me of something you said about all people—present, future, here, faraway—counting equally. Should we act to create as much happiness for human beings as possible? Without worrying about how equally it's shared? Should we make whatever sacrifices are needed to ensure that the most fundamental human rights are honored? At least to the extent we can. When I start to think in those terms, I feel I'm ignoring my special relationship with my boys. I wouldn't be caring properly for them if I treated them on a par with distant children. But then it seems to me that everyone's voice, everyone's needs, ought to count. Aren't I being partial, even selfish, in focusing on my boys as I do?

Joe: That's surely too harsh. (*Pause.*) Listening to you this evening, I've learned something about you. (*Very slowly.*) If you didn't give your kids a special place in your thinking . . . in your caring . . . you wouldn't be who you are. You wouldn't be you without your deepest . . . your closest . . . concerns. Maybe . . . I'm fumbling here . . . to be a person . . . an individual . . . is to care about some things so much . . . so much that you can't act to do a lot of good elsewhere. . . . There are limits to the demands on you.

Jo: Thanks. You've said the sort of thing I often say . . . when I try to reassure myself. (*Pause.*) There seem to be these two perspectives. One is partial. Centered on what you called my . . . closest concerns. The other one global, focused on humanity in general. How can I reconcile them?

(*She drinks the end of her wine. Then very slowly.*) Here's the best I can do. I imagine a gigantic conversation. Lots of people, including the ones around us who are in trouble, as well as all those distant people who suffer terribly. Future people who feel the impact of climate change are part of it, too. And people who might be able to help, like you and me. But others whose lives are a lot more secure than ours are also involved. And, of course, the boys.

We all get together and talk about what might be done, and how we can use whatever resources are available to address all the different problems. Everyone brings their own point of view. Their sense of what matters to them. *Their* closest concerns.

They learn about the situations of the others and about what's important to the others. They try to see things from the others' points of view, and look for a balanced plan for tackling the problems people face. One everyone can live with. Not necessarily anyone's favorite but something all can acknowledge as reasonable and fair.

So, in one sense, everyone gets treated equally. Their claims are recognized and discussed. On the other hand, the individual points of view are appreciated and retained. I hope that provides an appropriate compromise between the global way of thinking and the partial perspective.

Of course, it's really silly to think of a conversation like that as ever happening, but it sets a standard for balancing rival demands. We ought to be aiming for policies that would live up to that standard. Policies in harmony with what all those people would settle on.

Joe: It's an interesting idea. But mightn't some of your participants be greedy? They might favor a kind of life that demands a lot of the world's resources. Imagine—"My way of life, my identity, is bound up with owning palatial residences in a number of major cities, in having private jets, etc., etc." Would it be reasonable to treat that kind of attitude as sacrosanct?

Jo: Of course not. If all the discussants were trying to engage the perspectives of others—*really* trying to find a solution everyone could live with—people who began by saying that sort of thing would have to scale back. They'd come to see their demands as completely out of whack with those of the vast majority of human beings. They'd begin to recognize that they could have a meaningful life with far less.

Joe: But you don't think the same might apply to you? That as you presented your own perspective to others who have far less than you have—people who struggle for the bare means of subsistence—the kind of life you want for your boys might appear luxurious in similar ways?

Jo: (*Reflectively.*) I don't think so. I think even the poorest people in the world would understand what I want. They'd see themselves as hoping for the same—a secure, healthy, rewarding life for their own children. I hope they wouldn't want to take things away from me, but rather to ask me—and people like me—to take steps to provide them with the similar things they lack. I also believe it could be done, and that we could address their problems without sacrificing what's most important. We can avoid making life joyless and unsatisfying for everyone.

Joe: Even if we also take the steps you want to take to limit the threats from climate change?

Jo: (*Smiles.*) You're leading me towards the conversation we said we'd postpone. What kinds of actions are needed, and how much will they cost? But we shouldn't go there tonight. (*Glances at her watch.*) It's too late.

Yet I do want to say one more thing. Suppose I gave up volunteering at the climate center, and focused on some other problem. Or just stayed home with the boys. Then there'd be this different voice in my head, the voice of the people of the future, talking as they would in my imaginary conversation. I think I know what they'd say.

"Climate change has made human existence precarious for most human beings. And that's going to go on for centuries. Maybe as long as the human species continues to exist. Many of the world's economies are in ruins. Famine has taken the lives of billions. We're prey to devastating outbreaks of disease. These possibilities were clearly foreseeable, but you, who were warned of them, chose to do nothing. Minor disruptions of your comfortable habits were considered too large a price to pay to ward off "nebulous" threats to the lives of vast numbers of people you would never know. We don't suggest that you should have sacrificed the kinds of things you needed to live worthwhile lives, or crippled your own productivity so we could enjoy the kinds of ease you were unwilling to give up. Our demand is merely that the burdens stemming from climate change should have been fairly distributed across the generations. You should have done more, so we might suffer less. But you ignored the call to action, putting our lives at risk. Many of us have paid with everything we had for your indifference."

I just don't know what I could say in reply.

(*Pause.*)

Do you?

Joe: There's no short reply. (*Pause.*) It all depends on details. On what can be done to limit the dangers from climate change. On how we'd need to modify our lives to do what's needed. On what the consequences of those modifications would be. (*Pause.*) And that's the conversation we've decided not to have. At least for tonight.

(*He stands up.*) But I should go.

(*They walk together to the apartment door.*)

Thanks for this evening. As you said, it wasn't what I'd anticipated. (*Pause.*) But good. Really good.

(*He presses her hand. She returns the pressure.*)

Till tomorrow then. At work.

Jo: Yes. (*Pause.*) Thanks for what you said. For being frank and sympathetic. And for listening. (*Pause.*) Good night.

Joe: (*Opening the door.*) Good night. (*He goes out.*)

(*Jo bolts the door behind him. She returns to the living room. Picks up the wineglasses. Looks down at the coffee table. Straightens the picture. Smiles.*)

Jo, Conflicted

Jo is torn between two perspectives. The partial perspective, from which she begins, directs her care for her boys. Providing that care is not only the center of her life, but also what structures her life. Without it, she would be a different person. And if she had no similar alternative structure in her life, nothing to center what she wants, she would have no identity. She would hardly be an individual person at all.

Yet she feels the pull of the global—humanitarian—perspective. From that perspective, her boys have no greater claim on her than any other human being. Her conflict lies in the difficulty of reconciling these two perspectives.

Many religions develop the wider perspective by demanding sacrifices. They ask their adherents to devote themselves to alleviating the sufferings of others, even at great personal cost. Famous passages in the Gospels, for example, urge followers of Jesus to give up everything they have and to minister to the least fortunate. Ties to particular people, to parents or to children, apparently play no role. Yet, in practice, very few Christians, even those who are most devout and whose conduct consistently appears most admirable, live up to so demanding a standard.

If Jo were a religious person, she might base her concerns for the future on a much less exacting precept. The major religions often articulate views about the environment by appealing to a notion of stewardship. We are responsible for protecting the planet (perhaps the planet that has been "given to us"). We are temporary guardians, whose care for our earthly home will enable later generations to live in it and to take their turn in the work of stewardship. Failing to take steps to prevent it from becoming unsuited for human habitation would be to neglect the task we are asked to fulfill.

As she tells Joe, she is not a conventionally religious person. When she wrestles with ethical questions, she doesn't appeal to the doctrines presented in any sacred scripture. In trying to formulate the global perspective, she follows the lines of well-known secular ethical theories. She considers the idea that right actions are those producing the greatest amount of human welfare—where the joys and sufferings of future generations are to be included in the enormous sum. She reflects on an alternative approach, one acknowledging fundamental human rights, where people as yet unborn are viewed as having the same rights as those who live now. Whichever of these frameworks Jo might adopt, indifference to future people would be forbidden. We ought to care about our descendants and the world they will inhabit.

These ethical approaches emphasize a compelling idea—the idea of equal moral standing. It doesn't matter where, or when, somebody lives. That person should count equally in moral deliberation. So, it seems, justified concern for others should be impartial. We should respond to those with the greatest need. Yet that conclusion can easily appear too demanding, too abstract, too impersonal, even inhumane. It troubles Jo.

Nor is it hard to see why. Personal projects, typically including special ties to particular people, matter to all of us. Abstract "concern" for humanity that ignored or overlooked these specific relationships would miss the point. To care for another is to be committed to making that person's life go well—and for the life to go well the relationships at its center must grow, blossom, and bear fruit. The partial perspective, which focuses care on particular individuals, giving them priority, cannot be overridden by a lofty universalism in which what is most deeply human vanishes.

What makes a human life a meaningful one, a life that goes well? As ancient thinkers in many traditions already saw, an existence of uninterrupted pleasure isn't enough. If you spent your days, months, and years inside your very own orgasmatron (the machine from Woody Allen's *Sleeper*), your life wouldn't amount to anything worthwhile. Doctors cannot provide the most severely disabled children with worthwhile lives simply by palliating their pains and stimulating whatever pleasure centers remain in their disrupted brains. Human lives that go well are those in which people *achieve* something, something that matters to them and to others.

Many philosophers have viewed the worthwhile human life as centered on a project, something a person aims to accomplish. It is also widely agreed that further conditions are required to develop the approach. First, it's important to avoid taking the only worthwhile projects to be exceptionally large ones. Your project doesn't have to be to change the political direction of your country or to write the great novel in your language. Jo's project of providing her boys with opportunities for meaningful lives of their own is quite worthy enough. Second, the project isn't decided once and for all at some moment of great resolve in late adolescence or early adulthood. It can be, almost always is, something that evolves and grows throughout a lifetime. Third, the pursuit of it must meet with some success. A life devoted to worthy aims that are always frustrated would be sad, and often tragic. Fourth, the life must be the person's own. When people are forced into particular forms of existence, especially when the coercion arises from traditional expectations about what human beings "like them" should do—when options are sharply narrowed on the basis of gender or ethnicity or class or caste—something important is lacking. Even when those who are coerced profess happiness with the roles thrust upon them, they have been deprived of the chance to make up their own minds about how to live. Finally, a meaningful project must be one conceived as making a positive difference to the lives of others. It should be connected to other people, typically to some who will continue to exist, even after the life is over. Jo recognizes this point. Part of the worth of her own life consists in its resonances in the future. Like a stone thrown into a pool, her doings will cause ripples in the lives of others after her death. Of course, as Joe sees, the ripples will not—cannot—persist forever. But they will last for a while, and that is enough.

Projects meeting these five conditions are crucial for human lives to be valuable. If lives centered on such projects vanished from the Earth, the loss in value would be immense—indeed, it would be hard to identify anything valuable among what remained. So, while Jo appreciates the idea that each person counts equally, has equal moral standing, she cannot abandon the stance from which her boys are special. Her conflict arises from the pull of the universal and the contrary pull of the partial.

How, then, are the two perspectives to be integrated? The ethical approach Jo sketches grounds the correctness of ethical judgments in the fact that they would emerge from a particular procedure. To act rightly is to behave in a way that would be endorsed by a special sort of deliberation. If the course of action you would follow would be one commended by a group of people, sufficiently inclusive to represent all points of view, equipped with the best available information, and committed to find policies for conduct that all could accept, that is the best you can do. In the imaginary conversation about what is to be done, the projects of the participants are taken seriously. They are not automatically asked to abandon their personal ties in the interests of contributing to some panhuman enterprise. The global perspective becomes fundamental to the *procedure* for working through ethical questions: all affected parties have equal standing in the ideal conversations that set the standard for ethical decisions. But the participants bring to the conversation their own structured lives, their individual projects, and their special relationships.

Behind the speech Jo imagines the beleaguered future people as making lies a recognition of this fact. Conversationalists represent the various points of view, each embodying its particular partialities. Their varying projects, with their ties to different people, give rise to specific needs and claims. The discussion seeks a way of treating all the claimants fairly. It looks for a distribution of benefits and burdens with which all are prepared to live. Thus the representatives of future generations do not ask us to give up everything so that they may live in ease, but simply to undertake a share of the sacrifices, one that we and they can accept.

Yet, as Joe points out, although the personal projects people bring to the discussion are not automatically dismissed, they are not immune from revision. The distant poor and the people of the ravaged future should not ask us to abandon pursuing *some* worthwhile project. But they might inquire whether the projects we have framed for ourselves require everything we deem necessary. Perhaps they could be scaled back and remain valuable. Perhaps by reducing them or modifying them in some respects, we might demand less—and thereby be able to contribute more to allowing others opportunities to live worthwhile lives.

Everything depends on the details—details about what is needed to secure the future and what it will cost (the issue Jo and Joe agree to postpone). Yet the (sometimes difficult) conversation in Jo's apartment yields important lessons. The people of the future do have standing in our ethical life. We should try to summon up their voices and listen to what they say. On the other hand, we—and they—should appreciate the human ties in our lives, the personal projects people have. The partial perspective must be given due credit, for it grounds the value of any human life. Finally, our connections to others, especially to those who will outlive us, are the sources of significance in our finite lives.

So, from both perspectives, we should care about the future. The human future.

FOUR

WHAT CAN BE DONE?

Greek Idyll

A balmy September evening. A taverna at the edge of a wide bay. A few tables are occupied by Greek families, who are enjoying leisurely meals. Jo and Joe, a couple in their early seventies, sit at a table adjacent to the sand. Both appear fit and active. They have finished eating, and look over the water.

The moon has risen. Its shimmer stretches from a distant islet towards them.

Joe: I love this place. Never tire of it.

Jo: I know. I feel the same. (*Pause.*) It's always wonderful to come back.

Joe: It really is. We should come more often, and for longer. (*Pause.*) I had thought . . . when we retired . . .

Jo: . . . that we'd have more time. Travel more. (*Slyly.*) But don't you want to visit the grandchildren?

Joe: (*Smiles. He has heard this line before.*) Of course I do. (*Pause.*)

I want both. More visits to Greece, more time with the little ones.

Jo: And what gets cut out? Less gardening? Giving up your big plans?

Joe: You know that's not it. Sure, I've always loved growing things. (*Pause.*) But the big projects—the rock garden, the rose garden—were a reaction. Things I threw myself into because you were out so much.

(*He looks at Jo.*)

Since you really started to be active with this climate business.

Jo: Joe . . . don't be angry . . . please. We've had such a lovely time here. And this evening is especially beautiful. Let's not spoil it.

Joe: I'm sorry. I didn't mean to sound resentful. It's not that I'm dissatisfied. I just wish we had more time to see the grandkids . . . *and* to visit our favorite places . . . to come here, most of all . . .

(*Pause.*)

You know, I'd be happy to scale back and stop being so fanatical about the garden. If you did the same. (*He looks at her.*) Can we make a deal?

Jo: You mean "Spend less time on climate action"? I'm sorry, Joe. Much as I'd love to travel more . . . have more time with you . . .

But it's too important. If I cut back, I'd feel guilty, as if I were indulging myself. Partying while the planet sizzles. It sounds a bit melodramatic, I know, even silly. But I can't give up. I have to go on. For the people who will live after us.

(*Pause.*)

You know what I'd really like. If you *did* scale back on the gardening. If you joined me . . .

Joe: (*He looks at the moonlight on the water.*) Jo, you've asked that before. And I don't see how it's any different now. You know how I feel.

(*Pause. He glances back to the sea.*)

I really admire the dedication you show . . . you and your friends in the movement. Your perseverance. But it seems . . . quixotic. Hopeless, even.

(*He looks at the sea.*)

You know we agree about the problem. This place . . . this lovely place . . . who knows how long people will come here? Maybe in thirty, forty, years it'll be sunbaked . . . arid . . . withered trees . . . no flowers . . . charred hillsides where the fires have swept through . . . all the people gone. And similar changes . . . awful changes . . . in so many other parts of the world. So much disruption of people's lives. Poverty. Squalor. Misery.

But a political movement can't help to stop that. Nothing to be done. Nothing people like us can do. Nothing our political leaders can do. We can only hope. Maybe there'll be some technological breakthrough. Something to fix the mess. We can only hope and wait. Cultivate our own garden.

Jo: So gloomy, Joe? That's not like you. Especially not when you're *here*.

Joe: Well . . . maybe I sound too pessimistic. I haven't completely given up hope. But I don't think the problem's going to be solved in your way. Grassroots political action. Pressure on world leaders. Summit meetings and international agreements. Pledges to eliminate our use of fossil fuels. You're asking for fundamental changes in the ways people live.

Even if it happened, I suspect it would be disastrous, and send the economy into a tailspin. We'd leave our kids and grandkids even worse off, with nothing to draw on to adapt to a warmer planet.

Sorry! I'm sounding gloomy again. But I'm really dubious about that way of tackling the problem. If we have a chance . . . and maybe we do have a chance . . . it's going to come from science, from research. Don't you remember the big fuss about ozone and how we'd have to give up aerosols? No more deodorants, no more clean kitchen counters. And then it turned out the problem could be solved quite simply, by changing the technology.

So maybe there's a fix for the climate. That's where I'd put my money. Or my time, if I had the right training. Not in trying to get the politicos to work out a climate treaty.

Jo: (*She turns to look at the sea. Then, slowly, quietly.*) That's a bit more upbeat. More like my Joe. But not in another way. You've never been so blunt before.

(*She looks back at the sea.*)

(*Very slowly and quietly.*) So . . . you think what we're trying to do is counterproductive. Well-intentioned, but harmful. The cure we're trying to find would be worse than the disease. (*Pause.*) I . . . have to . . . answer that, . . . say why I think you're . . . profoundly wrong.

We have to talk this through. Even though it's a beautiful evening . . . in Greece . . . where our thoughts should be . . . happy . . . joyous . . . as they've so often been.

So let's try. May I . . . ?

Joe: (*Chagrined by his previous tactlessness, and impressed by her restraint.*) Of course. (*Pause.*) I'm sorry. I *was* too blunt. I should have realized how much this cause means to you. How much effort you've put in. Even if I disagree, I do want to . . .

Jo: . . . understand. Thanks, Joe. I'll try to explain, and you should tell me where you think I'm going wrong.

Joe: Clearly . . . but with a little tact . . .

Jo: Yes. (*She reflects.*) Well, let's start with your faith in a scientific solution. Why do you think there's *any* chance of a technological fix?

Joe: Aren't there all these ideas in geo-engineering? Like sucking carbon out of the atmosphere? Carbon capture and storage.

Jo: CCS.

Joe: And aren't there other possibilities as well? Shooting particles into the atmosphere? So it's not all pie in the sky.

Jo: Not all *pie*, no, but much less promising than you think. Actually, these are two very different types of program. *Negative* climate geo-engineering tries to prevent greenhouse gases from getting into the atmosphere. Or, when it's more ambitious, to remove some of the carbon we've already emitted. *Positive* climate geo-engineering accepts the existing level of carbon concentration. It usually tolerates increasing it, even increasing it indefinitely. We adjust the atmosphere to counterbalance the greenhouse effect.

And you're right. It's not all pie in the sky. The most popular approaches—negative and positive—rest on physical processes we know about. You were right to start with CCS. It's the main negative approach, and it's based on well-known facts. You know how deforestation makes climate change worse. Well, that's because trees absorb atmospheric carbon.

Joe: So maybe if we planted a whole lot more trees . . .

Jo: Oh Joe . . . you have no idea of the scale at which it would have to happen! Every year we emit a really large amount of greenhouse gases into the atmosphere. We'd have to plant trees over a lot of the Earth's land surface. Of course, the trees wouldn't instantly start to absorb a lot of carbon, and it would take plenty of extra energy to plant them and nurture their growth. You'd also have to keep planting, since the maximum rates of absorption tend to be while the trees are growing, usually when they're between ten and fifty years old. Reforestation can help a bit—a little bit. The real promise of CCS comes in finding ways of doing what the trees do, but on a far grander scale. Ways of sucking the carbon out, or preventing it from getting in in the first place.

Joe: OK. But there have been successes in doing that. CCS actually works.

Jo: On a small scale, yes. For a long time—nearly a century—people have been trying to reduce all sorts of emissions from industrial plants. Some gases you can force through a wet mix so that what eventually escapes isn't noxious. But if you want to reduce the emissions of carbon dioxide, from factories and, even more importantly, from power plants, you need a different method. The carbon dioxide must be captured, either before or after the fossil fuel is burned. Then it has to be compressed, transported—typically by pipeline—and buried in some safe place where it won't leak back into the atmosphere.

People know how to do this on a small scale. There are techniques for capturing the carbon—some before you burn it, some afterwards—and for compressing it. The best sites for burial are deep geological strata. If you dumped carbon into the sea, you'd accelerate the acidification of the oceans. Anyway, land deposit is more convenient for most of the sites at which large amounts of CO_2 are emitted.

CCS can help in limiting climate change. But it can't do the whole job, or even that much of it. For starters, the known CCS systems are imperfect. Running a power plant with CCS uses more energy, and a small percentage of the CO_2 escapes the trap. On the—small—scales so far attempted, between 80 percent and 90 percent of the carbon dioxide is caught. Welcome, but not something we could tolerate forever. More importantly, nobody knows how to scale CCS up, to build devices to handle the emissions of all the world's major power plants, and couple them to a network of pipes to provide a secure burial for the concentrated gases. And even if we could set up that system, the global cost would probably be enormous.

Joe: Now who's the gloomy one? It sounds to me like a promising approach. Why not have faith in human inventiveness? Scientists and engineers are always finding ways to do things people thought would never work.

Jo: Well, I don't believe it's a law of nature that, if we need it, science and technology will produce it. Maybe it will happen . . .

maybe not. I don't want to bet the future . . . our grandchildren's future . . . on the hope that science will provide.

We should be pragmatic. Experimental. We're facing a real mess. Our best strategy is to try a number of options. And phasing out fossil fuels is more promising than you think.

Joe: I'm dubious. But I'll wait to hear what you have to say. At least you seem open to some alternatives to the radical changes that disturb me. What about positive geo-engineering?

Jo: Oh no! That's a terrible idea. When you do negative engineering you're trying to return the planet to a condition we know about. We've been there before. We can be confident about what it'll be like. No nasty surprises.

But positive geo-engineering goes for broke. It launches us into a space we've never inhabited. Who knows what could happen?

The most popular idea is to "seed" the atmosphere with sulfur particles . . .

Joe: (*Excitedly.*) Yes. I've read about that. And it's not just fact-free speculation. We know volcanic eruptions spew out ash. And the ash contains sulfur. And there's a cooling effect because solar radiation is reflected. So the process *is* understood. Why not try to manage it?

Jo: Because we haven't a clue about how to strike a reasonable balance, and get the levels of cooling we need. The geo-engineers would have to experiment. They'd play around—like cooks. Add a bit of sulfur. No, that's too much. Now add a bit more carbon. Whoops! We've overdone it. Hoping all the time there's no unanticipated side effect.

So our descendants . . . our grandchildren . . . have to hold their collective breath while they wait to see how the experiment turns out? Remember, we're in this mess because people didn't know the consequences of what they were doing. They didn't know how industrialization would alter the climate.

Many of our past experiments with the environment haven't been rousing successes. Remember when we were young—all those dead rabbits on the hillsides? How did that happen? Because, decades before, Australian farmers saw the native animals, the marsupials, as annoying pests. So they introduced rabbits, who beat out their marsupial competitors, just as the farmers had hoped. The trouble was the rabbits bred . . . like rabbits. So then they wanted to control the rabbit population. They introduced the myxoma virus. It worked. Vast numbers of rabbits died of myxomatosis, all over the world. Leaving corpses on the hills we walked as children.

The same goes for the use of chemical pesticides. Things we don't know in advance come home to haunt us. Sulfur–carbon cookery is highly likely to turn up unintended consequences. Experiments that end badly. (*Pause.*) And we have only one atmosphere.

Joe: OK. I take the point. Better to stick to negative geoengineering. Hope we can scale up CCS. (*Pause.*) But what you've just said about our ignorance, about the dangers of experimentation, seems to me to undercut what you and your friends want to do. Aren't you trying to launch a massive *social* experiment? One that could easily backfire and wreck the economies of nations—if not the whole world. Suppose we try to give up coal and oil and gas, all those fossil fuels you hate so much. Aren't you worried about the changes that will result? Effects you haven't foreseen?

Jo: Oh, Joe . . . that's why I love talking to you . . . even when we disagree . . . you get it . . . see where the nub of the issue lies. (*Pause.*) Of course, I'm worried. That's why I emphasize being pragmatic. We have to experiment. But it's not *one* experiment. It's lots. And we can introduce safeguards, if we do the experiments right.

That's the short answer to your questions. But of course, it's too short to be convincing. You'll want details—and you shall have them.

(*She glances at the sea. The moon has shifted. The shimmer on the water is reduced.*)

But maybe it's too late? Enough for one evening?

Joe: No. Let's continue. It's a good conversation. So far. (*Pause.*) The night is yet young. And so are we . . . at least, young at heart.

Jo: (*Smiling.*) I hope so. (*Pause.*) So should I . . . ?

Joe: Yes. Go on.

Jo: Our group has a campaign. We advocate a transition to a state in which the emissions of greenhouse gases are cut to zero. Or maybe to something very close to zero. Maybe we should allow a little carbon indulgence—like an occasional fatty dessert. We can't know in advance, since we can't be sure whether there will be technological advances allowing for some small level of emissions. We think of the end-state as the sustainable world.

In this transition we have to eliminate the activities that cause the emissions. It might be done by simply giving up some way of behaving—"reducing" we call it. Or it could happen through finding a different way of doing things we want to do, one that avoids spewing out greenhouse gases. That's "replacement." You might reduce by giving up certain forms of travel—no longer spending your holiday on a Greek island, for instance. Or you might replace, by traveling to the same places, but finding a way to get there that doesn't involve fossil fuels—or, at least, considerably cuts down on the amount of fuel. Instead of going by plane, you sail.

The transition is going to involve some mix of these approaches. You have to reduce demand, replace the supply, or both. The more you reduce, the less you have to replace. And vice versa.

Joe: So what's the right mixture? How much should people give up? How can we replace our use of coal and gas and oil? And how quickly can we do that? What's the time frame for your transition?

Jo: Good questions. Just the right questions. I can't answer them. Nobody can.

Joe: But . . . but . . . but . . . that's just what frustrates me about this whole movement! I'm sorry, Jo. I know how committed you are. But how can you work for change whose consequences you just can't foresee? These are people's lives you're playing with. The lives of our kids and grandkids. You're telling me . . . telling them . . . "The future dangers of continuing as we have been are so bad, so terrible, that you should go in this direction, even though I don't know what the route will be or what the journey will be like." I don't understand how you can say that. How can you ignore the possibility that your transition might make things far . . . far . . . worse?

Jo: So let me try to explain. More carefully. (*Pause.*) You've given me a good analogy with your talk about routes and directions. I know how you love to hike. So imagine you've gone on a long hike, and have lost your way. You've found yourself in a dark wood, hemmed in by dense trees and bushes. Night is coming on, and the temperature is dropping rapidly. Maybe there are predatory animals around. In any case, it's very dangerous to stay where you are. You have to find your way out—before darkness falls.

Surely you'd look for some promising path. For glimmers of light through the foliage. You'd set out, and see how it went. All the time, you'd be assessing your situation. In light of what you found, you might change course. Perhaps you'd hear noises suggesting dangerous animals nearby. Or reach a dead end. So you'd adjust and try to find another way.

There wouldn't be any guarantee of succeeding. But you'd probably be better off than staying where you are, and trying to survive the night in a cold and dangerous place.

Actually, for my case, for making the transition to a sustainable world, human beings can do better than that. We're not restricted to a *single* way of trying to solve the problem—to choosing just one path out of the wood. Let me change the story. There are *lots* of you, together, lost in the wood. It's still just as dangerous—no safety in numbers. Now individuals and parties can try different escape routes. And suppose—this is where the story gets a bit fantastic!—you can all communicate with one another, and almost instantaneously regroup on any really promising path. The chances of getting out of the wood become much, much higher.

When you think about climate change, it's not a fantasy. It's really possible to try lots of things, communicate with others, and regroup quickly. Different countries can look at different ways of reducing and replacing. Even within a country, local communities can explore different possibilities. People can take stock of the successes and failures, and they can broadcast what they've found out. So the promising ways of handling the transition can be adopted everywhere.

Joe: But aren't the failures costly? And don't you assume unrealistic levels of international cooperation? Why should a country that's hit on some clever means of reducing or replacing share its secrets with its economic competitors?

Jo: Bravo, Joe! Once again you go to the heart of the matter. Those are real obstacles for the strategy of pragmatic experimentation we recommend. So, we have to find ways of overcoming them. I'll try to say how in a bit. But first, I'd like to be a little more concrete about how some parts of the transition might go. I want to identify some possibilities, not to chart a definite route, but to point in directions where there seems to be a glimmer of light between the trees.

So, can I dodge your questions for a while? Is that OK?

Joe: Yes. (*With mock sternness.*) But I shall want answers eventually.

Jo: (*Laying her hand on his arm; they smile at one another.*) And you shall have them, my dear. (*Pause.*) We'll get there. But let's talk for a little about reduction. People could do quite a few things to change their ways. To avoid emitting so much bad stuff into the atmosphere.

We could redesign cities and make buildings more energy efficient. We could introduce or upgrade systems of public transportation. We could change our roads so that solo commuting was much more unpleasant and carpooling or traveling by bus more efficient. People could be encouraged—or required—to limit their travel, and even substitute virtual conversations for face-to-face interactions. Governments could discourage living in monstrous apartments and houses. They could slap on a huge tax if you occupied more than so much square footage. Existing villas and mansions and estates could be turned into housing shared among a number of families. That's already happened in places like Berlin. All those things would decrease the energy budget.

Of course, I don't think we know which of these will work. Work, in two senses. First, make a real difference to our emissions. Second, be a change people could live with.

And there's a real biggie: agricultural reform. All around the world meat consumption is increasing. I know you worry about the conditions in which the animals are raised, but it's bad for the climate, as well. Some experts estimate that the emissions from meat-eating in 2050 could exhaust our budget of greenhouse gas emissions for that year. Our methods of raising animals as sources of food, particularly cattle, contribute at least 10 percent of the annual emissions right now. More than a few experts would put the fraction as high as one-third. The problem comes from using nitrogen-rich fertilizers to grow the feed—and from the waste the animals produce. Big Agriculture generates two potent greenhouses gases, methane and nitrous oxide. Give up meat and dairy products, unless they come from more traditional ways of farming, and the concentration of greenhouse gases in the atmosphere would increase at a significantly slower rate. Even if we did everything else the same. Which we shouldn't, of course. Agricultural reform would solve part of the problem—but only a part.

Joe: I'm glad you brought up this example. It's one of those ideas people often float in discussions about how to limit climate change. But—I'm sorry—I think it's out of date. It's been refuted. I read about a study done by really reputable researchers. It turns out that vegetarianism is worse for the environment than eating meat. Lettuce is three times worse than bacon for emissions.

Jo: (*Grins.*) Oh, Joe. You've been taken in. It's so easy in this general area, where there's so much spreading of misinformation. (*Pause.*) The leader of the team of scientists who did the work explained how it had been misinterpreted in the press. Here's what's true. If you ate the amount of lettuce that would contribute the same calories as a slice of bacon, the emissions involved in growing that lettuce—a *mountain* of lettuce—please don't try it!—would be extremely large. Whether they're three times as large as what it takes to breed and fatten a pig is disputed. But, of course, that's a *crazy* way to be a vegetarian. Nobody ever thought that *any conceivable* vegetarian diet would reduce emissions. Any sensible vegetarians would get their calories, protein, and essential vitamins in more efficient—and more tasty—ways. *Some* vegetarian diets can reduce emissions by a lot compared with *any* diet in which livestock are bred and treated in the ways Big Agriculture currently goes about things. Other vegetarian diets—like the silly "lettuce only" one—don't. In any case, if everyone's meals turned into exercises in tackling mountains of lettuce, the planet wouldn't be big enough to grow all the lettuce we'd need.

Joe: Fine. I was conned. But I have serious problems with some of the other things you said. Especially about travel and transportation.

Start off with the commuters. Workers have a hard enough time these days finding jobs, making ends meet, traveling to shifts at odd hours, being on demand when the bosses send for them. I wouldn't want to narrow their options.

Maybe you can *reduce* driving. Or *solo* driving, at any rate. But I don't think you can eliminate gas-fueled vehicles entirely. What about emergencies? No fire trucks? I also like having ambulances around. Especially as we get older.

And will air travel have to go? Jets, I'm told, contribute quite a lot of carbon. How will people move across long distances? Trains? So there'll be a railway line linking Paris and Vladivostok? Cape Town and Helsinki? Rio de Janeiro and Fairbanks? That doesn't help with some journeys people might want to take. Like across the Pacific. Or will there be a bridge across the Bering Strait? Does the expatriate South African who now lives in Rio have to go back to visit his family by taking the train through Alaska and Russia?

You did suggest substituting "virtual conversations" for the real thing. Talking to people through two computer screens. Of course, that works well—for some purposes. But not for all. Won't there be high-level negotiations requiring personal contact? Diplomacy? Or just keeping up with friends? (*More slowly.*) People we love. We talk to the grandkids "virtually" every week—sometimes more. But I wouldn't . . . you wouldn't . . . want that to be our *only* way of making contact with them. No chance to hold them . . .

Well, *we* could travel by train. The real loss would be for people on islands. And those who have left. (*Pause.*) As you know, I grew up on an island. Not many close ties any more. But some . . . friendships . . . deep ones. When I think about not being able to go back . . . it's a loss . . . a real loss.

(*Pause.*)

Jo: You're right, Joe. These are problems. Real problems. Maybe we can solve them in imaginative ways. (*Smiles.*) Bring back wind power. Bigger and better sailing ships. (*Pause.*) I don't know. That's why I keep harping on experimentation. Some group of people tries a particular change, and they see how it is to live with that change. Perhaps some things are real losses, while others can be accepted. Maybe a few are surprisingly better than things were before. In either case, they take stock of the savings in terms of emissions and assess whether the carbon reduction is worth the sacrifices they're making.

But it has to be hard, clear thinking all the way. If an approach to changing our lives seems intolerable in some respect—even though it delivers a lot of energy savings—we ought to ask if the problem can be overcome. Not simply give up, but build on partial successes. We should keep trying lots of experiments, exchanging information on how well or how badly they work—and then adopt and refine the better ones. But always with the goal in mind. We must make the transition. We have to get out of the wood.

Of course, reduction isn't the only approach. We can also try replacement.

Joe: You didn't say anything about the workers' commutes. Are they forced to use public transport? Or arrange car pools? Or will they all have electric cars? And can we rely on electric fire trucks and electric ambulances?

Jo: I hope so. I hope we'll see the day when the technology is good enough to make worries about electric ambulances seem as unfounded as thinking the plane is really likely to crash.

But your point about the workers is an important one. Whatever we do we mustn't make life much harder for people who are already struggling. On the contrary, it's important to combine our policies for the future with attempts to make their lives better. We're responsible not just for the world our grandchildren inherit—but also for improving the world in which people live now. Especially for the least fortunate.

I hope we can do that by a variety of means. Insisting on better wages and work conditions. Measures to debar bosses from summoning workers on a whim, or at the drop of a hat. And, in thinking about how they get to work, we could try making public transport really good. It's not impossible. But it will take work—and many more experiments.

(*She looks at Joe. Gravely.*) At bottom, though, we shouldn't think about these things in economic terms. What will generate monetary profit, what will incur financial loss. But always in *human* terms. (*Quietly.*) As you did with your questions.

Joe: Thanks. But you wanted to go on to talk about replacement. It's easy to see why. Replacement looks easier. We don't have to give up activities we value. Instead, we just do them using different sources of energy. No messy questions about what sacrifices we can tolerate and which ones we can't. Or taking an experiment with some pluses and some minuses and adjusting it.

I went in the direction I did because reduction sometimes seems impossible, or really costly in human terms. That's why I brought up the islands and the demise of air travel. (*Smiling.*) You mentioned silly worries about plane crashes. I guess I'd worry about the wind-driven or solar-powered airplane. In the end, then, certain kinds of visits won't be possible . . . not even for people who have migrated on the assumption they'd always keep in touch with those they left behind. Unless, of course, we go back to sailing ships.

Jo: You're right. For some things, all our experiments may fail. How to arrange travel to and from islands, for instance. Our best solutions might be far from perfect.

Joe: But I haven't yet expressed my real worry about replacement, and its effects on the economy of a country. Our country, say. Suppose we start to cut down on our use of fossil fuels. To keep things simple, I'm going to suppose we reduce a bit, cutting our energy demands by 20 percent. We'll then need to find clean energy replacements for 80 percent of the power we're currently using. We decide to spread that evenly over four decades. So we have to replace 20 percent of what's presently powered by coal and gas and oil during each of the next four decades. It's going to cost a lot.

Jo: Not as much as you may think. The costs of solar collectors and wind farms are dropping all the time. There are also possibilities for using water as a source of power, as well as geothermal energy. If all else fails, we might build some nuclear power plants . . .

Joe: But I thought you were adamantly opposed to nuclear power! Think back fifty years. The placards we carried, the demos . . .

Jo: I haven't forgotten. That was then. Now there's a bigger threat. Of course the risks we worried about should still be taken seriously. But they pale in comparison with the dangers from climate change. I've looked at the statistics. (*Pause.*) But I do feel a bit like Churchill and Roosevelt, picking Stalin over Hitler. I hope it won't come to that. People who know a fair bit about the technology tell me that solar energy and wind power are going to get cheaper and cheaper.

Joe: Who's the technology optimist now? (*Pause.*) Sorry. I couldn't resist. But mentioning nuclear power diverted us from the main point. Even if solar collectors and wind farms become a lot less expensive, the costs of storage and distribution—so electricity remains available when the sun isn't shining and the wind isn't blowing—are still going to make the switch expensive. People disagree about what the price tag is going to be, but nobody thinks these changes will be free.

Now let's compare us with another nation—one of our economic competitors. Suppose at the moment they aren't doing as well as we are. Their economy is sluggish. In lots of sectors their products aren't selling. We make similar things more cheaply—or provide higher quality for the same price. Their businesses are laying people off.

Our expensive program of phasing out fossil fuels is a boon to them. Our costs of production go up. Their products start to sell better. Unemployment for them declines—and increases for us. Now we're the ones with the sluggish economy.

What happens next? Do we stay the course? Keep going with the replacement program? If we do that, things are bound to get worse and worse. Our economy will collapse. Think massive unemployment, poverty, misery. Do you want that for our grandchildren?

Jo: (*Sharply.*) No. Of course not. (*Pause.*) I think you're missing a central point. Governments have to coordinate their actions. There have to be agreements . . .

Joe: More international cooperation!

Jo: Yes. That's an essential . . . an inevitable . . . part of the program. Some people might worry about that.* But surely not you, Joe. (*She pauses, regretting her previous irritation. Affectionately.*) As long as I've known you, you've wanted more cooperation among nations. Why so cynical now?

Joe: I haven't changed. I still prefer cooperation to competition, and I'd still like international agreements. But the agreements have to be enforceable. There must be ways of detect-

*As Joe does in Chapter 6.

ing nations that cheat, and punishing them—especially when the temptations to cheat are really strong.

As they are in this case. Suppose we make an agreement with our rival, so that we're both replacing fossil fuels on schedules we've negotiated. Maybe at the same rate, maybe at different rates. They start to do better than us. We suspect they aren't living up to the bargain, or are doing the truly easy things first. Picking the low-hanging fruit. Building solar collectors in the sunny places and wind farms on their exposed coasts. The least costly way to meet their targets for the first decade, but not something they could sustain for forty years. So we decide to shave a little, fudge the numbers, and pretend we're phasing out at the agreed on rate.

Lo and behold! Our economy starts to improve. Now, as their sales fall off, they're the ones to be suspicious. They think—rightly—that we're cheating. Quite probably they believe we're cheating more than we actually are, so they start fudging the figures and failing to do what they'd pledged.

You can see how this goes. It's a race to the bottom. And it would go faster, I think, if more countries were involved in the competition. In the end, the original program breaks down. Perhaps everybody discovers the continued high levels of emissions. When you add up the total from all the nations, there's lots of finger-pointing about who's responsible for how much. No real progress on the transition to the sustainable world. Just a political climate of reproach and suspicion.

Jo: You're right. It's a real problem. There *will* be temptations not to go along and to break the commitments you've made. But it's not insoluble.

Joe: I don't see how you tell who's cheating and who's not. Maybe you can measure what's happening in the atmosphere as a whole. How do you localize, and figure out that's it coming from here and not there?

Jo: That's really hard. Too hard, in fact. It can't be the right way to tackle the problem. But there's an alternative. Suppose we had a public signal, something that would reliably indicate whether or not a nation was doing its bit. It needn't be any direct effect of lowered emissions. Like local pollution going down.

Some economists who've thought really deeply about the problem have a promising idea. They imagine economically competitive nations forming a "climate club." Club members agree to phase out fossil fuels on a particular schedule—like the one you made up. The job gets done by changing the conditions of the marketplace. Each member imposes a tax on fossil fuels—a carbon tax. The tax has to be paid as the fuel is purchased. Consumers pay it when they fill up their cars or buy heating oil. Manufacturers and utility companies pay it when they order fuels for their factories or electrical plants. Of course, the costs are absorbed into the prices for all sorts of goods—food, housing, computers, tickets to sporting events . . . just about everything.

The economists sometimes justify the tax by saying it represents the "true price" of goods, a price that takes the "social cost of carbon" into account. I'm puzzled by that. Shouldn't the tax level be set so it makes the transition work? So it changes incentives encouraging individual people and nations to phase out fossil fuels at the agreed-on level? And isn't a specific rate of taxation justified, in the end, because it produces those effects?

But I'm getting out of my depth here. The main point is: the tax is public. Countries can tell when their competitors are imposing the tax, and when they're not.

Joe: Can they? In the relevant sense? Maybe the tax is on the books—signed into law and discussed in the newspapers. But everybody winks or looks the other way. Some of the time it gets collected—most of the time not. Consumers have more money. They buy more stuff. The economy booms.

So the "public signal" doesn't work. Cheating is still possible.

Jo: Maybe on a small scale. But you wouldn't need foreign "observers" as moles inside factories to expose widespread tax-dodging. Any typical stream of visitors from other countries would be able to tell. It's not so hard to discover when tax collection has broken down, or when governments and businesses are allowing that to happen. (*Pause.*) As all our friends around here have discovered. To their cost.

And that's another part of the story. Cheating nations get punished . . . and the lives of their innocent ordinary citizens are disrupted. For a climate club, the punishment would be really severe. If a country is expelled, it can still trade with the remaining members. But *everything* outsiders sell to members of the club is subject to a hefty tariff. Because the consequences of being caught are so awful, and because you're quite likely to be caught if you cheat, you have a strong incentive to live up to what you've agreed to do.

Joe: (*Reflectively.*) A clever idea. But will it work in practice? Won't the people who live in all the nations that join the club really suffer? And do all the members set the same rate for the carbon tax? I can imagine that could cause a lot of hardship. Suppose all the industries of one country are heavily dependent on coal. Wouldn't the citizens of that country suffer more?

Jo: Really important questions! Once again, I'm going to be evasive—annoying. I don't know the answers. Nobody does. Nobody can—at least, not in advance.

So climate clubs are going to have to experiment. Like ordinary clubs, there'll have to be rules. You start off with one set of rules and see how those rules work. You see if you're achieving the things you want, and whether there are bad effects you hadn't anticipated. If the rules don't work, you change them.

Maybe the club members begin by agreeing on the same taxation rate for all the countries. They put that into effect, and see how it goes. Of course, they need a standard for when things are working and when there are real problems. After the tax is imposed, some countries may thrive, and others struggle. The ones doing poorly are likely to plead for a lower tax rate. When would allowing that be fair, and when not? Is the right standard that all economies grow at roughly the same rate? Or that the relative ratios of growth remain constant? Or that the countries whose economies were more sluggish before they imposed the carbon tax should now grow faster than their more fortunate rivals?

All these matters need to be negotiated—worked out in continuing discussions among club members. Always with attention to the goal of phasing out fossil fuels *and* to the needs of people living now, especially those who struggle most. Obviously it won't be easy. Sitting here . . . in this country . . . recognizing the harshness . . . of the judgments of outsiders . . . supposedly fellow members . . . (*Pause.*) No. It won't be easy. The important thing will be to focus on the *human* consequences. On alleviating suffering, for today and for the future.

(*Pause.*)

What happens to ordinary people, depends on how their governments use the revenues from the extra taxes they collect. Do they just give it back to the citizens, as some economists suggest? Maybe divide it equally? Or give more to those at the bottom of the economic ladder—even though those people have probably bought less, and therefore paid less in carbon taxes? Or should they hold back a part of it? Invest in public goods? In improving their infrastructure? Or in education? Or in research to develop better climate technology? Or to build more wind farms?

You can probably guess what I'm going to say . . .

Joe: I think so. Experiment, experiment. Right?

Jo: Right. I'm sorry. I know I sound like a broken record. (*Pause.*) But it's the best way of finding the answers we don't yet have. The club can try out different ways of using the tax revenues and see what works. Again, the goal is to help the citizens *and* to ease the transition.

Joe: It's a rosy vision. I can't help feeling there's bound to be more suffering than you acknowledge. A serious dislocation of the job market. When you phase out fossil fuels, lots of people are going to be thrown out of work. Coal miners, for a start.

What are those people going to do? You keep talking about experiments. But the kinds of experiments you're talking about—social experiments—produce large changes in human lives. And you're proposing *lots* of them. Change on a large scale at a rapid pace. We've already seen the reaction to the "war on coal." The people protesting that "war" have a point. Social experiments have human costs. Any scientific experiment involving people has to protect the human subjects. *You* need to do that, too. How are you going to do it?

Jo: I agree. Something has to be done. That's why I said earlier that the experiments have to be carried out properly. Safeguards have to be built in, not only for citizens but for nations, too.

Actually, none of this is new. Workers have often been laid off. They've found themselves displaced because of foreign competition or technological change or shifts in tastes and attitudes. This case might be a bit better. After all, the experiments in climate action will be deliberate. Nations can try to anticipate what's needed to protect the likely victims. We surely want a "war on coal"—it's the worst of the fossil fuels. But we surely don't want a war on the miners.

The work environment is always changing. Sometimes it's because of a new technology: copyists went out with Gutenberg—and Xerox; blacksmiths declined with the arrival of cars; bookkeepers after computers. Sometimes fashions change; there aren't a lot of milliners around any longer.

Maybe orchestral musicians are an endangered species. The miners are joining a long historical parade of the displaced.

So how do we help them? Obvious answer: job retraining. Any humane society should have a safety net for the victims of changing circumstances. Part of that net must be effective programs for helping people learn new skills and find new jobs.

Joe: Nice in theory. But in practice it doesn't work so well. Job retraining has a very low success rate.

Jo: In some countries, but not in all. Sweden has a pretty ambitious program that seems to work well. Not perfectly, but a lot better than the efforts made in other places. We can try to build on that and . . .

Joe: Experiment. OK. OK. But I'm worried about all the people left behind. The people who struggle to find work. We're talking massive unemployment, particularly among young people. (*Pause.*) Look at the situation here in Greece.

If I were in my twenties, and not already committed to some safe line of work, I'd be *really* worried by your plans. The future you're shaping looks horribly insecure. How do I know there'll be a job for me? The sort of job I could do, or be trained to do.

Jo: (*Excitedly.*) Because there's so much to be done! Think of all we're going to need. Lots of solar collectors to be built and installed. Same for wind turbines. Maybe new dams. Desalination plants. On top of that, a whole new infrastructure has to be set up. Buildings to be reinsulated. Greatly extended systems of public transportation. You're pessimistic because you misread the lessons of the last recession. I know—in lots of countries, especially here in southern Europe, job retraining hasn't worked well. But the trouble lies with all this economic austerity. What we should do is *stimulate* economies. Provide public funding for the many—*many*—construction projects needed to cope with climate change. Retrain the workers for all these new jobs. The miners should have opportunities galore—and for much safer work.

Joe: Well, maybe. But will it go as you predict? I know some economists would agree with what you've said. Others see this sort of massive investment as burdening future generations with huge amounts of debt.

(*Pause.*)

Would you be willing to bet the lives of our children . . . and our grandchildren . . . on the success of your . . . optimistic . . . vision?

Jo: (*Pauses. Then quietly, but firmly.*) Yes. (*Pause.*) I would. (*Pause.*) So, I think, should you. For two reasons. First, there's a downside if you don't take the bet. You'd condemn them to a pretty awful future. Not only because of the direct consequences of a warmer planet, but also because of the shocks global warming is likely to bring to every nation's economy. Second, because it looks like a great investment. Creating so many opportunities for productive—and *necessary*—work.

But suppose your gloomy economists were right. We start to go in the direction I'm proposing, and it turns out badly. Then we change course, by learning from our mistakes.

Joe: Possibly costly mistakes. Maybe irreversible damage.

Jo: Not if the countries of the climate club hedge their bets. Remember, I allowed for different experiments in different places. So, if you think there's a genuine question about the value of stimulating the economy, creating lots of climate-oriented jobs, retraining people—all the things I've imagined—vary the policies across the member nations. Stimulus here, "fiscal responsibility" there. See which works.

And nobody has to suffer too much! Not if you have a safety net within each nation. And a safety net *across* the nations. Whatever you think about other institutions, nation-states are surely "too big to fail." The club rules have to include a section requiring the other nations to bail out members whose experiments have gone badly. Protections at different levels. For individual citizens and for whole countries.

(*Pause.*)

But I'm willing to bet that the stimulus approach will work. It'll create jobs, reboot economies, *and* provide a sustainable world for those who come after us. (*Pause.*) I'm willing to bet the future on it. Our children's and grandchildren's future.

(*Pause.*)

I think I've come to the end. Run out of words. Have I made any headway?

Joe: Some. (*Pause.*) More than I expected. (*Pause.*) But I wish you had been more specific. Told me exactly what's likely to happen.

Jo: I couldn't have done that. It wouldn't have been honest.

Joe: I know. And the uncertainty nags at me. I'm still bothered by the idea that your plans will end in disaster. Maybe the best I can do is to cultivate my garden.

Jo: (*Tenderly.*) Of course you're bothered. Success isn't assured. And it's so important to succeed. (*Pause.*) But even without knowing how things will turn out, we have to try. Not just retreat into the garden.

(*Pause.*)

Remember my hiking story? (*He nods.*) Imagine yourself in the wood. Staying still is *really* dangerous. If you strike out along a path, it may end up badly. You'll end up exhausted and forced to rest overnight in some other place. Maybe you'll be exposed to even greater dangers. There are no guarantees.

You know all that, as you stand, thinking about what to do. Perhaps that path, over there, will lead to safety. Or maybe to a better path. You can't tell.

(*Slowly.*) So . . . what would you do?

Joe: I'd try. Look for the most promising path. Follow it. Reevaluate as I went. (*Pause.*) Just as you said.

Jo: I thought you would. And I bet you'd succeed.

(*Silence. Joe looks down at his watch.*)

Joe: It's late. I should pay up. We should go to bed.

(*He goes into the taverna. Only one party remains, a large Greek family at a long table, evidently enjoying a celebration. The lone waiter sits at the back, watching a soccer match on a small television set. Joe approaches him. They exchange some words in fragmentary Greek and broken English. Joe pulls out a bill from his wallet. He indicates by waving his hands that he doesn't want any change.*

Jo has left their table. She has walked out to the edge of the sand, and stands looking at the sea. The night is very clear. Stars twinkle. Moonlight still shimmers on the water. Joe joins her.)

Joe: Shall we go then?

Jo: Let's wait. Just a moment or two. I want to fix this scene. In my memory. In case . . .

Joe: In case we don't come back again. (*Softly.*) So do I.

(*They stand side by side for a short while. Then, spontaneously and simultaneously, they turn to one another. They embrace.*)

Grounds for Hope?

Joe is frustrated by Jo's unwillingness to be definite. He wishes she could be more specific. In her view, however, giving more detail would be pretending to have more knowledge than she has. It would be irresponsible and dishonest.

But maybe, away from the taverna, with books and articles at her elbow and a computer in front of her, she could have done better? She could have cited the estimates given by the most insightful economists, people who have devoted decades to forecasting the social impact of climate policies. We agree with Jo's emphasis on experimentation. She is correct in suggesting that this is the best way to learn what we need to know. We endorse her pragmatism—try things out, and change course if necessary. Nevertheless, the estimates are worth the labor invested in producing them. Not because they tell us what is going to happen, or even what is likely to happen, but because they provide reassurance. Tackling the problem of climate change is not hopeless or inevitably counterproductive—not (in Joe's characterization) quixotic.

Proposals to replace reliance on coal, oil, and gas with renewable sources of energy provoke an obvious question: How much will it cost? Unfortunately, answering the question isn't entirely straightforward. One obvious difficulty involves predicting the likely course of technology in coming decades. There's been a welcome recent trend. Renewable energy technology has evolved at a rapid rate: the costs of photo-voltaic cells have dropped by 33% over the past few years, with a projected further drop of 25% by 2020. Analysts differ on whether we should rely on that trend continuing.

It proves to be tricky even to estimate replacement costs assuming the *present* level of technology. Much depends on what resources a nation has. Is there ample sunshine? Or areas subject to constant strong winds? Are there large, rapidly flowing, rivers available for generating hydroelectric power? And, even if the resources exist, is it *politically* possible to use them? Opposition to wind farms or large new dams is often fueled by strong desires to save the environment. One environmental cause—preserving a habitat for wildlife and conserving natural beauty—is given priority over another—limiting the impact of climate change. How these causes are eventually balanced affects the possibilities for replacement and thus the costs of a switch to renewable energy.

A second difficulty in measuring the costs lies in the varying needs of energy supply. Installing solar panels to provide electricity for individual homes in areas with abundant sunshine is relatively cheap. Providing a reliable supply of electricity to a large city, full of factories, office towers, public buildings, and blocks of apartments is quite another matter—even if abundant sunshine reigns. The technology for large storage of energy is still under development, and "reservoirs" for delivering electricity on demand to an urban megalopolis are expensive (to the extent that they are available at all). Hence, when experts consider the costs of replacement, they typically differentiate cases in which storage is only needed on a small scale (home production of electricity) and those where a large influx of power might suddenly be needed (supplying industrial areas or cities).

Finally, how do you measure the costs of a dam or a wind farm or a solar collector? A standard—and entirely sensible—approach is to consider the construction costs in the context of the lifetime of an energy delivery system. Analysts amortize the initial investment across the life of a wind farm, for example. But it would be cheating to consider just the turbines, the "windmills" that have increasingly dotted landscapes in the world's more prosperous countries. Parts of the storage and delivery system, the newly rebuilt electrical grid, also need to be included. But how, exactly? It depends on the number of renewable sources that will eventually be hooked up to the wider system. Just as it would be wrong to count the price of the roads and the water pipes and the power lines in the cost of the first house to be built in a new development, so too the first wind farm in a region should not automatically be "charged" with the entire amount of the delivery system on which its value depends.

Because of all these considerations, Jo's unwillingness to offer hard figures is perfectly reasonable. Yet something more can be said. Despite the recent drop in price for solar voltaic technology, in which light from the sun is converted directly into electricity, solar power would still be more expensive for any nation than using either natural gas or the cheapest (dirtiest) coal. Nevertheless, using solar voltaic technology in places where the sun always shines and where large-scale storage is not required would be relatively cheap. The increase in costs over the least expensive fossil fuels could well be below 10%. Indeed, in some circumstances, the replacement program might even save money. For many countries, there are "low-hanging fruit," replacement projects available at very low cost. Typically, however, the transition will involve meeting harder challenges. Some of the plants to be replaced must serve factories or residential areas with quite variable demand. Ancillary systems must be introduced to allow for a flexible supply. In assessing the costs for these cases, large uncertainties loom again. The best estimates suggest a price increase of 50% for replacements of this type. Because the technology is still under development, even the best estimates provide only soft figures. The costs might well be higher—although only a few pessimists would demur at taking a doubling of the price to be an outer limit. Given the information currently available, Jo's combination of optimism and pragmatism looks just right.

Yet one important issue about the economic future remains unaddressed. Joe's questions focus on the fortunes of an individual nation. He worries about the economic decline of their country, if it commits itself to making the transition. A stretch of the dialogue revolves around finding a way to international coordination, so that reduction and replacement can be carried out globally. (We'll ignore, for the moment, the fact that Joe and Jo are concerned with economic rivals, affluent nations that have already undergone industrialization. Developing nations will have their turn shortly, in the next chapter.)

Let's suppose global cooperation has been achieved. All nations have signed on to climate action. Doesn't Joe's worry about the *relative* wealth of nations now have a counterpart, an anxiety about the *absolute* prosperity of our descendants? Instead of asking a comparative question—"Will our country be able to keep up with its rivals?"—Joe might wonder whether the resources demanded for forestalling the perils of a warmer world are too vast. The transition Jo envisages would condemn our species to a radically impoverished way of life.

That global question isn't one for a late evening by the Aegean. We'll pose it more precisely. How much of the wealth produced worldwide is needed to make a transition to a zero-carbon state? Economists have offered calculations, using two different approaches. One is to think generally about global economic growth and about emissions worldwide, averaging over the effects of different schemes for replacing sources of energy. The other proceeds by dividing the economy into sectors and the world into regions, considering the costs of replacing fossil fuels by renewable sources across the various domains and for the different parts of the globe, before aggregating to compute the bottom line. An analysis of the two methods undertaken by Nicholas Stern (arguably *the* most distinguished economist in this area) and his colleagues suggests that they generate similar conclusions.

Stern's thorough exploration of the global costs originally set a figure of 2% of the world's wealth (the global gross domestic product [GDP]) per annum. In his assessment of the situation in 2009, he wrote:

> Many people, including myself, think 2% of GDP per annum is well worth paying to reduce the chances of temperature increases above 5°C from around 50% to around

> 3%. This is a dramatic reduction of the risk of genuinely disastrous outcomes for the planet, and the cost should not be viewed as large relative to the reduced threat it buys. Such a payment is not very different from the premium to insure against the probability of a disastrous outcome.

He goes on to remark that the "insurance payment" is equivalent to a "one-off 2% increase" in a price index, and that the effect of instituting an increase of this type would be to delay reaching the level world income would otherwise attain in 2050 by approximately six months.

The estimate is reassuring. Unfortunately, it is subject to debate. More recent analyses offer a more dismal assessment of the costs. They claim that a program adequate to keep the temperature in 2100 from being more than 2°C above preindustrial levels would reduce overall global consumption in 2100 by between 2.9% and 11.4%. That is, the people of 2100 will have (on average) between 88.6% and 97.1% of what they would have had, if business had continued as usual. The assessment obviously depends on figuring out the amount of wealth that would have been generated if business had continued as usual. It simply extrapolates growth for an increasing human population. Supposing annual growth rates of between 1% and 2%, the expected increase lies between 300% and 900%.

This is a perfectly reasonable way of trying to estimate global wealth in 2100, *given a determined effort to limit the effects of climate change*. But it's important to appreciate how optimistic it would be to suppose the rival total, *given business as usual*, to be 100% of what would be obtained from smooth extrapolation. After all, if we don't change our ways at all, the global economy will be affected by climatic shocks. Nobody can say what the costs of these will be. Any serious comparison of the global wealth given climate action with global wealth under business as usual should recognize how coping with the future climate will cut into economic growth—and how the cuts will be deeper if we continue our current practices of emissions. Quite possibly the actual resources available under business as usual would turn out to be less than 88.6% of the extrapolated figure: the world would be poorer in 2100 if nothing were to be done.

But we wanted to know the likely global wealth, taking account of the costs of climate action. Plainly there's a range of possible values—there is, after all, considerable daylight between the bounds given in the estimates of the percentage costs and of the rate of growth, between 2.9 and 11.4, between 300 and 900. We'll assume the worst-case scenario: take the lower value for the business-as-usual growth rate and the higher value for the percentage loss. A reasonable estimate of current global GDP is $75 trillion. Global wealth at the end of the century would then be around $200 trillion, given climate action, rather than around $225 trillion given a highly optimistic business-as-usual scenario (optimistic because it ignores climatic shocks to the world's economy). Surely this "all adds up to real money."

The important point for our purposes is that the world of the future is a long way from penury. Given the current global population (somewhat more than 7 billion) and the estimates for the population in 2100 (11.2 billion), global wealth per person would increase from under $11,000 to nearly $18,000. Hence it is possible to respond to the threats of climate change *and* to leave our descendants richer—although they would not be as rich as the figures of fantasy in the fiction that supposes continued dependence on fossil fuels, and continued economic growth untouched by climate change.

Yet we should be honest. Most of this is (informed) guesswork. As many economists have pointed out, the costs of adapting to a changing climate are impossible to assess with accuracy and precision. The estimates for business-as-usual scenarios are equally uncertain. Nobody knows exactly how rates of phasing out fossil fuels will affect increases in gmt; nobody knows whether there will be economic complications leading to periods of reduced growth, or whether technological developments will both lower the costs of replacing coal and oil and provide an extra boost to the world's economies. Existing macroeconomic models drown in assumptions—entirely reasonable, given the extent of our ignorance, but speculative nonetheless. The differences in the estimates of the bounds reflect this uncertainty. Reductions of 2.9% or of 11.4%, like growth of 300% or 900%, suggest rather different futures. Our descendants of 2100 would enjoy different lives if their average wealth were around $60,000 rather than $18,000. As many who have reviewed the calculations agree, it's clear that climate change poses a threat, and, unless we are badly mistaken, that it can be addressed without impoverishing those who will come after us. The obvious policy is to act as Jo recommends. To aim for a rapid transition to the sustainable world, and be prepared to modify our course if we encounter unanticipated difficulties (or, perhaps, unhoped-for successes).

The uncertainties are even greater if, as Jo maintains, addressing climate change is entangled, ethically and politically, with discharging responsibilities to people who face other urgent problems. Attempts to think through the social details of the transition, considering how to provide protections as people have to change jobs or to abandon things that matter to them, plunge discussions into areas where there is scant theoretical basis for calculating costs. We don't know what will need to be done; for many potential tasks we don't have reliable methods for discharging them, and we can't compute how much must be spent on solutions we cannot foresee. Adding these layers of indefiniteness to those already present in economic modeling, the idea of a clear plan whose costs and benefits can be identified in advance is a sham. We should stop pretending.

Yet one simple calculation might properly guide our thoughts as we consider the human future. The current global GDP allows between $10,000 and $11,000 to each person. That is roughly the level of wealth per capita available to citizens of countries like Namibia, Egypt, and Ecuador. If the per person GDP were to increase to $18,000—as in our worst-case scenario—each of us could live at the average level available in Bulgaria, Lebanon, or Mexico. For the entire human population to enjoy life as the Canadians, or the Finns, or the Australians do, each person's share of the global wealth would have to be four times as high as it actually is ($44,000 instead of $11,000).

If the (soft!) estimates of the analysts are right, that is not out of the question. We focused on the worst case. We might have considered the best. Suppose the economic growth is 900%, and the cost only 2.9%. Then the per capita wealth in 2100 rises to $60,000. Joe's unvoiced challenge—global economic decline—would be decisively answered.

What good are these figures, hedged as they are with provisos, imprecision, and uncertainty? They don't give Joe the guarantee he wants. They don't rule out the possibility of economic losses. But they do support Jo's optimism. The transition might turn out very well, and even the worst case is by no means disastrous. The prospects look better than allowing climate change to produce the effects we can reasonably expect. And the softness of the figures supports her pragmatism. There's so much we cannot yet know. Let's try it—experiment—and see.

FIVE

WHO PAYS?

Firebrand

Early afternoon. An office on a high floor of a multistory building. Joe, a well-dressed man in his early forties, sits at an elegant desk. He is reading the documents in a file, occasionally making annotations. Behind him large picture windows show an impressive urban skyline, currently bathed in warm sunlight.

There is a knock at the door.

Joe: Come in, please.

(*The door opens and Jo enters. She is a slender Nigerian woman in her late thirties. She is dressed in Western clothes—jeans, a plain T-shirt, and a worn denim jacket. Her only jewelry consists of three bangle bracelets on her left wrist. She moves gracefully, but rapidly, to the desk. Joe stands up, extending his hand.*)

Jo: Good to meet you, Mr. . . .

Joe: Joe. Call me Joe. Very good to meet *you*. I've heard a lot about you.

Jo: Oh . . . from the boys' network? (*Pause.*) Probably not flattering.

Joe: On the contrary. Several friends . . . (*with a slight emphasis*) not all male . . . suggested we should talk. (*He indicates a chair facing the desk. She sits.*)

Jo: (*Obviously regretting her bluntness.*) In any case, I appreciate your seeing me. I'm sure you're very busy. (*Joe nods.*) I haven't had many chances to make my case to people like you—especially in places like this.

Joe: How long have you been in this country?

Jo: Eight months now. But I've been in the North much longer. Almost three years. I spent a couple of years in Paris, but I made virtually no headway. So I decided to move here. It's been a bit better. (*Pause.*) Only a little, though. Sometimes I think I should give up and go back home.

(*Pause.*)

Then, out of the blue, I got your e-mail. (*She smiles. Her face lights up.*)

Joe: As I said, I've really wanted to meet you. To talk about your organization. What you're trying to do. But I'm being inhospitable. Would you like some coffee? Tea? Water? (*Jo shakes her head.*)

So tell me about your group.

Jo: (*Nervous; her sentences spill over one another.*) We're from all over Africa. We now have members from all the developing countries on the continent. We began early in 2011. After it became obvious that there wasn't going to be a serious aid program. Not one generous enough to help us develop using green technology. Some of our political leaders kept trying. They made the case for help. So we could grow economically. Provide all the things our people clamor for. The sorts of things that are so obvious . . . here. (*She gestures towards the window.*) Prosperity. Good jobs. Education. Access to everything the West has enjoyed for so long. Electricity. (*Pause.*) Especially electricity.

And we don't want to achieve that . . . some of that . . . by making the climate worse. We know what's coming. It'll hit us harder than most of the world. Droughts. Famines. Extreme heat. Probably plague. So we resist popular voices in our countries. You know—the ones urging us to forget about climate change and develop using coal and oil. As all of you did. (*Firmly.*) That can't be the answer.

Our leaders have tried to persuade . . . but yours have refused . . . again and again. No help . . . at least not on the scale we need. So it seemed to us, to some of us, that we had to do something different. Not to abandon the goals of development. But to work through different channels. To try to find allies in the affluent parts of the world. People who might exert political pressure, and make the case for a serious aid package. What we think of as a new Marshall Plan. But with no strings attached.

It was all very modest at first. Just a small number of us, in a few countries. Now we've grown. And there are similar movements in Asia and in South America. The basic idea is quite simple. Send representatives to the big cities of the North. After all, that's where the money is . . . and where there are organizations—like yours—concerned with development *and* with climate. To try to make the case to you . . . so you can make it to others. So, in the end, your politicians hear our voices. As they haven't heard those of our official ambassadors.

(*Pause.*)

You can imagine how excited I was when I saw your message.

Joe: (*Cautiously.*) But perhaps I should say . . . from the beginning . . . that's not quite our sphere of operation. We don't deal so much with politicians. The aim is to work around that process. With all its tangles . . . special interests . . . horse trading on votes. We think we can help most by dealing directly with investors, and trying to guide them to ventures that will do good. We want to encourage them to boost economies like yours—in ways that also limit climate change.

Our strategy is to identify places in the developing world where local groups might enter into profitable partnerships with corporations—and sometimes foundations—in affluent countries. We try to help them discover possibilities for the benefit of all involved.

Jo: Some development, some economic growth for us. (*Pause.*) Profits for them.

Joe: Yes. (*Pause.*) From what I've heard . . . and what you've already said . . . you seem to want something more radical.

Jo: I do. We do. (*Pause. With a deliberate effort to be gracious.*) Of course, we appreciate the kinds of activities you engage in. They do offer us *something*. But not enough. And in the wrong way.

(*Pause.*)

That was too harsh. I know I'm inclined to put these points too strongly but . . .

Joe: (*Gently.*) . . . the feelings moving you are very strong. You think about your homeland . . . and other countries like it. You see vividly what the lives of your countrymen are like. How difficult . . . how confined . . . they often are. And you come here. See how different things might be. So you feel anguish . . . indignation . . . even resentment. I can understand that.

Jo: Can you?

Joe: I think so. You see, I've been there. Not to your homeland, but to others nearby. I spent two years there. Nearly twenty years ago, working with the local people, building schools, and teaching. (*Pause.*) It's what inspired . . . inspires . . . the work I'm doing now.

I go back often. I've been to many parts of the developing world—sometimes at times of great suffering. I was in Haiti just after the 2010 earthquake. I saw for myself the kinds of things I suspect move you.

"Especially electricity," you said. When you said that, I thought—of course. No power. No refrigeration. No lights. Food spoiling. Hygiene breaking down. Desperate people looting under cover of darkness. Shortages of medicine. A black market. (*Pause.*) So I have seen a little—but only a little. You've seen much more. (*Pause.*) It's quite natural . . . quite reasonable . . . to react as you do.

Jo: (*Clearly moved.*) Thank you. I know . . . I already knew . . . what we have in mind isn't quite your line. But I wanted the chance to make a case to you, by offering our perspective. After all, you're closer to us than almost everyone here. You do understand . . . at least some of the important things. And that's rare.

(*Pause.*)

So I'd like to persuade you to go a bit further. To see things as we do. (*Pause.*) To adopt a more . . . radical . . . view. (*Pause.*) May I try?

Joe: Of course. I want to listen. That's why I invited you here.

Jo: Let me start by explaining my reaction . . . my harsh reaction . . . to your description of your organization and what it does. Why shouldn't we just be happy, and appreciate the opportunities for development you provide for us? (*Pause.*) Because they feel like bits and pieces . . . leftovers offered by generous people who sit at the rich man's table. The generous ones decide . . . they say who gets what. There's no systematic attention to our needs. Some areas of some countries might get lucky—simply because they happen to be places where investors can turn a profit. (*Slowly but firmly.*) And, in the end, given all the history, that way of doing things is unfair . . . deeply unfair and unjust.

(*Pause.*)

I know. I've used strong language again. But it's the *right* language. I'd like to show you that. (*Pause.*) From what you said . . . about your own involvement in our world . . . I think I might have a chance. It'll take time. Is that OK?

Joe: Yes.

Jo: So let me start where I think we'll agree completely. Surely we're both delighted by some recent developments. At last, there's some progress on climate change—although who knows how long it will last? Climate clubs to coordinate action. At least among prosperous nations and some "threshold" countries.

But what happens to those of us lower in the economic order? From India on down. If we went ahead with our economic development in just the way the rich countries have done, it would be a disaster. Britain, the USA, Germany . . . those countries led the way. Industrializing, becoming wealthy . . . very wealthy . . . by burning lots of coal and gas and oil. And now, of course, they are cutting back. Pledging to make the transition to a carbon-free world. China is on a similar curve, but a bit behind. Maybe by mid-century their emissions will be tapering off.

But what about us? We haven't really started yet. Does India now get its turn? Indonesia? Brazil? Central Asia? All of South America? All of Africa?

Of course not. We're denied the opportunity others have had. We're in a bind. We can't afford to develop using green technology. Not unless we receive aid. A lot of aid. So should we follow your old path and burn coal? Knowing, of course, that when the consequences come, we'll be hit hardest. Some leaders in our countries advocate doing that. Our movement thinks they're wrong. There has to be a better way.

Joe: And, of course, my colleagues and I agree with that. We're trying to find that better way. Yes, I know you don't think it's that much better. But it may be the best anyone can do—at least in the world we currently live in. (*Pause.*) Sorry. I interrupted. Please go on.

Jo: Of course, in the end, if we did opt out of the global attempt to limit climate change, you could easily stop us. You have the wealth . . . and the power. You could make us an offer we couldn't refuse. Just invade and shut down the coal-fired plants. Or do it in a softer way. We'd be flouting the rules of the climate club. So we'd be pariahs. Outsiders. Forced to pay heavy tariffs if we tried to sell to you.

So are we coerced, one way or the other? By the guns and the tanks or the soft power of unfavorable trade? Our local champions of coal don't think so. They think the developing world could form its own club. After all, there are enough of us. We could follow the course you did . . . burning coal . . . industrializing . . . and then trade with one another. Who knows if that's feasible? Even if it is, it doesn't matter. We can't afford the consequences of doing that, of all those extra emissions. *We* can't especially. And that dog-in-the-manger attitude would be wrong. Willfully destroying the planet for our descendants.

So there's our bind. It seems we have to give up on development and resign ourselves to being left behind. Always left behind. Us, our children, our grandchildren . . . down the generations.

(*Pause.*)

Our movement was born in realizing we couldn't accept that. We have to try to do better.

Joe: You've put it eloquently. It's the same bind that's moved me as an outsider . . . an observer . . . of course. Not, like you, from the inside.

I wish I had an ideal solution. I wish I could do better than set up some deals . . . here and there. "Leftovers" from the more generous people at the feast. (*Pause.*) We share the same goals—and to you the solution seems straightforward. The rich countries pay for global development on the basis of renewable sources of energy. A new Marshall Plan, as you called it. (*Pause.*) It's not so simple. The world doesn't work that way. We have to be realistic, and understand what can be done and what can't.

You want to persuade me that your solution is the right one. I *don't* want to convince you that my colleagues and I have the answer. I'm sure we don't. But maybe you can help us do better. You can help us improve our efforts to help you. Together we might be able to achieve something . . . not something perfect . . . but something better than what we've offered so far.

Jo: (*Very firmly.*) Not yet. I can't give up yet . . . I can't compromise before we've worked it through. That would be a betrayal. Of billions of people, and of justice. It would violate principles . . . deep principles . . . that we have to honor.

(*More quietly.*) And, in the end, I don't think I'm being unrealistic . . . or any less realistic than you. Your assumptions about how people will behave may be as off-target as you think mine are.

Joe: (*Plainly a little irritated.*) I don't see why . . . but go on.

Jo: I've spoken too forcefully. I get carried away. A bad habit.

Let me start more slowly. There's a simple idea on which people agree. You see expressions of it all the time. Like in the shops here. When they sell fragile things, they often put up a sign. "If you break it, you own it." More generally—if you mess something up, you ought to fix it. To the extent it can be fixed. Well, as we agreed, your nation, other rich nations, got to be wealthy by messing up the climate. Now you have the responsibility to do something about it.

Joe: And we're now trying. Once it became completely clear . . .

Jo: "Once"? You only just noticed? Hasn't it been clear for quite a while now? Clear . . . but inconvenient.

Joe: You're right to chide us. It *did* take us too long to face up to the problem. But we *are* trying to solve it.

Jo: But surely you don't think a "solution" involves causing harm to innocent parties? Depriving them of chances for a better future? You get rich by mucking things up. You then realize the mess you've made. So you start to limit the damage. You lay down rules for how everyone's supposed to act from now on. Rules that confine people who were no part of the cock-up. They suffer. Meanwhile you hang on to your entire ill-gotten gains . . .

Joe: Not us! We *are* trying to help, you know.

Jo: Yes, you're right. I've done it again. Forgive me. But I think you see the point. Why the ones who suffer might think they'd been treated unjustly. Might think reparations are due.

And there's another simple idea, leading to the same conclusion. Imagine a situation in which a whole group of people's lives are threatened. Say they're on a ship that hits a rock and starts to sink. Some of them have the skills and strength to slow down the rate at which water is pouring in, or to help the less able ones into lifeboats. Others don't. You expect the vigorous people to do the bailing and the lifting. A general thought—when something goes badly wrong, people who *can* do something about it *should*.

So let's forget about who caused the climate mess. Just focus on which countries have the resources to do something about it. You get the same answer as before. The rich nations can solve the problem without too much pain. The poor ones can't.

Joe: That may be too quick. Affluent societies have their problems, too.

Jo: I wouldn't want to overlook that. Of course, there are *many* different sources of trouble, all around the world. We're going to have to talk about how to balance competing demands. Later. (*Pause.*) But all I want to claim for now is that the entire burden can't be borne by us. Those whom your road to wealth has left behind.

I think I can make this clearer if I show you some figures. (*She reaches into a pocket of her jacket, and pulls out a piece of paper. She slides it across the desk. Joe picks it up, and finds Table 5.1.*)

Joe: (*After a few moments studying the table.*) I don't understand. What do these numbers mean? What's the point?

Jo: They show the extent of what's happened—how a few countries overexploited a resource that should have been fairly shared, and how they left too little for others.

Joe: Take it more slowly, please. What resource? What's this talk of a "reservoir"? What's this multiplier?

NATION	TOTAL EMISSIONS IN TONNES	PERCENTAGE OF RESERVOIR SPACE USED (F)	PERCENTAGE OF GLOBAL POPULATION (P)	PER CAPITA MULTIPLIER ($\frac{F}{P}$)
USA	3.4×10^{11}	31%	4%	7.75
UK	6.9×10^{10}	6%	0.88%	6.82
Germany	8.1×10^{10}	8%	1.14%	7.02
China	1.05×10^{11}	10%	20%	0.5

Table 5.1

Jo: Right. I do need to explain. Let's start with natural resources. A lot of them get assigned to particular countries. Saudi Arabia owns the oil under the sand, Brazil owns tropical forests along the Amazon, and so on. But some we don't treat that way. Instead we see them as belonging to all of us. To be shared. The atmosphere is like that.

We'd be appalled if some technological innovation allowed one group of people to deny air to members of another group. If they charged for the ability to breathe. Nations aren't allowed to pollute so they choke their neighbors who live downwind. The air above us is a resource to which we should all have equal access.

Breathing isn't the only way in which we make use of the atmosphere. Discovery of the greenhouse effect showed that. The air is a sink into which we can pour the gases we emit. As we drive and fly, as we breed livestock, as we generate electricity. We should think of the atmosphere as a reservoir, a waste dump, if you like. It's a container of finite size, capable of absorbing just so much carbon.

How big is it? Well, that depends. The size is fixed by the concentration of carbon in the atmosphere we consider safe. A decade ago, the scientists would probably have agreed on 400 ppm as the appropriate target. Today, as we're passing 400 ppm, many of them would take 500 ppm to be a realistic—but dangerous—level. I chose 450 ppm because that gives us a greater than 50 percent chance of keeping the increase in gmt by 2100 below 2°C. Even that seems to me pretty risky.

Joe: I agree with you there.

Jo: OK. As you probably know, in 1850, the concentration was 280 ppm. So our chosen reservoir size allows for the dumping of carbon up to an increase of 170 ppm. That's the total from 1850 to the end of the transition, the moment when we reach the sustainable world—no more emissions. Who knows when that will be?

An increase of 170 ppm allows for emitting 1.06×10^{12} tonnes of carbon by the time everyone stops emitting. I calculated the fraction of the space in the reservoir taken *so far* by each nation since 1850. But it seems only reasonable to give large nations bigger shares of the reservoir than smaller countries. So I divided the percentage of the space a nation has used up by the nation's population considered as a percentage of the global human population. That gives my numbers for *F/P*, the entries in the final column. It represents the multiple of its fair share the nation has used so far.

You can see what the pioneers in industrialization have done. The USA, the UK, and Germany have already used around *seven* times their fair shares. And that would be true even if they stopped emitting tomorrow. Which isn't going to happen, of course.

China, on the other hand, a country often criticized for its emissions, has used up only about half of its share. Maybe the Chinese will even go through the transition without consuming their whole allowance. They'd be the good guys.

Joe: Now I understand. It's an interesting way to dramatize the history. But I have some worries. First, explain your standard for what's fair. Why should I calculate the "fair share" as you've done?

Jo: Well, imagine food is quite scarce, and there's a village full of hungry people. Now someone arrives with a consignment of things to eat. Every family sends one of its members to the distribution center. Wouldn't it be fair to allot each family a share according to family size? Each one is given the fraction of the food that represents its percentage of the village population. If my family is 10 percent of the village, it's given a tenth of the food.

I think we should divide up—or should have divided up—the reservoir in the same way. Each nation gets the fraction of the space that represents its percentage of the global population. If my country contains ten percent of the people living, it gets one tenth.

Does that help?

Joe: A bit. But sometimes we think we shouldn't just apply such a simple formula. Some people—and some families—might have greater needs than others. (*Pause.*) You're also talking about a long period of time. The relative sizes of nations change. A country's fraction of the global population might be quite different in 1850 and in 2015.

Jo: You're completely right on both counts! We might want to adjust the principle for assigning fair shares. Plead that some nations have especially large needs. That isn't going to bring much comfort, though. The three over-users are very rich. They've been rich for a long time. So why do they qualify for receiving more? "To him that hath, it shall be given"?

My calculations are based on the population percentages as they are today. I did look at the values for earlier times. In 1850, the USA had roughly 2% of the world's population, compared to 2.3% for the UK, and 3% for Germany. That means the fair share for America is *smaller* than the value I've given, and the fair shares for Britain and Germany are bigger. So the UK and Germany have over-used a bit less than my figures suggest—and the USA has over-used more. Possibly it's even used up ten times its fair share. Already.

Joe: I think your dismissal of special needs is a bit hasty. You're ignoring a really important feature about industrialization, and about what the first major industrial nations contributed. They haven't just made themselves rich. They've produced things that have changed the world. Inventions that have transformed human life, making it better in all sorts of ways. Don't we want them to keep providing more things like that? And isn't that sufficient reason to keep the factories going? They get a larger share of the reservoir because they keep developing new benefits for all of us.

Jo: I thought you might say that. But it doesn't get them off the hook. Think about it this way. Any nation's use of fossil fuels can be divided into two bits. One bit goes towards making that country and its citizens wealthier. The other contributes benefits to the world—or, to keep things simple, to the non-industrialized world. (We'll suppose that what a nation gives to its industrial rivals is canceled out by what it receives from those rivals.) In the spirit of your suggestion, we now only "charge" countries for that part of their emissions associated with the "selfish" benefits—the bit that makes the country richer.

How big is the selfish part? Even if it were only one-half, the countries would still have been over-using. Not as dramatically, of course. And can you really claim that it's less than one-half? Surely if it were, the world would be a *much* more equal place! All those goodies flowing out to the developing nations. In fact, as you know, the main benefits of contemporary production in the affluent countries are distributed very unequally.

What's the largest benefit stemming from the Industrial Revolution? Surely, it's electricity. That's what's really transformed the lives of people in prosperous countries—and what has the potential to transform our lives too. And we're desperate for it. For reliable electrical power, available to all of us. You said you understood that. So you should also understand that the goodies haven't yet flowed smoothly and evenly around the world. So it's false advertising to pretend that we've all shared equally in your overuse of the atmospheric reservoir.

Not to mention the history of interactions between the affluent and the world's poor since the industrial revolution began. Colonialism. Exploitation. Disruption of many people's ways of making their livings. Far from a pretty story.

Also your point about continuing to fuel the production in the already industrialized world backfires. Past decades have taught us something. The benefits you see as flowing round the world can come from many different places. So there's no good reason to provide the prosperous nations with an extra share of the reservoir. Why not spread the wealth by giving other countries their turn, and let them produce for a while? It might be a better strategy from the environmental perspective. You might even be able to set up plants based on renewable energy, to get more production for less emissions.

Joe: You're at least partly right. I can't wave away the charge of over-use—significant over-use—by airily gesturing at "benefits to all mankind." The distribution of goods—of electricity, as you said, and, more importantly, of quality of life—around the world gives the lie to that. (*Pause.*) Yet it still seems to me you're too harsh. After all, nobody knew what was happening. Not until recently. They acted in ignorance.

Jo: But they didn't stop! Even when they knew! And they're not stopping now. What do the agreements say? "We must phase out." And, by the time they've done it, they'll probably have used up their original share at least once more.

(*Her bracelets jangle as she digs in a side pocket of her jacket. She pulls out a small, wrinkled, scrap of paper.*)

Take the USA. It's been thirty years since James Hansen briefed Congress about the danger posed by climate change. And the scientific advisors to the president surely knew well before that. So I did another calculation. In 1980, the concentration of carbon in the atmosphere was 340 ppm, allowing for the further emission (worldwide) of 6.85×10^{11} tonnes. Let's follow your generous suggestion. Nations aren't responsible for their emissions before they find out the consequences of what they're doing. In 1980, the USA starts with a clean slate. Its share of the global population was 4%. Hence it's given 4% of the remaining allowance of global emissions. That's 2.7×10^{10} tonnes. Now how much carbon do you think America emitted between 1980 and 2010?

Joe: I don't know. But you wouldn't have brought up this topic unless it were more.

Jo: You're right. The actual emissions from the USA in that thirty-year period were 3.3×10^{10} tonnes. Twenty percent over budget. So, even when you're generous—forgiving *and* forgetful—they're still guilty of overexploitation. And, as I keep saying, they aren't finished yet.

But there's another point I wanted to make. Ignorance can serve as an excuse. You do something that makes a real mess for others. You plead—sincerely, correctly—that you didn't know how it would turn out. What do you think you should do next?

Joe: Apologize. Change your ways.

Jo: Right. That's what people—at least morally sensitive people—do. So, if you've taken more than your share of something, you express your regrets for what's been consumed, for what can't be given back. If there's some you've left unused, you give it to those who haven't yet had any. You don't keep taking . . . and taking . . . and taking . . .

Joe: Wait a minute. I distrust this analogy. You're abstracting from important features of the political situation. Large nations aren't exactly like over-greedy people. They're complex. Governments have duties to their citizens. They can't just say sorry, close down their industries, make the reparations you think appropriate. That would be irresponsible.

Jo: I don't deny that! They're in a bind, too. They have duties, as you say. I'm going to get to that. I really am. But it has to come later. (*Pause. She realizes how much control of the discussion she has taken. In a more conciliatory tone.*) I know. I'm only giving one side of the picture. The other has to be presented too. That's only fair. (*Slowly.*) But we do need to see the whole . . . and that's why I emphasize things most people here don't seem to recognize . . . things they overlook.

You see . . . all this . . . overuse of what should have been a shared resource . . . all this is the background . . . to what we . . . the poor nations . . . are now asked to do. There's a big problem. You made it. A lot of the time . . . but not all the time . . . you didn't know what you were doing. But now you have to change your ways and make the transition. We don't have to change. But we do have to . . . alter . . . what we hoped to do . . . planned to do . . . to move to lives like yours . . . or, at least, in that direction . . . with some of the things you enjoy. Because you won't pay. You won't give us aid so we, too, can grow . . . with green technology.

You ask us to sacrifice the future we wanted—even though you made the mess. Even though you'll continue to live high. That seems to us unfair . . . deeply unfair . . . *unjust*.

And it's not a hard point to see. Almost all of us see it. Very clearly.

And because it's so clear to us, we resist. We keep asking you . . . begging you . . . for help. Which . . . you . . . refuse. (*Pause.*) Some of us . . . as I said . . . think we should just ignore your agreements. Develop in any way we can. (*Pause.*) That's foolhardy. Counterproductive.

You accused me of being too idealistic. Of ignoring the politics of the real world. I threw the charge back at you. That's because your vision supposes politics can be divorced from justice . . . from morality. But it can't. Not when the injustice is so glaring . . . so obvious to those who are wronged. In the real world, people won't behave in the . . . agreeable . . . way you suppose. Simply lying down when they see what's been done . . . is being done . . . to them. (*Pause.*) They won't give up. They'll continue to ask for justice. Maybe fight for justice.

Joe: That's what moves me . . . moves us . . . to try to do something . . .

Jo: But it's not enough! It doesn't acknowledge . . . (*Sensing that her vehemence may be counterproductive.*) But, as you said, I feel strongly . . . (*More quietly.*) Do you mind if I tell you a story? A parable? It might help make my point.

Joe: Go ahead. These questions are hard, and parables sometimes help us see things more clearly.

Jo: Thanks. You *are* being patient with me. (*Pause.*) I'll call it "Exodus." It's set in the future. At a time when the effects of global warming have become really bad.

It takes place in . . . or starts in . . . what was once a city. Almost all of it has been ruined. Great buildings shattered by wars . . . fights between people desperate for the necessities of life. Battered by terrible storms. The population reduced to just two hundred. Living on the edge, scavenging for food and water, ransacking the ruins to form makeshift shelters.

The story begins in a time of severe drought. The last nearby water sources are drying up. So the people get together to decide what to do. There are leaders among them—a group of about thirty. The Elite. They're the ones who've kept things going during past disasters. The strong ones who've put out the fires—the clever ones who have organized the food and water supply. The rest, the Commoners, defer to them. And now, with the reservoirs almost empty, the Elite announce that it's time to leave. The journey ahead is likely to be hard. Nobody knows how long it will take to find a new place to settle. Everyone should travel light.

The party sets off in the evening. Going through the night is better because the heat of the day is so intense. They head off in a promising direction, but all the old watercourses they find during the first two days are completely dry. On the dawn of the third day, one of the Elite spots two bodies of water, glistening in the distance. They head for the nearer one.

As they come closer, the path they are following narrows. Everyone has to go in single file—and the order reflects the social hierarchy. The Elite lead the way and the Commoners trail behind. There's a bit more space at the water's edge. Room for ten people to drink at once. The Elite go first. They drink . . . and drink . . . and drink. After all thirty have drunk their fill . . . and more . . . a lot more . . . in three shifts . . . it's clear to everyone that there isn't much water left. Maybe enough for twenty or thirty Commoners to have restorative drinks.

You can guess what happens next. The Commoners are angry. They seize a couple of the Elite who have foolishly allowed themselves to be separated from the rest. They start to beat them up. Until a shot rings out. A warning shot.

Everyone was supposed to travel light. But the Elite had foreseen the possibility of needing to maintain order. They had packed weapons—for just this sort of occasion.

One of the Commoners quickly intervenes. She reminds the whole party of the second water hole. She suggests that they may have brought enough bottles and containers to carry water for those who haven't yet drunk. A quick check shows that she's right. The Commoners are exhausted . . . dehydrated . . . some are in real danger. They can't make the further journey. But, as they point out, the Elite are thoroughly refreshed. The Elite could go and bring back the water the Commoners need.

And they agree to do so. But not during the heat of the day. They promise to set off as soon as twilight comes. Then they retreat to a cave on the hillside. The Commoners find shade where they can.

When the evening comes, a few of the Commoners—the fitter ones—go up the hill to the cave. It's empty.

That night, one hundred and seventy parched people set off for the second water source. Sixty of them make it.

(*Pause.*)

So—what's your judgment?

Joe: (*Exasperated, but obviously trying to control his temper.*) Do you need to ask? It's obvious. What the Elite did was wrong. They shouldn't have taken more than their share. Maybe they didn't know at first that they were drinking too much. But they should have paid attention to the amount they were leaving. Then they should have apologized for their negligence, and *volunteered* to go—at once—to fetch the water.

But, of course, what's really bad . . . morally monstrous—is breaking the promise. Sneaking off and leaving the Commoners to their fate.

(*Pause.*)

It seems to me you're flogging a dead horse. You don't need this parable. You're just repeating what you already said more clearly . . . more directly . . . without the need of any story. I've already conceded the point the story makes. I've recognized our responsibility to help countries like yours. Our whole organization is founded on that recognition. *We* aren't like your Elite. We're trying to help. To fetch the water, if you like.

Jo: (*Quietly.*) I think I do need the parable. We agree about this version of it. I expected that, and I'm glad we agree. But there's a variant of "Exodus" with a different ending.

This time, when the Commoners go up to the cave, the Elite are still there. They've gathered all the jugs and bottles together. They're ready to set off. But before they go, one thing has to be settled. An agreement needs to be signed. It sets a price . . . oh, a truly tiny price . . . for the service the Elite are about to perform. From now on, in the new settlement the party eventually reaches, Commoners will be required to perform some small services for the Elite. Maybe only a few hours of labor per year. Or one percent of the crops they grow. It is a very small fee, really minute. It's to be paid by each Commoner now and through the coming generations. Indefinitely.

(*Pause.*)

How do you judge the Elite now?

Joe: They do better. (*Pause.*) But I see your point, it's not good enough. (*Pause.*) Does your new parable really apply to us? To organizations like ours? Or to the entrepreneurs we recruit to invest in the developing world and to support some of the things you need.

After all, the people who make these deals today aren't the ones who originally took more than their share of the "reservoir." We've arrived late on the scene. The crucial action is long over. We're doing what we can to fix the mess. Do you think the sins of the fathers should be visited on the children?

Jo: Sometimes. When the children continue to benefit from the wrongdoing of their parents. When they go on doing the same things on a smaller scale.

(*Pause.*)

Maybe I should extend the story further. It's half a century later—fifty years since the Commoners signed the agreement. The whole party set off, and settled in a new place. Their lives there aren't easy, but they get by. The descendants of the Elite manage a bit better than the others. That's partly because the original Elite were more refreshed during the journey. They went faster at the end and arrived before the others. They took the better land. (*Pause.*) And partly because the Commoners continue to have to pay their small . . . tribute.

Fifty years later the Commoners question the agreement. Why should they keep paying . . . and paying? The Elite reply:

"We're not the ones who took more than our share." (*Pause.*) Is that good enough?

Joe: No. I see your point. (*Pause.*) So when we set up a venture . . . a partnership between some corporation or foundation here and a local group in your country . . . you think we're doing the same. Requiring a fee . . . an illegitimate fee. Say the corporation finances setting up solar collectors for the local group to run a factory. It's a success. After ten years or so, the profits are flowing in. And in, and in. Most of them go to the local economy—the corporation has been generous in its terms. But some go back to the affluent world and fill the coffers of those who caused the mess—or add to the wealth of their heirs. People who have benefited from the mess-making.

Jo: Yes. That's just what I had in mind. As I said near the start of our conversation, I worry about the fact that the interventions come from the outside. They're dictated by what strikes entrepreneurs as profitable, not by what we need. We owe everything to the largesse of strangers.

But I went further. I said it was the wrong way to do things. Deeply unjust. Strong words. (*Pause.*) But not strong enough, maybe. Sometimes, when I think about our needs for development . . . needs to develop using renewable sources of energy . . . this patchwork of partnerships . . . with some of the profits siphoned off . . . by people from the countries . . . that got rich by causing the situation . . . that makes our lives so hard . . . "unjust" seems too mild . . . it seems . . . *obscene.* (*Pause.*) Can you see why someone might think that?

Joe: (*Slowly.*) Yes. I believe I can. (*Pause.*) I wish we could do better. And perhaps with your help we can. You . . . people like you . . . might show us how to set up better arrangements. More attention to your needs. Possibly smaller . . . "fees."

But I don't think we can change the fundamental structure. This is the real world. It's not a moral philosophy seminar room. We have to work within existing constraints and attend to the bottom line . . . to profits. Even if, from a certain perspective . . . a morally sensitive perspective . . . it's . . . unjust . . . obscene.

Jo: No, we don't live in a seminar room. Most of my people will never sit in one—or even know what goes on in one. They don't need any of that—they can judge . . . correctly . . . without it. The injustice they suffer is evident to them.

We have a history of dealing with your . . . investors. Most of it is not exactly benign. Now, thanks to the support of organizations like yours . . . the *good* work you do, moved by sympathy for us . . . they come to us again. We are in a bind, and they offer to free us. But for a small price.

How can we not understand what is going on? See it in the way my parable does? And not resent the system that exploits us?

Joe: What's the alternative? Your Marshall Plan isn't going to happen. (*Sadly.*) I wish it would. But it's politically impossible. Beyond the horizon of our policy discussions.

I know what people . . . even the most progressive people . . . would say. They'd like to help and wish we could provide more aid. But there are so many problems at home. So much of our society needing to be rebuilt. So many people in trouble. Our government has a duty to provide for them and to offer them better opportunities.

Jo: I . . . we . . . don't deny that duty. During the time I've lived here, I've learned something about the plight of people in some parts of your country. And they *should* be helped.

The trouble is with the whole political discussion. It's . . . morally . . . flawed. In a subtle way. Your "progressives" see a clear duty at home. What's provided—or not provided—to us appears differently to them. Not a matter of *justice*, but of generosity . . . of benevolence. An optional extra. Something good to do, if you can do it. Not something you can be faulted for not doing.

Everything I've said this afternoon tries to undermine that. Your government has *two* duties. One is the duty you mentioned. A duty at home. The other is the duty to repair . . . to pay for . . . the mess the rich countries made in the course of getting rich. Neither can be neglected. It's a matter of justice and injustice. *Glaring* injustice.

Joe: You're actually supporting my point. We just don't think about things that way. A lot of our citizens . . . and a lot of our politicians . . . don't appreciate the duties you and I see. No duty to the poor at home. No duty to our descendants, to limit the impact of climate change. Certainly no duty to help faraway people develop using green technology.

Some, maybe a growing number, have started to recognize the need to do something for our poorer fellow citizens. To do something about the lack of jobs, for instance. Probably many of the people who think about climate change, who recognize our duty to preserve the planet for our grandchildren, also belong to the group that worries about inequality in our society. And vice versa. But I don't think many of these people would see us as having the same kind of obligation to the developing world. They might agree it would be a good thing to do—if we could. But we can't. At least, they think we can't.

That's why I see your movement as unrealistic. It has no chance of succeeding. Not in this political climate.

Jo: Then we must change that climate. That's why I'm here. Why I was thrilled when I heard from you. Because you could help . . . could help us. I firmly believe that.

Joe: How? It looks impossible to me.

Jo: You have standing . . . moral standing. And political clout. You could persuade important people. Politicians. To see our point of view.

Joe: By telling stories? Parables?

Jo: (*Quickly.*) No. (*Pause.*) Maybe. It might help.

Joe: But before I could do that . . . even if I came to see it as having the slenderest chance of success . . . I'd have to know . . . *exactly* . . . what you want.

Jo: You're right. I haven't been completely clear. The Marshall Plan is only a label. A gesture towards our aims.

(*Pause.*)

What we really want is a conversation. A *different* conversation. One that includes us—and our perspective. One that corrects the flaw in the political discussion. One that recognizes *all* the duties.

I said: We're in a bind. We face a dilemma. So do you.

An ethical dilemma. Your government has several important duties. One is to act to limit the impact of climate change—to participate in a global transition to a sustainable world. Another is to take better care of its own disadvantaged citizens . . . the poor people here . . . the many who lack opportunities. Yet another is to help preserve all the important things human beings have accomplished . . . all the contributions that make life today . . . at least for the luckier people . . . so much richer, more rewarding, than it was for our remote ancestors. And then there's the duty I've been insisting on. To help us be part of that global transition without giving up our hopes for a much better life. To give us the resources we need to grow . . . without bringing more ruin to the planet. So . . . four duties in all.

It's not easy, of course, to discharge all these duties. Impossible, perhaps. Surely impossible in the short term. But there has to be a policy . . . a global policy . . . for making progress on all of them. None can be slighted completely, or given absolute priority. There has to be negotiation. Compromise.

We think the climate duties have a lot of weight. The longer we delay with them the harder the dilemma will be for future generations. But they can't override all the needs . . . all the suffering . . . of people who live today.

Your country has joined with others to recognize the need for coordinated action on the climate. There's bound to be a series of discussions . . . negotiations . . . about just how it should be done. And we want those conversations to be completely clear about the duties. That all four are *duties*. That the concerns of developing nations can't just be written off . . .

dismissed . . . seen as having a different status. You can't . . . can't *justly* . . . ask us to postpone our development forever. Or to accept whatever scraps accord with the ideas of your entrepreneurs . . . as they seek partnerships to make profits for themselves. Our voices . . . our demands . . . must have equal weight in the negotiations.

We know we can't have everything we want, all at once. Just as you won't be able to solve your domestic problems overnight. But your poor . . . and ours . . . have to see you as paying attention . . . as committed to doing something . . . as making progress on these fronts. We must have . . . *hope*. Real hope and not just hope based on wishful thinking. Reasonable hope, the kind that's grounded in your visible efforts at helping us.

(*Pause.*)

That's what we want. That's the message we'd like you . . . and people like you . . . to take to your political leaders.

Joe: So not a definite plan? Not contributions at some particular level. But a process that brings your perspective into the climate negotiations in a different way. By making . . . all the duties . . . transparent.

Have I got it?

Jo: (*Warmly.*) Yes. We need acknowledgment. Of what your country and the other rich nations have done. And where that has left us. (*Pause.*) Will you deliver our message?

Joe: (*Reflectively.*) I don't know. I can't say right now. I need to think about the message. Whether I agree with it and whether I'm an appropriate messenger. (*Pause; very firmly.*) But I *shall* think. You can rely on that.

Jo: Thank you.

Joe: Thank *you*. (*Pause.*) I'm very glad you came.

(*They both sense that there is nothing further to be said. Jo's bracelets clatter as she rises from the chair. She reaches out her hand. They shake hands briefly. She turns and leaves.*)

Joe: (*Remains still for a moment; then picks up the phone; dials.*) Hello. (*Pause; he listens.*) Good that I caught you. (*Pause.*) Yes, I've just seen her. (*Pause.*) As you told me . . . intelligent, forceful . . . *very* forceful . . . something of a firebrand, actually. But she made me think. You and I should talk about what she said. (*Pause.*) Maybe tomorrow? Lunch? (*Pause.*) OK. Noon? The usual place? (*Pause.*) Right. See you then.

(*He replaces the phone. Swivels in the desk chair. The light has shifted. Some of the surrounding buildings are now in shadow. Joe looks over the city, thinking.*)

A Many-Sided Dilemma

Our atmosphere doesn't much care where the greenhouse gases come from. So long as they continue to accumulate, the planet will warm and adverse effects on human life will follow. Securing the human future is impossible unless there is full cooperation across the human population—including the world that was left behind by the Industrial Revolution. This means that everyone's energy needs—needs both for survival *and* for development—must (somehow) be met.

Climate clubs offer a way to coordinate a part of the global effort. They might be set up to adjust incentives, so prosperous nations could navigate their way through the transition. Unless some form of coercion is used, however, developing nations have no motive to join. As Jo sees, the poorer nations of the world—whose citizens collectively make up the majority of the human population—are in a bind.

The bind is apparent in recent decisions by countries destined to suffer the most from climate change. India's emissions trajectory is on course to make it the global champion in coming decades—by mid-century it will surpass the United States (long the leading supplier of CO_2 to the atmosphere) and China (the latest emissions superstar). As of this writing, India's current government (under Prime Minister Modi) has repeatedly emphasized the need to provide all Indians with reliable electricity, 24 hours a day. To this end the Modi government has supported policies to increase the use of coal (indeed, a cheap and available form of coal, rich in potential for emissions).

Like India, neighboring Bangladesh seems to have excellent reasons to reduce emissions from fossil fuels. Roughly a quarter of its population lives along the flood-prone coast. Yet in February 2016, the government decided to stick with an earlier decision to build coal-powered plants for generating electricity on the edge of one of its last remaining forests.

Plainly, in both instances, the felt need for electricity and behind it the yearning for economic development override the climatic threats. Nations desperate for development see themselves as having no good options, and they choose what appears as a lesser evil. They embody the bind Jo describes.

So she asks for aid. The developing world would escape the bind if affluent nations financed the construction of an infrastructure based on renewable sources of energy. Developing nations would then be able to grow without contributing further to the concentration of greenhouse gases.

Joe presses her—what exactly does she propose? At that point, she doesn't make the definite requests nations desperate for growth have sometimes put forward—requests affluent nations have consistently refused. Instead, she asks for a procedure. The rival claims of different constituencies are to be heard. In the subsequent negotiations *all* duties have to be acknowledged. The comfortable idea that prosperous nations owe nothing to the many countries the Industrial Revolution left behind has to be abandoned.

Jo recognizes a many-sided—four-sided—dilemma. Our decisions should respond to four groups of claimants. First, there are our descendants, people who will suffer terribly from our inaction. Second come the struggling citizens in the rich countries—people in the predicaments from which the Joe and Jo of Chapter 3 have, at least temporarily, escaped. Third are the world's poor, hundreds of millions of people whose situations are even more desperate. (These are the people whose plight moves Jo to her more vehement outbursts.) Last is a more general human interest. Even if the benefits of past human accomplishments are currently badly distributed, available only to a privileged few, it would be wrong to discard or wreck the valuable products of our cultural traditions. Instead, we should try to preserve them, to bequeath them to a future in which they may be far more widely enjoyed.

If there were some identifiable way to craft a policy discharging all four duties—meeting them *completely*—there would be no dilemma. Our difficulty resides in our inability to find any such policy. The best we can hope for is to make some progress on each of the fronts. Jo sees the appropriate policy as resulting from discussions among representatives of the different constituencies. It will involve negotiation—and compromise.

She offers the outline of a plan. How can her suggestions be implemented, developed as a series of steps? We'll offer *one* way to do so. It is intended as a *proposal*, an attempt to make the suggestions more concrete (and thus more comprehensible.) There may well be better alternatives.

The climate change problem sets the time scale. Jo and Joe agree in recognizing its urgency. Delay would exacerbate the problems of the poor, making fulfilling the other duties even harder than it already is. So we elaborate Jo's procedure by starting with climate policy. A global transition is needed, and it should proceed as rapidly as possible, *given the importance of attending to the three other responsibilities*. The question for international discussion can be framed: What is the best way to make a rapid transition, while responding to the needs of poor nations for development, the needs of the disadvantaged members of prosperous nations, and the need to preserve the major accomplishments of our species?

Our answer begins with the approach to ethical decisions outlined by Jo in Chapter 3, and taken up here by Jo's current avatar. The standard for properly resolving an ethical question is that the decision accords with what would emerge from a particular type of conversation. What is ethically justified is what would be endorsed in deliberations among a fully representative group of people, equipped with the best available information, and committed to finding a solution all of them can live with. If the global cooperation we need is to be achieved, all nations must view the demands made on them as reasonable and fair—unless, of course, the powerful ones have their way through the exercise of brute force. The obvious way of convincing people that they have been given a fair deal is to make it clear that the deal has emerged from negotiations, in which they've been properly represented and in which all parties have sought an outcome all can tolerate. So we propose a transparent procedure approximating the ideal conversation that sets the standard for ethical justification.

We need a global forum. The participants must include people who can speak for each nation and for each of the world's major cultures, as well as advocates for the future inhabitants of our planet. It is important that the disadvantaged citizens of both the developing world and the affluent world have voices in the conversation.

The first phase of the discussion would involve climate experts, energy experts, representatives of developing countries, and economists. They would present a range of possible programs. These programs should fit a schedule for limiting the expected warming by 2100 to no more than 2°C (as well as some that strive for less than 1.5°C—assuming that goal remains possible). They should specify detailed targets for each country to replace fossil fuels with renewable resources. They should also offer developmental paths for the poor nations and programs for funding the construction of the systems of renewable energy those nations will need. Although it is important to have a diverse set of options, discussion can only be fruitful if the number of possibilities considered is not too large. The aim of the first round of the discussion is to narrow the field to a small number of candidates that can then be refined.

The surviving options would then be considered by the individual nations, and particularly by those from whom large transfers of funds are required. Intranational discussion also requires representation of the affected parties. Each national forum should include people who are currently disadvantaged and people with many different views of what is important in their lives. The discussants need expert advice. They need to learn about potential plans: plans for reducing energy demands, for modifying budgetary allocations, and for engaging in social programs (some of them probably experimental). They will have to know how much difference the plans make to the global climate effort (both through domestic replacements and the funding of growth among developing nations). They must be told about how the plans allow for improving the situations of the disadvantaged and preserving the things that give value to people's lives. They will also need assurances about what will be done to ensure that the aid provided by wealthy nations will be used for its intended purpose. Throughout the discussion, consideration of the "sacrifices" required should be couched in terms of what makes human lives go well, not in potentially misleading reflection on monetary losses and gains.

Once the actions required of individual nations are clearly in view, the conversation returns to the global level, seeking an option with which all can live. Almost certainly there will be no consensus on a *preferred* program. Probably, for any of the possibilities, some discussants will resist that proposed course of action. Given this failure to find a solution tolerable to all, the conversation should proceed in two directions. First, the parties explore any option proving acceptable to a large number of them, trying to find ways of refining it to produce a version with which all could live. Second, those who resisted this option explain the grounds of their sense that the burdens imposed on them would be too great. In light of that discussion, alternatives previously rejected might appear more promising; or perhaps resisters would come to recognize the large demands made on them as legitimate.

Of course, there can be no guarantee that actual exchanges of this form would arrive at a plan to which all could assent. The practical prospects for successful convergence are, however, greater than in the climate negotiations of the past. *When moral responsibilities are clearly in view, when the bearing of alternative policies on human lives can be recognized and appraised, and when ethical grounds for favoring or objecting to the proposals can be put forward and debated, discussants move beyond assertions of clashing self-interest.* There is pressure to explain why acceding to the demands of others would be unacceptable. Where ethical debate seems destined to end in irresolvable conflict, especially when the urgency of finding *some* solution is widely appreciated, parties are often moved to negotiate and compromise.

The process we've sketched is intended to bridge the gap between an ethical ideal and the complexities of the real world. As Jo pointed out in Chapter 3, it's silly to think of bringing together all human beings—let alone the generations to come—so they can work things out in discussions with one another. Yet the ethical ideal supplies important pointers for real conversations. Actual negotiations often break down because one (or more) of the ideal conditions on discussion is violated. Sometimes future generations or people now living in poverty are left unrepresented. Often some or all of the participants are misinformed. We have tried to correct for these defects by demanding fuller representation and by recruiting expert witnesses. If our procedure runs aground on insuperable disagreement, the most likely culprit will lie in failures of mutual engagement.

How, then, to foster sympathy for others' positions? How to produce a motivation to seek compromise? We offer some possibilities. Give discussants the opportunity to explain why they take some burdens to be intolerable. Require positions to be defended by considering what is most ethically significant, the consequences for human lives. Remind participants of the need not to ride roughshod over the demands of others. Above all, make the structure of the ethical dilemma transparent from the beginning—be clear that there are *four* obligations that are not easily fulfilled together. This is Jo's central point. She pleads for standing in the negotiations.

Rome wasn't built in a day. The forum will have to meet again and again, on a regular basis. Any plan emerging from the conversation at any stage serves as the basis for the next steps in a program extending across decades. It should constantly be reappraised and adjusted in the light of new evidence.

Scientists may make new discoveries in understanding climate dynamics. Engineers may offer new advances in technology. A dangerous increase in episodic shocks could inspire accelerating the pace of the transition. Agricultural innovations could point the way to achieving dramatic reductions in emissions through changes in the handling of livestock. Carbon capture and storage might become viable on a significantly larger scale. Surely some modifications of policy will come from the results of social experiments. A variety of schemes for introducing renewable energy into the economies of developing countries will teach policymakers which ones work best. A similar diversity of efforts at addressing social problems—unemployment, education, health care—could provide similar lessons. We may also learn what features of our lives can be given up without any fundamental cost.

The imagined procedure combines readily with the pragmatism we've emphasized (Chapter 4). The decision-makers know they can try out multiple possibilities and absorb the successes at the next stage of the program. As we have said, they are better off than the lone hiker in the dark wood. They can divide their efforts, learn, and improve the chances of success.

Joe regretfully concludes that ethically justified policies must bow to the constraints of political life. But some facets of global justice are too evident for *realpolitik* to ignore. Repeated evasion of moral responsibilities has complicated climate negotiations. Better by far to acknowledge the legitimacy of demands for aid, to explain the difficulties of acceding to those demands while addressing other urgent problems, and to try to negotiate a solution all can tolerate. Even in global politics, honesty is the best policy—especially when the chances of a cover-up are slim.

Jo is right. Joe isn't the political realist he takes himself to be.

SIX

A NEW POLITICS?

Power Lunch

A little after noon. An upscale restaurant near the Capitol in Washington, D.C. Joe, a man of about thirty, sits at a table for two. He is wearing an expensive suit, tailored to fit his athletic frame. Very much at his ease, he leans back in his chair, reading and sending messages on his phone.*

Jo, a woman in her mid-twenties, approaches the table. She is slightly out of breath, and has evidently been hurrying. She wears an inexpensive suit and an unstylish blouse. Both sit a little awkwardly on her. Joe looks up. Sees her and smiles.

Jo: Hi, Joe. So sorry I'm late. The Metro . . .
Joe: No worries. I had plenty to do. Texts coming in all the time. The senator is really busy with the environmental debate.

*The conversation could occur in a similar place in any capital in the affluent world. The titles of officials and the references to political details would, of course, be different. But it should be easy to make the substitutions.

Jo: I know. It's so good of you to make room on your calendar for me—especially during such a busy time.

Joe: Well we wanted to touch base with your group. The senator is intrigued. It's important to her to represent the people actively interested in climate policy. Knowing more about you will help us, as we try to do whatever we can.

Jo: Oh yes! She's been so energetic on the issue. Such a strong voice for defending the environment.

Joe: We think so. (*Pause.*) But from reading some of your group's literature, I suspect you think we don't go far enough. Too conservative for you?

Jo: A bit . . . we do want changes . . . serious changes . . . we think it won't work without them. We must seem radical . . . maybe utopian . . .

(*A waiter appears. Joe is familiar with the menu and orders at once. Jo scans it and makes a quick choice.*)

Joe: You do seem to be asking for quite sweeping economic and political reforms. Far, far more than is realistically possible. Remember—on this issue, the senator is at the progressive end of the spectrum. Even she wouldn't support some of the things you recommend. (*Pause.*) Of course, you're a young movement—started and run by young people.

Jo: But we *have* talked with distinguished scholars! We're well grounded in political and economic theory, and we've studied these questions carefully. We've discussed them thoroughly with some of the best minds in the country.

(*She looks directly at Joe.*)

I know we don't have your background in practical politics. That's why it was so great when you invited me. It gives us a chance to explain to someone who might make a difference. Someone with the ear of an important senator.

So . . . can I tell you why we think as we do?

Joe: That's why we're here.

Jo: (*Takes a deep breath.*) Let's start with the need for global action. We have to make the worldwide transition to a zero-carbon state. Phase out fossil fuels and reform agriculture. That's going to require a sequence of international agreements. So far the senator is on board, I think?

Joe: Right.

Jo: And it can't be done while avoiding our other obligations. Climate policy has to be combined with fixing the problems in our society. The crumbling infrastructure. The awful schools many kids have to go to. Unemployment and underemployment. People who can't find *any* job. People who can't find jobs suited to their qualifications. People who have to work two or three jobs to make ends meet. All that has to be attended to. While we try to preserve a habitable planet for future generations.

Joe: Agreed. So far, we're with you.

Jo: And we mustn't wreck the valuable things we have. We can't let our national parks, our cities, our museums, our art, our music, our science, our libraries, our universities decay—we can't allow them to fall into disrepair. (*Pause; slowly.*) But the climate effort has to be global. All nations have to participate. Even the poor ones . . . the ones desperate for development. And we can't just say no to their yearning for economic growth. We've created the bind they're in. So we have to help them out of it, and support them in developing on the basis of green technology. (*Very slowly.*) We have an obligation . . . a duty . . . to give them aid . . . to pay our debt . . . and give them what they need. At least to make some progress . . . (*Her voice trails off. She has seen Joe's skeptical expression.*)

Joe: It's there we start to be dubious. That it's a *duty*, a *debt*. Sure, it would be a good thing to do. But is it on a par with what we owe our citizens?

Jo: Should I say why we think . . .

Joe: No. Not now. We've read some of the things you . . . and others . . . have written about this. They've made me reflect. Made the senator reflect, too. We're still discussing the question. We haven't made our minds up yet. (*Pause.*) Let me concede that point for today. Suppose we do have the obligation to give aid, even on the scale you propose. What really interests us is where you go next—the politics you have in mind and the economic changes you make room for. That's where we're *more* dubious. Much more dubious. Is all that necessary? And, as I said, we're pretty sure it's not politically possible. It's so far beyond where the country is now.

Jo: I know. That's why we started the Movement for Global Democracy. To change people's hearts and minds at a grassroots level. We want there to be conversations among ordinary citizens. We hope they'll talk through the issues, so they'll come to see what's needed. So that what's currently beyond the horizon comes to seem the right . . . the necessary . . . thing to do.

Of course we have a long way to go. A very long way—we know that. Who knows if we have a chance . . . any chance . . . of succeeding? But after we'd analyzed the problem, worked it through . . . thoroughly . . . it seemed as though starting this movement was the only option.

Joe: So exactly *what* has to be changed? And why are the changes necessary?

Jo: We need structures for global democracy, and a global social contract. It's agreed—right?—that there have to be regular meetings, to work out the details of how we make the transition. To get the poorer countries on board, the phasing out of fossil fuels has to be combined with ways to help them develop. Our group has argued that affluent nations—the ones responsible for the current climate mess, the ones wealthy enough to solve the problem—have a duty to provide serious aid. And . . . at least for today . . . you're conceding that.

So how can we set up a structure to make all this happen? We think a new kind of global governance is required. An institution dedicated to this particular complex of issues. One charged with the task of working out the agreements . . . of revising and refining them . . . of monitoring what's happening. And it must have the power to enforce. It has to be able to impose penalties on nations that don't live up to their commitments.

Joe: The United Nations? With more teeth?

Jo: I know. You're going to remind me how unpopular the UN is. How it's failed in so many ways. How some countries resent it. How smaller-scale projects of the same kind—like the EU—provoke similar antipathy. How nationalism is resurgent. I know all that. And it's important. It has to be addressed. (*Pause.*)

Behind the League of Nations was a splendid idea. Of

course, the League itself failed. Spectacularly. Catastrophically. The UN has done better—but not as well as its architects hoped. Not well enough to offer much encouragement. (*Pause.*) If we had that model in mind, there wouldn't be a serious basis for hope.

But there's another way to think about global governance. The League and the UN emerged after devastating wars. Wars in which nations had worked together as allies and supported one another in a common cause. We believe we should see our situation today in just that way. We need an alliance . . . a global alliance . . . an alliance of all humanity . . . to combat a new enemy. Atmospheric carbon. It threatens our future.

Joe: Of course you're right. Nations do ally together. They make deals and support one another. But only while the threat endures.

Jo: And . . . you'll say . . . nobody will sign on to a *permanent* global structure. It's a good objection. (*Pause.*) But can I set it aside for the present? I promise to come back to it. OK?

Joe: Sure. Go on.

Jo: What does this alliance need if it's going to defeat the enemy? First, it must have what previous international climate meetings . . . climate summits . . . have already provided. A forum for discussion, and for making commitments. But what we've had so far isn't enough. The threat to the future is so large . . . so urgent . . . we can't settle for periodic meetings. You need constant review. You need a body that meets all the time and is always equipped with the latest . . . the best . . . information. And, as I said, with enforcement powers.

Its scope is limited. After all, it's set up to win a war. Anything not relevant to winning that war is no part of its purview. But more falls within its scope than you might initially think. Policies for helping developing nations. Global population policy. Not just schedules for phasing out fossil fuels.

That's because you can't have a stable alliance unless the terms of cooperation are recognized as fair. Seen as just by all the allies. So, as we've argued . . . in writings I think you've read . . . (*Joe nods*) . . . green development must be part of the package . . . and aid for developing countries to do that . . . with a system of monitoring to make sure the aid is used for its intended purposes. Also the problem is hopeless . . . the war will be lost . . . unless there are agreements about population growth. We just can't expand indefinitely.

(*A waiter arrives with food. An elegant salad for Joe, a simple salad for Jo.*)

Jo: Oh . . . I'm rattling on . . . bombarding you with bits and pieces of our ideas . . .

Joe: Don't worry. I'm listening. Give me the whole picture.

Jo: Well, there's more. We think there's no way to plan the transition in advance. It's too complicated. Too much we don't . . . can't . . . know. Too many consequences for people's lives. So the policy has to be pragmatic . . . experimental . . . constantly adjusting . . . with information about successes and failures flowing freely . . . to help with the next decisions . . . that's why the body has to meet all the time.

And the experiments pose dangers. People . . . and nations . . . need protection. There has to be a safety net—a real commitment of resources . . . wealth . . . to guard against the disruption of lives . . . the decline of national economies.

The sorts of supports allies have given one another in times of war.

So you see . . . (*apologetically*) global democracy does require a new kind of politics. A politics of cooperation.

Joe: (*Setting down the fork with which he has been unhurriedly eating.*) It's a very ambitious program and, of course, I can see how it might lead to large economic changes. You know, the kinds of things your group talks about—the "transformation of capitalism," as you call it. We'll probably get to that.

I have lots of questions, though. Let's begin with the most obvious. Where does the money come from? How do you pay for this system of support . . . these safety nets?

Jo: Well, if you're fighting a war, shouldn't your military budget be spent on providing the weapons you need? Many politically savvy people—including the senator, I think—worry that we're not spending wisely. Of course, there are questions about whether building so many weapons, especially nuclear weapons, makes the world safer. But if you think the largest threat to safety comes from terrorism, does it make sense to invest in even more sophisticated fighter jets? And if the enemy is the atmosphere, shouldn't we pay for what's needed to limit the concentration of carbon?

I suspect you know how much the ten nations giving the most to their armed forces collectively spent in 2015. Over a trillion dollars, right? The US contributed more than half. China was second with over 150 billion. Then—and this surprised me—Saudi Arabia came ahead of the UK. 57 billion to 55 billion. If you add the expenditures of a hundred more countries, you get a global investment of one and a half trillion dollars. Couldn't we make better use of all that cash? Use it to wage the war we really need to win?

Joe: Hang on. You can't give up international policing entirely. Are you thinking of waving a magic wand? The age of cooperation dawns, and the peaceable kingdom arrives? Old hostilities are forgotten? Not every sword can be turned into a ploughshare . . . not every missile can become a solar collector.

And you're adding on extra expenses beyond those climate economists foresee when they calculate the costs of the transition. You need to fund the replacement of fossil fuels with renewable energy *and* provide aid so developing nations can do that too *and* construct a safety net to protect those who take part in the experiments you're so keen on. The bill is huge. Far bigger than even the whole military budget.

Jo: I don't think we know that. But you may be right. (*Pause.*) You surely are right when you say that international policing will be necessary. Of course, the policing might go better . . . might be more just . . . if it were carried out by some designated international body. But maybe that's a step too far. We simply think the amount spent on weapons could be considerably reduced. Deployed in the war against the atmosphere.

So where else could we look for funds? Like the pope, we think the environmental crisis—that's what he calls it—is entangled with problems of global poverty. And with what he sees as the dominance of materialistic attitudes that sap real meaning from people's lives. We don't necessarily go along with his particular views about what's most important for a human life to go well. But he's got a real point. And if you approach questions of climate policy with that point in mind, lots of possibilities for paying the bill emerge. Higher tax rates to support public goods. Safety nets to protect people who are most in need—to help them get back to work, and to be productive.

All this has to go along with a deeper form of democracy at home. I haven't talked about that part of our program. But I should have. It's really important for there to be places where citizens can come together and talk. They need opportunities for figuring out what they can't live without and what can be given up. It's like rationing in wartime. Some sacrifices must be made so the war effort can be sustained. Which ones? We think that's determined by democratic discussion. It's why we insist on conversation . . . more conversation and better conversation. Why a crucial part of our program is a grassroots movement.

(*Increasingly animated.*) Don't you think there are *lots* of opportunities for using our wealth . . . our national wealth . . . better than we do? And shouldn't we face up to the need . . . to the urgent need . . . to spend more wisely? So we can win the war against the atmosphere? And shouldn't we work out what counts as wiser spending by talking together? By a deepening of democracy . . . in fact, a *return* to the kind of democracy that once inspired people to try to govern themselves.

Joe: (*Genuinely impressed.*) I think some of the things you've said would resonate with the senator. I suspect she's thought along the same lines, particularly when she was younger. But she . . . and I . . . given our experience . . . would have to question some of your optimism. Why do you believe there's a chance, even a small chance, of agreement on anything substantial, in any diverse international body? The track record isn't good. And even within a society . . . a complex society like ours . . . how can people come to agree on what can be given up and what mustn't be touched?

Jo: (*Surprised by his tone; awed by a sense that she might be taken seriously.*) Because . . . I think there are two important changes. I keep using this metaphor of a war . . . but it helps. When the threat becomes clear, people can overcome past differences and see the need for agreement. They come to feel new forms of solidarity. That in itself can be very rewarding—I've heard that many Londoners looked back to the Blitz as the most meaningful part of their lives . . . how there was a . . .depth . . . to their working together . . . like New Yorkers . . . for a shorter period after 9/11.

Now the climate threat *hasn't* been so clear. But it's becoming more . . . palpable. And our movement tries . . . tries very hard . . . to spread the message . . . to show that it's real . . . that it must be taken seriously . . . even more seriously perhaps than *any* past war.

The other change . . . really important, we think . . . is in making responsibilities transparent. The duties you and I agreed on. (*She smiles. Joe is struck by the radiance of her expression.*) Well, almost agreed on. The global parliament is founded on recognizing our fourfold obligation—to preserve a habitable world for our descendants, to do so in a way that allows the poorer nations to develop, to attend to the sufferings of those all over the world who have been left behind, and to preserve the valuable accomplishments of our species. Acknowledging that is crucial. If a rich country . . . if the US . . . says, "We have no obligation to give you anything" . . . that closes off negotiations. On the other hand, it might say something different. Like: "Of course, we should help you with this; but here is the full range of sacrifices we are demanding of our own citizens; that's why we are offering you less than you ask for, and less than you fully deserve." Talking like that opens the way for a discussion about the strengths of competing claims. No guarantee of agreement, but it helps.

(*She smiles again.*) Do I still seem . . . such a . . . wide-eyed . . . optimist?

Joe: (*Returning her smile. He hasn't resumed eating. She hasn't touched her food. Both are caught up in the unexpected intensity of the conversation.*) Less . . . you've obviously thought . . . thought hard . . . about these questions. (*Pause.*) I'm still a bit troubled by an obvious reaction from American citizens, even the most progressive ones. The ones we count as the senator's staunchest supporters. Isn't it all give on our side? We pay the bill for the whole world? What do we get in return?

Jo: (*Excitedly.*) Oh, I have *lots* to say about that! First—what do we get? A habitable planet. For our children . . . grandchildren. I don't have any, of course. Not yet. Do you? (*Joe shakes his head. Smiles.*) And it's really strange . . . really ignoring history . . . to think we're now the ones making the big sacrifices. After all, we got rich . . . very rich . . . by filling the atmosphere with carbon . . . we created the enemy we now have to fight . . . and it's only fair that we . . . we and the other industrial countries . . . the ones responsible . . . collectively pay the bill. It's not just us on our own. Then there's another thing. We do ask something of the developing world. They have to join us in limiting population growth. I mentioned that earlier. It's relevant to what you just asked. (*Pause.*) Do you mind if I say more about it? Do we have time?

Joe: Of course. (*Pause.*) This is a useful . . . a valuable . . . conversation. More so—I'll be frank—than I'd expected. Don't rush. Say what you want to say. Take all the time you need. (*Smiles.*) You might even have a bite of salad.

(*Jo returns the smile. She takes one small bite. Lays down her fork again.*)

Jo: It's really clear that the human population can't keep growing—at least not at the current rate. Even if we limited the impact of climate change . . . if we won the war . . . we wouldn't have the resources . . . not for everyone to live a worthwhile life. So we have to persuade the developing countries to do what the affluent world has already done—coax them into going through the demographic transition. They'll need to reduce birth rates, so they're more or less at replacement levels. Maybe a little higher. But not too much.

How does that happen? Through education. Particularly education of girls. So part of the policy package . . . the agreement . . . has to be for them to make universal education a high priority. Even if they don't currently view that as important. Or, in some cases, as a good thing. (*Pause.*) There are demands on them, too. It isn't as one-sided as you suggested.

Joe: But surely you expect resistance. There's so much suspicion of international institutions. People see the threat of interference in their lives, in what matters most to them. Confinement of their lives. Dictated from afar.

Jo: Yes. Of course we understand that. Nationalist voices are so loud today—they're impossible to ignore. And there are obvious reasons behind all the shouting. (*Pause.*) I'm not sure if what I'm about to say will allay people's fears, or simply make them feel worse.

In today's world our lives are intricately interconnected. Linked in inscrutable ways . . . ways whose workings are impossible for ordinary folk to fathom. So they can't control . . . or even detect . . . the major forces that shape . . . and sometimes confine . . . their lives. Distant actors can change . . . or destroy . . . things on which they rely. Think of what transnational corporations can do, or the havoc cybercrime can produce. It's not silly to feel powerless.

The right response to the threats . . . or so it seems to us . . . is to broaden . . . and deepen . . . democracy. The deepening comes from creating new channels for citizens to explore and express what's really important to them . . . what matters most in their lives . . . or maybe revive old opportunities for doing this . . . local conversations . . . community-wide discussions . . . like the town meetings some theorists have seen as the heart of democracy. The broadening comes from building a democratic framework on a larger scale. A global scale. The scale on which it's needed to tackle the large issues that cut across national lines. Like cybercrime. And, first and foremost, the dangers coming from climate change.

We *have* to make global democracy work. There's no other way to address the global problems. (*Pause.*) I'm afraid that isn't much consolation.

Joe: No, I'm afraid it isn't. Government can seem so remote and uncaring. It can easily become indifferent to predicaments it only dimly understands. (*Pause.*) The senator has tried to address the concern. She looks for ways of giving people chances to speak—so she can listen.

Jo: I know! That's one reason we admire her so much. That and her recognition of the climate problem. In fact, our program for deepening democracy tries to take her approach further. We want to help the people speak, encourage them to talk together, and to discover . . . in the exchange of ideas . . . what most needs to be said.

Here's the way we see it. If a particular problem . . . like climate change . . . can only be tackled through cooperation . . . through collective action at a particular level . . . there's a danger . . . a real danger . . . of government coming to seem remote . . . alien . . . indifferent. But you can't simply decide to make all the decisions at a lower level . . . to leave it to nations . . . or to smaller groups. That would create chaos . . . not the coordinated action that's needed . . . so the problem will remain . . . or probably get worse. Instead you have to keep the governance at the right level . . . take steps to bring the deciding body closer to the people it represents . . . to enable all the people to recognize that their concerns . . . for the things mattering most to them . . . can be heard . . . can be weighed . . . when decisions are made.

(*She looks directly at Joe.*)

I know I sound idealistic again. Maybe I am. But I have this picture of how democracy . . . real democracy . . . works. May I . . . ?

Joe: Yes. I'm getting a sense of how you . . . you and your colleagues . . . think. (*Pause.*) It's deeper than I'd thought.

Jo: (*Reassured; smiles.*) Thanks. I see democracy as taking place at many different scales. Let's start with the family. (*Animatedly.*) Oh, I know, families have often been *really* antidemocratic. But not the best ones, not today! Some decisions families make have to involve others. The actions required go beyond what a single family can do by itself. So you join with neighbors. There's community discussion. Hopefully it's democratic. You see where I'm going, I'm sure (*Joe nods; they exchange smiles*) . . . above the community there's the national level. Probably a number of levels in between. When you need all members of a particular group to come together in collective action, you have to involve members of the group. This should be done democratically—for the sake of freedom. The freedom of all of those involved.

Climate change requires all of us to act together. So the level has to be international. Panhuman. Ideally, it should involve conversation. A discussion that's inclusive, well-informed, and dedicated to find a solution everyone can live with. Of course, we can't bring all people together to talk. So we have to represent them. And not only those now living, but our children, grandchildren . . . it's really weird to talk about them so definitely! . . . future generations. They have an enormous stake in what we decide. And . . . those channels of communication—between the citizens and the decision-makers—are immensely important. Without them, how will the representatives know what most matters to those they're supposed to represent? What can't be given up? What can be tolerated?

Joe: But I'm worried about your confidence. You seem to think it's always obvious who the actors should be and who the stakeholders are. It isn't. In the real world, people disagree about that.

Jo: You're right! That is a problem. Two problems, actually. Things might go wrong because you don't include enough people. Surely that's often happened. In our history . . . in its darkest chapters . . . people have been excluded . . . decisions made for them. But there's the opposite mistake of including too many people. An issue gets resolved by folk who have no real stake in it—and who act against the interests of the ones for whom it really matters. That's a big part of the fear you mentioned. The remote dictator. The faceless bureaucrats of the UN . . . or Brussels.

Ideally, it shouldn't happen. If there are extra people . . . the don't-cares . . . and if they're really engaged with the other participants . . . concerned to find a solution all can live with . . . then they should step aside. They say "We're leaving the matter to you . . . you folk for whom it's serious." They leave the room. But . . . (*She grins at Joe.*) I do know the real world isn't like that. The don't-cares don't appreciate how serious it is for the others. No channels of communication! At any rate, not channels of the sort our deepening of democracy hopes to create. Or maybe the channels are in place, but the don't-cares really don't care. Too bad if some of the others have to lump it.

Joe: Right. And what do you do about that?

Jo: Provide recourse. Sometimes, in the courts, parties to a suit disagree about the level at which the case should be heard. Our legal system offers a procedure for deciding what kind of court has jurisdiction. Multilevel democracy can imitate that line of solution.

Suppose some country thinks our imagined global body has gone too far. In trying to work out a plan of attack in the war on the atmosphere, it's overstepped its proper limits. It's interfered in a matter that should have been left to individual nations. The aggrieved country can go to a second international body . . . a "court" . . . and present its case. I'm giving the same answer I offered before. You don't automatically reject the global level. Instead, you try to build in protections against abuse . . . ways of addressing the anxieties people have . . . that they *reasonably* have.

Joe: So you want to reassure people who worry about global government, by telling them about a *second* international institution? Don't worry about this fox guarding the chicken coop—there's a second fox to keep his eye on the first one!

Jo: (*Smiling.*) I know, I know! It sounds silly at first. But if they thought that way . . . consistently . . . they should be worried about democracy at all sorts of levels . . . well before you get to the international stage. When you unite . . . when you have to unite with others . . . to act . . . because what's needed couldn't be done at a smaller scale . . . you put your own interests at risk. You might be overridden. So it's very important to have protections. But the protections are *always* more of the same. There's always a question about who guards the guardians.

It's a lesson well-brought-up democratic children have to learn. You're not always going to get your own way. And sometimes that will happen when you *ought* to have received what you wanted . . . when the actual decision overrides your legitimate interests. So it's crucial that there should be protections, even though the protections are more of the same and even though they sometimes fail. Because there's no alternative. We have to act together . . . and the best we can do is to introduce democratic discussion . . . at many levels. Including, today, the international . . . panhuman . . . level. And to try to ensure that the protections work.

Joe: It's an interesting vision . . . a coherent vision. Effectively, you're posing a dilemma to the people who resist internationalism—go with democracy all the way, or reject it from the very beginning. If you don't like global democracy, go back to your remote hut and live in solitude. Probably a few loners would bite that bullet. But my guess is most nationalists would feel you haven't really addressed the heart of their point. They see nations as . . . *special*. You see it here in our own politics. All over the spectrum. A firm belief in American exceptionalism. What can you say to them . . . to the true believers?

Jo: Well . . . there are nationalists . . . and nationalists. It's perfectly OK to take pride in local traditions and achievements. (*Pause; with quiet emphasis.*) So long as you recognize the worth of what *other* people—people living at different times or in different places—have *also* accomplished. But if you see them as contributing valuable things . . . why not open yourself up to learning from them . . . acting with them . . . a joint effort to solve big problems . . . global democracy?

Nationalism goes bad when you contrast yourself with all the rest. You're better, they're inferior. You have a unique role to play in running the show. Your mission is to govern "the lesser breeds without the law" or bring the Pax Romana. Wealth and might and success can come to be viewed as outward symptoms of intrinsic superiority. If you have that attitude, it's easy to think your "inferiors" shouldn't be equal partners in making important decisions. So you reject global democracy. Not because a wider circle of deliberation might inevitably lead to compromises and losses of freedom. But because opening the doors of the council chamber would bring in people who are unqualified. Decisions are important, and only the best should make them. And we're much better than all the rest.

Is this what lies behind American exceptionalism? I surely hope not! If you think about it, it's implausible—even ludicrous. Do people believe we've been chosen to fulfill the Creator's plan for the creation? Is that belief any better grounded than taking the Romans to have been given a divine mission or supposing God to be an Englishman? I think those ideas . . . once very popular ideas in Rome and in London . . . sound a bit . . . quaint . . . today. And if people think things are different this time . . . Americans are the *real deal* . . . shouldn't they explain their grounds for believing that?

Joe: Probably some of our fellow citizens would take up your challenge. They'd appeal to their faith. (*Pause.*) And that's an area we have to explore. Maybe later. (*Pause.*) But I think you've made life too easy for yourself by setting up an extreme form of the position. Many Americans think there's something unique . . . and important . . . about our country. You haven't done justice to that.

Jo: No, I haven't. Actually, my plan was to proceed in stages. So let's ask what might make a country . . . any country . . . special. One answer . . . a terrible answer, I think . . . is that human beings come in grades. Some are simply better than others—nobler, stronger, more virtuous, more intelligent, wiser. I don't think anyone should believe in the superior native endowment of the people of any country. There's no basis for distinguishing "national genomes" . . . for thinking Americans or Armenians or Argentinians or any other group have the "best genes."

I was once tempted to write a parody of a scientific paper and supply the "evidence" for American superiority. We're a country of immigrants. That's increased interbreeding among historically separated peoples. We've reaped the benefits of "hybrid vigor." But there's a glitch . . . a problem with the hypothesis. How does our "hybrid vigor" sit with past laws against miscegenation . . . or present fondness for closing borders?

But that's a tangent. (*She smiles.*) The real position . . . the sensible idea is that some countries have made *social* breakthroughs. They've set up conditions under which their citizens thrive. So . . . in our case . . . people think American children grow into adults who tackle problems with a distinctive ingenuity. They work hard. They're inventive and rightly confident about exploring new avenues and overcoming obstacles. These people think moving towards global democracy would weaken all that. It would dilute what's best in our society. Maybe even accelerate a dismal trend that's already begun.

Joe: Fine. It took a little while. But I think you've now expressed the kinds of considerations moving thoughtful people. And you need to address them.

Jo: Agreed. So what exactly *is* this social achievement? Perhaps it's democracy . . . many people think of us as the birthplace of democracy. Of course, others can quibble . . . point to what happened in ancient Athens or on that little island off the coast of Europe. But I think it's perfectly fair to take pride in the great experiment launched in 1776 and see it as an *enormous* political step forward. For all its limitations and imperfections. So suppose it's creating democracy that makes us exceptional and sets us apart. Isn't it odd . . . ironic . . . to go on and say "And that's why we have to resist global democracy!"? If democracy has been the source of so much that's good . . . if our democratic experiment has encouraged so many of the world's nations to follow our lead . . . why wouldn't you think of global democracy as a further progressive step? We need to act collectively to solve a species-wide problem. Humanity needs secure forms of cooperation. (*With emphasis.*) Just as post-revolutionary America once did. You can't simultaneously see democracy as the key to a great political transformation and then denounce a proposal to extend it—especially not when the extension is needed in our current predicament. And aren't we in a situation just like the one the founding fathers faced?

Joe: But they rejected all sorts of extensions of democracy. Think about the people they included—and all those they left out.

Jo: You're right, of course. But we criticize them for that. We believe they should have gone further. As we should, too.

Joe: Agreed—we shouldn't imitate their *actual* behavior, but do the kind of thing they *ought* to have done. But your analysis is too simple. Of course, if the *only* social achievement were the invention of democracy . . . supposing we deserve all the credit for that . . . what you say would be a compelling answer. But there's more to it, and you yourself pointed to what's missing. All the stuff about ingenuity and perseverance and courage and a willingness to try new things. People see these virtues as threatened by the kinds of global structures you have in mind. Safety nets and regulations and smoothing out of inequality are bound to destroy some precious aspects of our society—including the bold style of initiative the world very much needs. That is, if the human future is to be a good one.

Don't you know how the charges will be presented? It's a return to socialism, or communism. You're going back to a form of economic arrangements that has failed—demonstrably and completely. Your kind of global democracy will be seen as undermining capitalism—the best economic system we know.

I'm not making those charges in my own voice. Just trying to predict how your global democratic movement will be greeted. Why I've seen what you're doing . . . and, as I've already said, it's more intricate, more sophisticated, than I'd thought . . . as politically unrealistic. Not something even a progressive political figure . . . like the senator . . . can press for. Not without losing all credibility.

Jo: (*Quietly.*) I know. I've heard that voice before. Inside my own head. (*Pause.*) We've come to the core of the serious opposition. It seemed right to get there by stripping away . . . all the other versions . . . the easily refutable ones . . .

Joe: And it *was* right to do that. So the debate doesn't get muddled up by irrelevant points.

Jo: Thanks. But now I have to say what I can . . . about why it's *not* socialism . . . or communism . . . but a *transformation* of capitalism. One the world needs.

Would international structures inevitably muffle our energy? Decrease initiative? I don't think so. We need to harness the talents of all our citizens. To do that, we have to provide all children, all adults, with opportunities to develop their talents. To find their own best path. Do we achieve that at the moment? Social mobility in the US is far lower than in many other countries. Because safety nets have been slashed, public goods underfunded. Horatio Alger should go back where he belongs—in the pages of fiction. We waste so much human talent as it is. The kind of global democracy we favor would correct that . . . or help to correct it. It would liberate more talent. So I don't think this version of the objection has any merit at all.

Joe: (*Teasing her.*) You're doing the same thing again. Starting with the less plausible ways of making the point. But I'm not going to let you get away with it. (*He grins; she smiles back.*)

The real problem . . . so your opponents will say . . . comes with all the constraints you place on markets. You shackle healthy capitalist competition. Lots of people who take climate change seriously think we shouldn't tinker with capitalism as usual. Scores . . . probably hundreds . . . of economists will rise up against you. And some of those who think . . . as you do . . . that tackling climate change entails modifying economic structures will go in the other direction. They'll prefer to settle for the climate risks if the alternative is to interfere with capitalism.

You know the line. For almost all goods and services produced within a society, it's better to leave the production to "the market" rather than to plan for providing and distributing them. Suppliers produce as seems best to them. Consumers select and pay for the goods and services they want. The market works. Other ways of organizing economies don't. If there were unbelievers before, 1989 taught everyone the true gospel.

Jo: I do know the line. But I don't know why it's supposed to be true . . . what the big virtue of the market is supposed to be. And, not knowing that, I can't tell if the things we propose interfere with what makes markets so good . . . so magically good . . . or whether they leave everything intact. (*She smiles; it is her turn to tease.*) So enlighten me, O most astute political savant . . . tell me the secret . . . so that I may learn and worship also.

Joe: Well . . . O equally astute political theorist . . . I can do no better than imitate your own approach to these questions. Start with ideas that are popular, but less good. Invite you to shoot them down. Until we get to the heart of the matter.

OK. First up—freedom. If you regulate the goods produced . . . or regulate how they have to be produced . . . or how they are sold . . . you're interfering with the liberties of producers and consumers. If you stipulate that goods must satisfy particular requirements, you dampen the initiative of people who supply them and you limit the choices of those who buy. Similarly, if you demand that particular things must be available to everyone at a specified price, or that everyone must purchase some version of a good or service. If you insist on safety nets, you interfere with healthy competition. Innovation declines. There's less experimentation. (*Pause.*) And you're very keen on experimentation.

Jo: So let's think harder about this "consumer" whose freedoms are threatened. Who is she? Where was she born? Where did she grow up? Where did she go to school? What opportunities did she have along the way? What chances did she . . . does she . . . have as a young adult? For lots of our fellow citizens . . . as the senator has been pointing out for years . . . the answers to these questions aren't particularly encouraging. If our society has let her grow up in poverty . . . in a decaying neighborhood . . . surrounded by broken families . . . by crime . . . if the schools she went to are unsafe . . . if the classrooms she sits in are overcrowded . . . filled with kids who need far more help than the teachers can provide . . . if the job opportunities for people like her are minimal . . . what freedom does she have to lose?

We think these questions ought to be asked about lots of contemporary Americans and about lots of people in affluent societies. Many economists would agree that the magic of markets doesn't extend to public goods . . . that markets aren't particularly adept at providing important things people need . . . education, health protection, job retraining. Others would argue that markets actually undermine these sorts of things. It doesn't matter. The necessities aren't there . . . they're not available for a significant number of people, even in prosperous countries like ours. So we insist on a safety net. To provide the basic capacities people need to be free . . . genuinely free. It's no consolation to my consumer, a *real* consumer, not the fictitious persona of market models, that "healthy competition in the free market" might produce a better brand of soft soap . . . or better cars . . . which she can't afford . . . or better building materials . . . for constructing houses . . . in which she has no hopes of living. Genuine freedom . . . the freedom that's most important to all of us . . . demands certain abilities . . . capacities. If markets don't provide those, if they can't provide those, then we serve the cause of freedom best by providing them in some other way.

And, as an afterthought, I don't buy your supposed connection between absence of safety nets and greater experimentation. I'd have thought it would go the other way. Don't you encourage people to experiment if there are limits to the price they'll have to pay if things turn out badly?

Joe: The senator would be proud of you. To be honest, I don't . . . we don't . . . understand why people associate markets with freedom. But people do. So the idea has to be considered and demolished. You did a nice job of demolition. (*They exchange smiles.*) On to a more serious point.

You know the explanation of why planned economies fail.

Centralized decisions about how much of some product to make and how to distribute it don't work very well. You get shortages of some things, and oversupply of others. Goods aren't available in the places where they're needed. Markets do much better. They provide information to producers. If something's undersupplied, there's an incentive to start making it.

Jo: I agree. Basically, it's a sound point. Although, sometimes, of course, there's a time lag. The needed goods can't be produced instantly. (*Pointedly.*) Like power plants based on solar or wind energy. (*Pause.*) But why think that regulated markets . . . or markets with safety nets . . . can't give information that's just as good? Or, if there's a difference, why not try to make it up . . . in the age of internet technology . . . with online surveys?

Joe: Because . . . and now we come to the heart of the case for the free market . . . markets are simply more efficient. The invisible hand works better than the central planners . . . even if the planners are thoroughly motivated by the public good. And that's a pretty big "if."

Jo: So what exactly *is* this "free market"? All economists know . . . and have always known . . . and will confess, if you press them . . . that markets work only if certain background conditions are present. You have to have a legal system, a transportation system, probably an educational system to provide the necessary workers. These things have to be there *before* the market starts to work its magic. And, as I already suggested, some of them may depend on constraints . . . on regulations and safety nets.

So here's a more cautious position, one that stands a better chance of being right than the usual hymns to the free market. A market subject only to the minimal set of constraints, the ones needed to provide the crucial background conditions, produces good outcomes more efficiently than one with extra constraints.

Joe: OK. And now you want to say that all the conditions global democracy would impose are already included in that minimal set?

Jo: No. That would be too cheap. *Some* of them are included. A safety net for education for example. But *all* of them? I don't know. (*Pause.*) Probably not.

This cautious position is still too imprecise. What's meant by "good outcomes"—and by "efficiency"? As I see it, the supposed efficiency of markets resides in their ability to deliver outcomes more regularly, more reliably, and more cheaply than alternatives . . . like planning and governmental regulation. And when economists think about good outcomes, they typically have some economic measure in mind. They're talking about *economically* good outcomes—greater productivity, lower prices, things like that. They're not talking in the fundamental terms . . . the human terms.

We want to talk in those human terms . . . to think about good outcomes as those in which human lives go well. Good outcomes are *ethically* good outcomes. Outcomes in which more people live lives that are more worthwhile. And, as I've said, worthwhile lives . . . lives that go well . . . depend on certain abilities . . . on capacities for which another set of conditions . . . a richer set of conditions . . . is needed. When markets fail to deliver those conditions . . . and hence those capacities . . . or even undermine them . . . we shouldn't leave everything to the market. The vaunted efficiency . . . the ability to produce . . . reliably, regularly, and cheaply . . . economically good outcomes . . . is irrelevant . . . unimportant. We're given the whole world . . . or, more exactly, a better TV set or smartphone . . . but we lose our soul.

Joe: Don't be so dismissive about smartphones, or TVs for that matter. They've helped lots of poor people get information that's helped them lead better lives.

Jo: At what cost? Importing Western technology has had its uses. But it's also disrupted the ways in which people lead their lives. (*She reflects.*) You have a point, though. We should look at the pluses as well as the minuses. I suspect the balance would be negative. (*Looking directly at Joe.*) But I don't *know* that.

I overstated. I couldn't resist the religious allusion. You see, I think the pope gets it. *Deeply* gets it. He sees that the current version of global capitalism is antithetical to lots of valuable things. Of course, I . . . we . . . lots of the folk in our movement . . . wouldn't share his way of thinking about values and the sources of value. But, like him, we'd point to failures to provide and sustain systems of education, satisfactory housing, opportunities for meaningful work, even nutritious food and clean water. Basically Francis is right. Efficiency in giving you the wrong things is nothing to shout about.

Joe: So maybe this is the moment for us to talk about something I see as potentially fatal to the success of your movement. You don't frame your proposals in the kind of language people understand. It's always so abstract . . . the ethical points you make have no connection with the religious language ordinary folk use every day.

Jo: It's a good question, and I do want to address it before we finish. But not quite yet. Can I say one more thing about the need to transform capitalism? (*Joe nods.*) It comes from a point you made earlier. When I called for an alliance to wage war on the atmosphere . . . or, at least, its carbon . . . you pointed out that alliances are temporary. On the other hand, as you rightly saw, the move to global democracy is supposed to be permanent. That's because, without an enduring change, we're bound to fail. Doomed to lose the war.

Lots of really brilliant economists, all the ones you said would rise up against me, want to set things up so market forces can steer the transition. I don't think it will work—at least, not as straightforwardly as they imagine—not only because it's hard to see how you include the developing nations in any "climate club" . . . without forcing them, that is. The trouble comes once you think of the terms of cooperation . . . all agreeing on rates of phasing out fossil fuels . . . as temporary.

As I see it, proposals to win the war, while preserving capitalism as usual, divide history from 1850 on into three chunks. In the first stage, nations compete. Some of them—the most successful ones—use fossil fuels to drive their production. Then comes the transition. Nations cooperate to reduce the use of fossil fuels to zero. After that's over, economic competition as we know it is supposed to resume. With the big difference that all production will depend on renewable sources of energy.

You have to arrange the cooperation in the intermediate phase. So economists ask: How can we motivate countries engaged in direct competition with one another to agree on terms of cooperation? Just as people who plan climate summits ask: How can we do it *this time* . . . change the dismal history of disagreement and get nations with conflicting economic interests to agree on the burdens they should assume in cooperating? The shadow of the future hangs over both questions. Everyone knows the third stage is coming. All of the constraints . . . the restraints of the intermediate phase . . . the things some "free marketeers" take to interfere with efficiency . . . will be discarded. Back to proper competition! And because all parties are aware of that future, they want to ensure they start it in excellent shape, without compromising their competitive advantages. They negotiate with that in mind . . . and it blocks the agreements the world needs.

So the cooperation . . . the alliance . . . has to be permanent. Capitalism must be transformed—it has to become more humane. So no country need fear a bleak future. So cooperation . . . and sharing . . . are assured.

Joe: You know, I think you're putting things too starkly. The language you use is likely to raise hackles, to be counterproductive. Why alienate people by talking about a "transformation of capitalism"? By dumping on "market forces"? What you're really asking for can be accommodated in fairly orthodox economic thinking. You have certain goals—humane goals, admirable goals—and you say we need sweeping changes to be able to reach them. I'm not convinced. Isn't it just a matter of introducing constraints to give people the right incentives? Can't we see the problem as one of harnessing self-interest? Of building the right sort of market? If you made your points that way, you might win more allies.

Jo: You may well be right. Perhaps we've let ourselves be carried away, by insisting on a radical program we don't need. (*She reflects.*) But it's important to put the human goals first. Whatever economic institutions we have, however we set them up, they're tools for preserving—improving—the conditions of human life. The tail can't be allowed to wag the dog. Economic dogma coming first, and dictating what goals we should be trying to achieve.

Joe: You're doing it again. Why "dogma"? Economists know some useful things. I agree with you when you give priority to human lives. But if you're clear about that, why pick fights you can avoid?

Jo: (*Smiling.*) I misspoke. Perhaps there would be less resistance if we focused on emphasizing our aims—making it clear how important they are. Once that's accepted, we'll welcome any good way to achieve them. Let economic institutions adapt so they achieve the crucial goals.

Joe: And, as I said before, language matters. You find the pope inspiring. His ideas about what needs to be done resonate with you. But you don't talk the way he does. All this stuff about responsibilities and abstract duties. Not the sort of language to be politically effective, perhaps?

Jo: I worry about that. We all do. (*Pause.*) We can't deliver the message . . . even if it's the same message . . . in a voice that isn't our own . . . pretending to beliefs we don't have. And there's another point. We want to address *everyone* . . . people of all religions . . . or of none. So adopting the language of any one religion . . . even the eloquent language of an extraordinary religious leader . . . wouldn't do. We need ways of making the case that cut across *all* the perspectives . . . that present the *core* . . . the shared line of argument people elaborate . . . oh, so much more movingly than we do! . . . in their different ways.

And it's so important to open the lines of communication. If we're to have a global alliance . . . if it's going to be strong enough to win the war against atmospheric carbon . . . we need to understand how . . . despite all kinds of differences . . . many of us share hopes for the human future. We present the issues as we do because we want to expose that commonality . . . because we want to . . . we *need* to . . . get lots of people, people with very different religious—or nonreligious—perspectives on board.

I feel it's not an adequate reply . . . but it's all I can give you today.

Joe: It's a start. Maybe we'll talk further . . .

Jo: Yes. (*Pause.*) I'd like that. You have been so patient with me. Wonderfully patient. I know how I must seem to you with all your experience. So thanks, thanks so much for listening. (*They look at one another.*)

You know (*she hesitates*) . . . I sometimes have this image of our politics . . . it's probably a silly image . . . but you've been sympathetic . . . so I'll share it. Our politics is like an enormous apartment in which many people live. It's full of furniture we've inherited from people who lived generations ago . . . the contents of our grandparents' attics . . . much of it in terrible shape . . . rickety . . . disjointed . . . piled higgledy-piggledy . . . at crazy angles. And, even though it's big, the apartment is stuffed. Large bits and pieces everywhere . . . precariously placed. The trouble is, our vision is really poor . . . we can't see at all clearly. We have to move about, to do things. But we're always bumping into this or that. Dislodging stuff. Sometimes with disastrous consequences.

The politicians have the task of doing something about this situation. They try to make clear paths and clean up some of the mess . . . to make the whole place less dangerous. Of course, their eyes are bad, too—they aren't able to see any better than the rest of us. When they start, they often think like me. They aim to make major changes and really improve *everything*. And those who've been there a while see the newcomers as silly blunderers . . .

Joe: . . . or sympathize with them . . . because the ones who've been around were once like those who've just come, and once tried to work on a larger scale. But they've bumped into too many sharp corners and brought down too many unsteady piles and caused too much damage and pain. So now their movements are small and stiff and slow and cautious. Sometimes, maybe, their limited efforts do a little . . . a very little . . . and they're glad of that. But often, even the small, timid, movements prove disastrous. Perhaps worse than a larger effort would have been. And they remember what they'd once hoped to do.

(Long pause. They look at one another. Then Jo stands up. Joe stands too.)

Jo: Thanks again. You've given me so much of your time. I feel I've kept you too long. And I should go back to our office.

Joe: It's been a pleasure. More than a pleasure. I hope we can talk again. Very soon.

(They shake hands. The handshake lasts longer than is strictly necessary.)

Joe: I'll be in touch.

(Jo smiles. She turns and leaves. He watches her as she makes her way to the door. Then he glances down at the table. Her salad is virtually untouched—only the single small bite she took at his urging. He sits down, lifts his fork—then replaces it and pushes the plate aside, signaling that he is done. As he waits for the waiter to bring the bill, he sits—and thinks.)

INTERVAL

Tea and Sympathy

Three years have passed. A very warm May afternoon in London, with the temperature above 90°F. From an imposing Georgian building, fronted by a colonnade, steps lead down to a small square. At one side of the square stand the outdoor tables of a small café. Only one or two are occupied.

A small group of twenty-year-olds bursts out of the building. They are led by Haroun, British of Pakistani descent. He is evidently very angry. The others are listening attentively, with sympathy for his com-

plaints. They are Rahel (a woman from Israel), Sumedha (an Indian woman who has spent most of her life in South Africa), Miguel (a Mexican man), and Ji-hoon (a South Korean man).

Haroun: (*At high volume and intensity.*) Sir Percival Pratt, Sir Percival fucking Pratt! Pratt's the name all right. What century does he think he's in? (*In falsetto, with mincing mimicry.*) "Ey-ah must-ah say-uh Mister Ick-bawl, ey-ah fai-ind you-ah lawst cawmment most-uh inawpwopwiett." Cutting me off. Cutting off all discussion.

Rahel: Yes. Just when we wanted to challenge you! Leap in and have the sort of exchange we came here for.

Sumedha: Right. It was so frustrating. What you said was really provocative. About Islam being the main target of prejudice. I was going . . .

Haroun: But no . . . Sir Percival looks at me . . . through his ever-so-dainty glasses . . . down his very long nose. What do you think he sees? Not me as I am. He doesn't see an undergraduate at Bristol, whose parents have lived here for nearly forty years. No. I'm a bloody jihadist, with a scruffy beard and a machine gun. With squads of women in burkas behind me.

It's 2020, not 1920. Britannia no longer even pretends to rule the waves, or the world. It's a different country now—the wogs are here to stay. You know, my mum and dad took a lot of crap after they came, and even for me, growing up in Bradford, there was a fair amount of shit. But it's all changing for the better. He just doesn't realize it.

And we're here to be international. Intercultural. We're supposed to be having dialogue across ethnic and religious lines. Then, when we start to say what we feel, it's (*falsetto again*) "inawpwopwiett." What a bloody farce! A complete sham. I tell you—I'm not going back. Not this afternoon. Maybe not tomorrow either.

Sumedha: I'm with you, Haroun. We can stay back at the hostel. (*She grins.*) Then I can explain why you're *so* wrong!

Miguel: Yeah. What Pratt said was completely offensive. We ought to protest and have ourselves a boycott. That might teach them how to run a real international dialogue.

Rahel: I'm not sure Sir Percival will turn out to be such an able student. Blunt instruments might be needed. But count me in. (*She turns.*) How about you, Ji-hoon?

Ji-hoon: Well . . . they have supported us . . . to come here . . . and not participating . . .

Miguel: Give peace a chance! But sometimes you have to take a stand . . .

Haroun: Not on the orthodox Buddhist line . . .

Rahel: So who's stereotyping now?

Haroun: (*Chagrined; suddenly less angry.*) Sorry, Ji-hoon. I didn't mean . . .

Ji-hoon: No, no. I understand. It's easy to do. We all do it. Without really thinking. (*Pause.*) But anyway . . . I'll join you.

Sumedha: One for all, and all for one!

(*They form a circle, extend their arms, and clasp hands. As they do so, Jo and Joe emerge from the building. Both are casually dressed. It's evident from their facial expressions and gestures that the relationship has blossomed.*)

Jo: What's going on? Is this the intercultural harmony we've been trying to cultivate?

Haroun: Not exactly. But in a way. It's a protest. A boycott. After what just happened. (*Apologetically.*) Not at your panel—that was really good. At the last one . . .

Joe: (*To Jo.*) You weren't there. You'd just stepped out. Sir Percival went . . . off script. It was bizarre—a throwback. Haroun had made a comment, a sharp one at that, about perceptions of Islam. It could have started a lively discussion. (*Sumedha, Rahel, and Miguel nod vigorously.*) But Sir Percival would have none of it. He reprimanded Haroun, and stopped the conversation—dead.

(*Turning to Haroun.*) So I understand why you're angry. He shouldn't have done it. But please . . . don't give up. (*Quietly.*) Some of us have worked hard to bring you all together.

Haroun: I don't want to go back. Not after that. Over three hundred people heard what he said. Only a few of them . . . the ones staying in our hostel (*he gestures at the others*) know me and know what I'm like . . . what I think . . . . The rest . . .

Jo: I'm sorry this happened. Believe me, it was definitely *not* what we had in mind. But, like Joe, I want you not to quit. (*Pause.*) I'm glad you thought the climate panel worked. We thought so too. There was real convergence. We wish we could have continued.

Sumedha: Well, the two of you are a *lot* better at chairing a discussion. (*Rahel, Miguel, Haroun, and Ji-hoon all nod.*) Maybe Sir Percival should take lessons.

Jo: Thanks. (*Pause.*) So why *don't* we continue? Have a nice cup of tea? (*She points towards the café.*) Let's change the subject. We could go back to the profitable exchange we were having.

Haroun: So I get censored? *My* perspective doesn't belong in "polite conversation"?

Joe: No. What you said was important. Jo didn't hear it, but the rest of us did, and it ought to be discussed. (*Pause.*) But maybe not right now. Perhaps we should wait for the cool hour. (*Mops his brow with a handkerchief.*) If it comes at all. In the meantime, it might be good to build on our successes. We *were* making progress in thinking about climate change together. A reminder of that might help us as we turn to other topics.

Jo: That's what I had in mind. Tea . . . and sympathy.

(*She smiles. The atmosphere has lightened. All of them walk the few steps to the café. They sit down at a large table. Joe disappears inside.*)

Miguel: One thing really surprised me this morning. How much we could agree on. I mean . . . we come from such different perspectives. All of us are religious . . . but who'd have thought a devout Jew would agree with a Muslim (*he waves towards Rahel and Haroun, who are sitting side by side*), or that Sumedha, a Hindu, would find common ground with me, a Catholic? Or that anyone would have any time for Ji-hoon's weird Buddhism? (*Ji-hoon grins. He and Miguel have evidently struck up a friendship.*)

So *why* did it work so well? What really strikes me, Jo, is that your way of framing the discussion was so strange . . . even weirder than Ji-hoon's ideas. All this abstract talk about duties and responsibilities. Ethical decisions coming out of conversations. Negotiation. Compromise. That's certainly not the way

I think about these questions. Morality as something completely separate from religion. I suspect we all feel the same. (*Nods all round the table.*)

Everything you and Joe have written about the climate, and the politics we need . . . well, all the things I've read of yours . . . sort of makes sense. But it's so relentlessly secular. No place for God. Or (*smiling at Sumedha*) Brahma. I'm on board with the various points you make about our responsibilities to future generations, to the members of our societies who find life a constant struggle, to the countries desperate for growth, and why we have to preserve the important things we've inherited from the past. But I just wouldn't put it your way. Morality for me is more . . . grounded . . . than you seem to make it.

(*He turns to the others.*) Do you agree with that?

Rahel: I think Miguel is right . . . although I couldn't have put it as well as he did. In the articles you circulated before we came, you often talk about ethical decisions as emerging from ideal discussions. As if we could make it all up as we go along. That's not the way I see it. It's more . . . objective . . . than that.

Jo: And you think the grounding, the objectivity, comes out of your various religious books? It provides something my approach can't have. That perhaps no secular view can have. (*Joe returns carrying a large tray with a teapot, teacups, milk jug, sugar, and a plate of small cakes.*)

Joe: Shall I be mother? (*The others nod agreement. He distributes tea and cakes to everyone's specifications.*)

Jo: While you were gone, Miguel brought up an interesting point about the way we frame the issues. He feels it's too abstract, too secular. (*Smiles.*) The same point you once made to me. He agrees with us about the responsibilities we think people have. But he worries about the way we arrive at our judgments. (*Pause.*) I should probably let him—and Rahel—say what bothers them.

Miguel: Or others? Haroun? Sumedha? Ji-hoon?

Haroun: (*He is beginning to recover his temper.*) I basically agree with you. Though of course for me it's the Quran, not the Christian Bible or the Torah. The word of God provides a . . . force . . . a weight . . . to our responsibilities. I don't see that in the way you formulate things.

Sumedha: Nor, to be honest, do I.

(*Pause.*)

Ji-hoon: I may be an outlier here. It's hard to put this into words. (*Hesitantly.*) Like the others, I do find the way you talk about morality . . . different. But, in a way, it's no more peculiar than what they say. (*Pause.*) You see, I don't see how *any* religious book, even the ones I value most, can do the work for us. There are so many issues and we have to figure them out . . . for ourselves. The books can help us get started. But the situations are . . . new. So we need ways of deciding these new issues. And once we start asking *how* we should decide, I don't see how can we do better than the kind of conversation Jo suggests. (*Pause.*) I'd never thought of it before, but . . . I think I see the point.

Jo: Thank you, Ji-hoon. I think you do grasp what we're getting at.

Miguel: But I'm still a bit puzzled. When you spoke this morning, I found what you (*he looks at Jo*) said hard to follow. For quite a while. Then, when you got to the specific things we have to do, it was all clear and exciting. (*Pause.*) I must say I found the other Joe easier to understand. He's closer to my language.

Joe: (*With a glance at Jo.*) Perhaps my Protestant upbringing?

Jo: Which will enable you to explain better than I could.

Joe: Actually, I think Ji-hoon's pointed us in the right direction. I remember as a kid thinking the Bible had all the answers. Until one day I faced a difficult choice. Two alternatives that both had something going for them. I can't remember exactly what it was, but two people . . . my brother and a really close friend of mine . . . were involved. One of them was going to be disappointed either way, whatever I did. I do know I asked my parents. I asked them what Jesus would advise. They told me they didn't think Jesus would have any particular view about this particular situation. They suggested I talk things over with my brother and my friend. That's what I ended up doing. It was a long time ago . . . but I *think* it worked.

You know, Miguel, I may sound a bit more familiar to you. But Jo's thought far harder about these questions than I have. It's probably better to let her try to address your concerns. (*With a smile.*) I'll translate if necessary.

Jo: Well, there's a lot that *could* be said about the idea of grounding ethics in religion and whether religion can add any extra moral oomph. There are plenty of intricate arguments, worked out by brilliant thinkers.

In my view, all that's pretty irrelevant. We don't need it to forge ahead with global democracy and to do the things that have to be done if we're to limit the effects of climate change. The crucial point is that people *can* reach consensus. Even though they start in different places. And I think we can understand *how* they end up agreeing. When they do.

It's pretty easy in our case. Joe and I share an attitude with all of you. You see . . . we read your application materials. We wanted people from lots of ethnic traditions, and from the major world religions. But we didn't want any old Hindu or any old Muslim. The people we selected practice *humanistic* religions—we could call them religious humanists. Religious humanists—like all of you—take human life, as we live it here on Earth, very seriously. It *matters* how people's lives go and whether they turn out to be worthwhile. Religious humanists don't think the sole point of the whole business is found in some afterlife . . . in some heaven . . . or whatever. And because of that, they don't think they have to go around converting people—by force, if necessary—even killing those who don't want to sign on. In each of your religions, there are some who aren't humanists . . . I think they're a minority . . . even a small minority . . . at any rate, I hope so. For them, nothing in the here and now matters. And some of them sometimes do terrible things . . .

Haroun: The way that bloody fool Pratt thinks of me. Any Muslim must be a terrorist . . .

Sumedha: (*Laying a hand on his arm.*) Oh, I'm so sorry, Haroun. That was an awful moment. But it's really not *just* Islam that gets caricatured like that. Sometimes when I tell people I'm a devout Hindu, they think I'm going to set fire to mosques. Or churches. I wanted to say that this morning, when Pratt closed down the conversation. You think it's just your religion . . . your culture . . . that gets dissed. But you're not alone.

And it's painful when that happens. I want to scream out, "I'm studying to be a doctor! I want to give my life to healing. I want to help restore people. So they can live well, have a good life . . ." (*Stops; realizing how she has phrased her thoughts.*) Oh, I'm starting to sound like Jo.

Joe: No great harm in that.

Jo: Thank you, Sumedha. You've made my point. It's the humanist in you speaking. And when your version of the humanist talks to mine, or to Joe's, or to Rahel's, or Ji-hoon's, or Haroun's, or Miguel's . . . we can converge, reach agreement, and then go forward together in the project of global democracy. That wouldn't be possible with the non-humanists . . . the anti-humanists . . . among the different religions. Or secular anti-humanists, for that matter.

But there's one more thing I want to say to address Miguel's troubles with my way of putting things. This may surprise you, Miguel. (*She grins.*) It won't surprise Joe, though. I'm a fan of the pope. A huge fan. He sees the climate issues . . . and the way they're tangled up with problems of poverty . . . with materialistic attitudes . . . he sees all that . . . pretty much as I do. And he says it loudly and clearly. That's why I'm such a fan. We're allies. And he's a very powerful ally for a movement like ours to have.

The Dalai Lama has also said similar things . . . important things. He thinks Buddhists ought to address climate change in tandem with issues of global poverty. And lots of other people came out in support of the pope. The archbishop of Canterbury and the patriarch of the Greek Orthodox Church. The International Islamic Climate Change Symposium made a forceful recommendation. Over four hundred rabbis signed a Rabbinic Letter on Climate. And the president of the Universal Society of Hinduism welcomed the pope's linkage of climate change to justice for the poor. *All* these people take different routes. They describe what leads them in different ways. But they all come out in the same place.

(*Turning to Miguel.*) I know the language I use isn't familiar. Talking about worthwhile lives, ideal conversations and all the rest of it *is* perplexing . . . especially to religious people like you. I talk that way because I want to present the core humanist position . . . the line of reasoning all of us can follow . . . in our own distinctive ways . . . to reach that common conclusion. Your religious leaders can express it and develop it further in the language of the faithful . . . language that moves the faithful . . . Francis speaks to them far more beautifully and effectively than I can! And that's terrific. Even when he uses parts of the Bible to support his message, I—a complete unbeliever—often find what he says inspiring. And when he writes about the need for a farsighted politics to handle all the aspects of our critical situation, I want to stand up and cheer.

In the end though, I think we need both the uplifting language of people like the pope and the Dalai Lama, and the sober . . . abstract . . . unlovely . . . language I use. Because we do need to see that humanist core. Made completely explicit. Does that make sense?

Miguel: Yes. It helps a lot. You want what you're saying to resonate with my inner humanist, and with Haroun's and Rahel's and Ji-hoon's and Sumedha's . . . maybe even with Joe's. And, as we go forward, working out the details of global democracy, it serves as a guide to the sorts of conversations we ought to be having.

Jo: That's right. If we are going to address the problems posed by climate change, we have to continue those conversations. This morning was a promising start.

Joe: I thought so too. Of course, it's *only* a beginning. But we need to forge an alliance—bringing together people all around the world, people from lots of different religions, as well as people who've lost their faith, or never had any to begin with. We have to work together . . . fight together to win the war against atmospheric carbon . . . that's the way Jo once put it to me . . . (*glancing at Jo*) in the first real conversation we had. What we've tried to do here is to take a small step in building that alliance—in hopes that all of you will continue the conversation with many others. So all the world's humanists . . . all those who care about the future of humanity . . . about the importance of preserving the only planet we have . . . can learn to understand one another . . . and raise their voices . . . so the message is finally heard. So something is finally done.

Haroun: (*Quietly.*) And you've inspired us to try.

Jo: Thanks, Haroun. I'm glad of that. (*A church bell rings the hour. She glances down at her watch.*) Whoops! We're going to be late. And Joe is part of the next panel. (*Pause.*) But are you coming back with us?

(*Everyone looks at Haroun.*)

Jo: We need you as part of the conversation. I gather it was horrible this morning . . . at the end. (*Joe nods.*) Maybe we can fix it. Perhaps Joe could say that Haroun's point was important . . . that discussion shouldn't have been broken off and that we need to take up the question he raised—perhaps at the final open session. Would you be willing to say something like that, Joe?

Joe: Of course. I wanted to talk about it publicly and express my feelings. (*He glances at Jo.*) But I had wondered if it might be out of line. After all, we invited Sir Percival to chair a session . . . in hopes of broadening the alliance. An experiment that failed. (*Pause.*) Yes, I'll be more than happy to say something.

Jo: What do you think, Haroun? Is that good enough? I know what's said can't be unsaid, but . . .

Haroun: Yes. It's OK. I was angry. Overhasty. This conversation has helped a lot. (*He looks around.*) And the solidarity.

Jo: Good. Let's go then. (*They all stand up and move towards the building.*)

Jo: You know . . . we need to talk. More. All of us. (*Pause.*) Yes—we need to talk . . .

EPILOGUE

. . . so we can avoid having a different kind of conversation.

The Banality of Suffering

A hot and humid evening in 2059. Daylight is fading. Jo, a woman in her late eighties, is sunk deep in an armchair. Like the rest of the furniture crowded into the room, the chair testifies to events that have reduced its former elegance. Water stains are clearly visible on the walls, on the carpeting, on the upholstery, and on the woodwork. Jo's cotton dress is faded and frayed at the hem. She fans herself with a folded newspaper.

An external door creaks as it opens, and then again, for longer, as it is carefully closed. Shuffling footsteps are heard. Joe, also in his late eighties, enters. He moves slowly and stiffly across the room to Jo's chair. He stands in front of her, a much-used shopping bag in his hand.

Jo: Did they have anything? Anything at all?

Joe: No. Not even aspirin. I'm sorry. The pharmacist says production has broken down. Only the most essential drugs are being supplied. Of course, people have been hoarding . . .

Jo: We should have thought of that. (*She grimaces.*)

Joe: Is it very bad?

Jo: A little worse than usual. (*Another grimace.*) And the heat.

Joe: I did find some food. A couple of oranges. Some cheese. (*He sets the shopping bag on her lap.*)

Jo: Maybe with something to drink? How's the water?

Joe: I'll look. (*He makes his painful way to the door. Then, loudly, from the kitchen nearby.*) Brown. Murkier than usual. I'll boil it. Make tea. (*He returns, carrying a pan of water and two cups. He bends awkwardly, setting the pan on a small camping stove that sits on an unsteady dining table. Carefully, he lights the gas. He opens a box of tea bags. Turning to Jo.*) New, or used?

Jo: How many do we still have?

Joe: Five new. Seven used.

Jo: It's so hot. (*She reflects.*) Let's have a new one. But share. (*The lamp beside Jo's chair suddenly flickers.*) Power! Maybe we can run the fan. (*The lamp goes out.*) Apparently not.

(*The water comes to a boil. Joe pours it into the two cups, places a tea bag in one of them. He waits, then transfers the tea bag to the other cup, and brings the first cup to Jo. He returns to the table and sits down gingerly on one of its chairs.*)

Joe: (*Removing the tea bag from his cup and carefully setting it in the box.*) How is it?

Jo: OK. (*She fishes in the shopping bag.*) Ugh . . . the cheese is hard, and the oranges are mushy.

Joe: It was all I could find . . .

Jo: I know. It will have to do. What would you like?

Joe: (*Getting up and going to her.*) You choose.

Jo: (*She breaks off a piece of cheese, and hands it to him. Then offers him an orange.*) OK?

Joe: Thanks. (*He moves slowly back to his chair. He takes a small bite of cheese, and sips his tea.*) I suppose you didn't hear anything . . . ?

Jo: No. They didn't call. (*Her face contorts with sudden pain.*) I just sat here. Worrying. Thinking. (*Pause.*) Remembering. All those evenings in this room. As it used to be. (*She glances round.*) And I thought of the conversations I tried to have with you. All the times you didn't . . . *wouldn't* . . . listen. How you mocked me. Laughed at my fears for our future. In this heat . . . in this pain . . . it's hard not to think of that. Especially when I sit alone, and see the marks of everything that's happened since. The things I . . . we . . . my friends and I . . . foresaw. And how you wouldn't listen.

Joe: I wasn't alone. (*Pause.*) I know we turned out to be wrong. But it wasn't unreasonable. Your campaigns . . . the demands you and your friends made . . . they sounded so exaggerated . . . so hysterical. (*Bitterly.*) Does it comfort you to know you were right? Does righteousness ease the pain?

Jo: Of course not. How can you ask that? Or fail to appreciate your own deafness, your obstinacy, your arrogance? You . . . people like you . . . could have reflected . . . could have thought hard about what was happening. There was evidence . . . yes, there always was . . . and we tried to present it to you. But you dismissed us. (*Emphatically.*) You refused to talk about it.

Joe: We did talk. You forget the many times in which we sat here . . . when you pretended to know all about the science . . . all about the economics . . . when you speculated about ways of saving energy . . . or about international agreements and a new global politics. Was I supposed to take all of that . . . or any of it . . . seriously? I did look at some sources. Incomprehensible stuff about tree rings. Claims and counterclaims. At economic forecasts predicting huge costs from the sorts of things you and your friends were recommending. Because it was *your* cause, I tried to explore . . .

Jo: But never seriously enough! You never read the materials I gave you. Or looked at the links I sent you. When I started to talk, that superior smile would come over your face . . .

Joe: Because you were so fanatical, so extreme. A true believer. With such zeal. Brooking no disagreement. While all around us . . .

Jo: People like you, people we knew, were sticking their heads in the sand. Insisting on "maintaining our way of life." Maintaining our way of life—what a joke! Look at us now. Look round this room . . . (*A cell phone rings. Joe picks it up from a nearby table and answers it.*)

Joe: (*Listens.*) At last! We've been waiting. But you're OK? (*Listens.*) You can't tell how much damage? But everybody's safe? You salvaged something? (*Listens.*) That's the main thing. I understand. Calls are tricky. The service is intermittent. But do let us know—whenever you can, however you can. (*Listens.*) I understand. We love you. (*He sets down the phone, and turns to Jo.*) They're safe. All of them. But it sounds really grim. I don't think they've been able to save much. They're in an evacuation center. I could hear the kids crying in the background . . .

Jo: Will they call again? With more details?

Joe: When they can. It's difficult. They keep trying.

Jo: (*Her face contorts in sudden pain.*) I wish I could see them. Hug them. Just once. (*Sobbing.*) What kind of a world have we left them? For the little ones. Especially for the little ones.

Joe: (*Moves painfully to the side of her chair, kneels stiffly, and takes her hand.*) Oh Jo, I wish I'd listened. All those opportunities wasted. You were right. You *are* right. I'm so sorry.

Jo: (*Quietly, taking his hand in both of hers.*) I know. It could have been different. (*She looks slowly around the room.*) So very different.

NOTES

PROLOGUE

xi **Violent conflicts:** Michael Klare has studied the ways in which warfare has been sparked by competition for scarce resources, including water: http://www.tomdispatch.com/blog/176063/tomgram%3A_michael_klare%2C_are_resource_wars_our_future. He has argued that climate change poses a severe threat to world peace. For an illuminating discussion of the connections between climate change and violence, with attention to problems posed by water shortages, see also Harald Welzer, *Climate Wars* (Cambridge, UK: Polity, 2012).

xi **New diseases are born:** Laurie Garrett, *The Coming Plague* (New York: Farrar Straus Giroux, 1994).

PREFACE

xviii **There are plenty of excellent books:** We especially recommend the following: James Hansen, *Storms of my Grandchildren* (New York: Bloomsbury, 2009); Naomi Oreskes and Erik M. Conway, *Merchants of Doubt* (New York: Bloomsbury, 2010); Michael E. Mann, *The Hockey Stick and the Climate Wars* (New York: Columbia University Press, 2012); Gavin Schmidt and Joshua Wolfe, *Climate Change: Picturing the Science* (New York: Norton, 2009); Joseph Romm, *Climate Change: What Everyone Needs to Know* (New York: Oxford University Press, 2016); Nicholas Stern, *The Global Deal* (New York: PublicAffairs, 2009); Stephen M. Gardiner, *A Perfect Moral Storm* (New York: Oxford University Press, 2011); John Broome, *Climate Matters* (New York: Norton, 2012); Dale Jamieson, *Reason in a Dark Time* (New York: Oxford University Press, 2014);

William Nordhaus, *The Climate Casino* (New Haven, CT: Yale University Press, 2013); Gernot Wagner and Martin L. Weitzman, *Climate Shock* (Princeton, NJ: Princeton University Press, 2015). In what follows, we'll sometimes refer to some of these books by using short phrases from their titles.

The most recent report of the IPCC is an indispensable source for any group of people who want to discuss what might be done about climate change. It is easily downloaded from https://www.ipcc.ch/pdf/assessment-report/ar5/wg3/ipcc_wg3_ar5_full.pdf. In *Dire Predictions*, 2nd ed. (London: Dorling Kindersley, 2015), Michael E. Mann and Lee R. Kump provide an accessible "visual guide to the findings of the IPCC."

Jeffrey D. Sachs, *The Age of Sustainable Development* (New York: Columbia University Press, 2015) is also a valuable source for many of the topics we consider.

xviii **just two characters:** We recommend thinking of them as (for example) "male Joe 2" and "female Jo 5."

CHAPTER 1: IS IT REAL?

3 **Meteorologists:** For example: Richard Lindzen (emeritus professor of meteorology at MIT), Roy Spencer (a research scientist at the University of Alabama/Huntsville, trained in meteorology), Brian Sussman (former meteorologist with KPIX [San Francisco]), Garth Paltridge (formerly a professor of Antarctic Studies at the University of Tasmania). Other prominent critics of climate activism—for example, Judith Curry (climatologist at Georgia Institute of Technology) and Freeman Dyson (physicist at the Institute for Advanced Study, Princeton)—accept the minimal claims, but argue that their significance is exaggerated.

3 **funded by people with vested interests:** Oreskes and Conway, *Merchants*, Chapter 6, discuss connections between climate change deniers and fossil fuel companies. The relations between Richard Lindzen and oil companies are matters of dispute; Lindzen is currently supported by the Cato Institute. Spencer's book *Climate Confusion* features endorsements from Rush Limbaugh and Glenn Beck on the cover of the paperback edition (New York: Encounter Books, 2009).

3 **hockey stick:** See Figure 1.1. Michael E. Mann coined the name, and his *The Hockey Stick and Climate Wars* (New York: Columbia University Press, 2012) offers an excellent discussion of the graph and the evidence for it.

4 **really hard to measure:** Mann and Kump, *Dire Predictions* (34–49), is a good source for understanding how the gmt is calculated.

5 **always the hockey stick:** The principal reconstructions of the temperature record were offered by Mann, Bradley, and Hughes (1999) and by Wahl and Ammann (2007). For a useful discussion, see Stephen H. Schneider et al. (eds.),

Climate Change Science and Policy, 2nd ed. (Washington D.C.: Island Press, 2010), 12–14.

5 **the corals and the tree rings:** For an accessible introduction to the use of proxies in reconstructing the temperature record see http://www.windows2universe.org/earth/climate/CDcourses_investigate_climate.html. Mann, *Hockey Stick*, also explains the basics. See also Peter de Menocal, "Taking the Temperature of the Planet" in Schmidt and Wolfe, *Climate Change*.

6 **Figure 1.1:** From http://www.ucar.edu/news/releases/2005/ammann.shtml. The figure is reprinted as Figure 9.3 of Mann, *Hockey Stick*, where Mann cites the Wahl–Ammann study as a compelling reply to criticisms of his work.

8 **all those wrinkles we don't know about:** A standard textbook on reconstructing the Earth's past climate is William F. Ruddiman, *Earth's Climate: Past and Future*, 2nd ed. (New York: Freeman, 2008).

9 **even more striking:** In fact, the temperature depends not only on the total concentration of greenhouse gases (including methane and nitrous oxide), but also on other variables. Among these are changes in the Earth's orbit and volcanic activity. In principle, a graph could include these other factors and thus show an even closer correlation. But focusing on carbon dioxide alone shows a large effect.

9 **Figure 1.2:** From http://www.futuris.it/public/eng/about_renewable.html. The figure is also given in the 2014 IPCC report.

9 **Methane has a more intense greenhouse effect:** Methane's impact on climate change over the course of a century is 25 times that of the same weight of carbon dioxide; see https://www3.epa.gov/climatechange/ghgemissions/gases/ch4.html.

10 **You measure the past:** Mann and Kump, *Dire Predictions*, 30–33; Schneider et al., *Climate Change Science and Policy*, 17–18.

11 **about 30° Celsius too low:** Archer, *Global Warming*, 19–23.

12 **Radiation of particular wavelengths:** Archer, *Global Warming*, 23–26, 29–39.

12 **Some Swedish guy:** Svante Arrhenius formulated a "greenhouse law" in 1896; he was awarded the Nobel Prize in Chemistry in 1903.

12 **Our distance from the sun varies:** For a good brief account, see Mann and Kump, *Dire Predictions*, 78–81, 86–87.

15 **97 percent of climate scientists:** The figure of 97 percent is given by various surveys, although there have been some criticisms of the sampling methods used. In a published critique of a 2013 survey (*Skeptical Inquirer*, November/December 2015), James Lawrence Powell attempts to estimate the percentage of dissenters among climate scientists by considering the papers published in refereed journals in 2013 and 2014. He counts 69,406 authors of whom only 4 reject anthropogenic global warming. He concludes that the correct figure for the consensus is 99.99 percent. Unfortunately, this computation faces the obvious rejoinder that dissenting climate scientists are radically underrepresented

in the refereed journals, either because their submissions are automatically rejected, or because they have given up hope of publishing in those places. So we have stuck with the sociological consensus in this area—97 percent—while allowing Jo to suggest that the estimate may be conservative.

16 **saints in lab coats:** The idea of scientists as members of a new priesthood was formulated by Francis Galton in *English Men of Science* (originally published in 1874). It has endured in many popular accounts of scientific work.

16 **A really eminent biologist:** Based on a conversation in the 1980s between Ernst Mayr and PK.

22 **Climate scientists have addressed:** See Hansen, *Storms*; Mann, *Hockey Stick*; Schmidt and Wolfe, *Climate Change*. These are only some of many excellent and accessible sources.

23 **particularly in Anglophone countries:** According to a 2015 poll, 70 percent of Americans now believe that the climate is changing. Those who believe that climate change is occurring are divided in their views of the principal cause. Some estimates suggest that around half of the U.S. population would claim both that the planet is warming and that we are primarily responsible. Figures for Australia, Canada, and the United Kingdom paint a slightly more positive picture of public awareness, although in each country, there is a significant body of doubters (40 percent or more). International comparisons are difficult because the questions posed in surveys vary from country to country. But it seems clear that the Anglophone acceptance of anthropogenic warming is less than that in such countries as Germany and Switzerland.

23 **based on *political* convictions:** See Dan M. Kahan et al.,"The polarizing impact of science literacy and numeracy on perceived climate change risks," *Nature Climate Change* 2 (2012), 732–5. This influential article offers evidence that attitudes towards climate change do not vary with level of scientific education and expertise. Rather, they tend to reflect social and political sympathies. We take this to indicate the fact that scientists who are not climate scientists are effectively in the same position as Jo and Joe. They, too, have to trust the experts. We conjecture that the kind of science education necessary to overcome the problem would pursue Jo's strategy: concentrate on the structures of scientific reasoning and consider social explanations of disagreement.

24 **advances human freedom:** Plato, *Republic,* Book IV.

25 **to live up to its billing:** The point is elaborated in Philip Kitcher, *Science in a Democratic Society* (Amherst, NY: Prometheus Books, 2011).

25 **most eloquent champions:** For example, John Milton, *Areopagitica*; Thomas Jefferson, *Notes on the State of Virginia*; and John Stuart Mill, *On Liberty*.

26 **can be carefully managed:** For this theme, see Oreskes and Conway, *Merchants*, which provides a clear and well-documented account of the ways in which the same cast of characters has figured in a sequence of public controversies surrounding science. The issue of climate change is one of the most recent battlegrounds.

26 **Perhaps money can be supplied:** Traceable donations from ExxonMobil and from the Koch brothers to fund the research and the public pronouncements of "climate deniers" have recently declined. Other major foundations associated with right-wing political causes are still contributing to efforts to deny the climate science consensus. For a brief assessment, see http://www.scientificamerican.com/article/dark-money-funds-climate-change-denial-effort/.

26 **rival websites:** Very different graphs of the temperature record of the planet are sometimes presented. See, for example, https://www.skepticalscience.com/10000-years-warmer.htm or http://realclimatescience.com/global-temperature-record-is-a-smoking-gun-of-collusion-and-fraud/. For patient explanations of the problems with these kinds of reconstructions, readers can consult realclimate.org.

27 **Perhaps by establishing public committees:** For a proposal along these lines, see Kitcher, *Science in a Democratic Society*. The proposal was inspired by ideas of James S. Fishkin, *When the People Speak* (New York: Oxford University Press, 2009).

29 **political or economic motives:** See Oreskes and Conway, *Merchants*.

CHAPTER 2: SO WHAT?

32 **There are so many big problems:** One prominent advocate of the idea that other problems have priority over climate change is Bjørn Lomborg. See his book, *The Skeptical Environmentalist* (Cambridge, UK: Cambridge University Press, 2001). An extensive critique of Lomborg's ideas is given in Howard Friel, *The Lomborg Deception* (New Haven, CT: Yale University Press, 2010).

33 ***far more* suffering:** Here and in what follows, Jo's diagnoses follow those given in the 2014 IPCC report. See also Mann and Kump, *Dire Predictions*.

34 **I wonder about two things:** Joe is pointing towards the two components of expected value (or disvalue), probability and utility (disutility). Readers familiar with cost–benefit analysis might think he could make his concerns more precise by using that approach. For discussion and defense (of Joe and Jo), see the final section of this chapter.

36 **precise estimates of the chances:** This raises the question of climate sensitivity: by how much does an increase in CO_2e of a given magnitude affect the gmt? Climate scientists differ in their answers. They agree, however, that well-established physical facts set bounds on any adequate answer.

36 **between 3°C and 7°C above the baseline:** See the MIT "greenhouse gamble" (http://globalchange.mit.edu/focus-areas/uncertainty/gamble), and the 2014 IPCC report.

37 **some bad stuff and some good stuff:** This is a popular idea about climate change. It has been presented, for example, by Matt Ridley in columns in the *Wall Street Journal*. Ridley has strong ties to the British coal industry.

38 **full effect of that concentration:** Climate scientists used to believe in a lag

between the time at which emissions stopped and the time at which the full effect of the emissions was felt. The atmosphere had to "come into equilibrium." Recent analyses that consider the absorption of carbon by the oceans suggest that that process balances the further warming of the atmosphere, and that there is no lag. Mann and Kump, *Dire Predictions,* 106–9.

39 **One respected group:** See the MIT "greenhouse gamble" (http://globalchange.mit.edu/focus-areas/uncertainty/gamble).

39 **a bit more cautious:** For example, the 2014 IPCC report.

39 **no ice anywhere:** See Mann and Kump, *Dire Predictions,* 41. The discovery was announced in Appy Sluijs et al., "Subtropical Arctic Ocean Temperatures During the Palaeocene/Eocene Thermal Maximum," *Nature* 441 (2006), 610–13. It's sometimes suggested that a warm period in the middle Pliocene, in which there was no ice in the Northern Hemisphere, provides a picture of what the future climate will be like.

40 **too hot for us to live on it:** The maximum temperature in which human beings can survive depends on the humidity, the length of exposure, and the availability of cold water. Estimates suggest that several hours at 47°C in tropical air would be fatal. A detailed analysis is given in Stephen C. Sherwood and Matthew Huber, "An Adaptability Limit to Climate Change Due to Heat Stress," *Proceedings of the National Academy of Sciences* 107 (2010). 9552–55.

40 **places where there's plenty of ice:** Jo's example is an optimistic fiction. In fact, many mountainous regions are becoming much warmer, and higher temperatures in the Arctic and Antarctic are causing the melting of ice sheets. Mann and Kump, *Dire Predictions,* 64-65, 110–11, offer an accessible account of what is occurring.

41 **some types of clouds:** For a brief introductory account of the difficulties clouds cause for climate forecasting, see https://www.nsf.gov/news/special_reports/clouds/question.jsp.

41 **climate models have to simplify:** For good introductions to climate modeling, see Archer, *Global Warming,* and (with more technical details) Kendal McGuffie and Ann Henderson-Sellers, *The Climate Modelling Primer,* 4th ed. (New York: Wiley-Blackwell, 2014). Eric Winsberg provides a valuable discussion of the features of climate models in *Science in the Age of Computer Simulation* (Chicago: University of Chicago Press, 2010). An excellent philosophical analysis of modeling in science is Michael Weisberg, *Simulation and Similarity* (New York: Oxford University Press, 2013).

43 **try to simulate:** See the books by Winsberg and Weisberg cited in the previous note.

43 **lots of gradations:** The 2014 IPCC report offers two kinds of assessments. Qualitative judgments about predictions are rated in terms of levels of confidence, from very low to very high. When probabilities can be estimated, predictions are assessed on a scale from exceptionally unlikely to virtually certain.

44 **the permafrost:** See, for example, the *Scientific American* report on the work

of Anton Vaks and his colleagues (http://www.scientificamerican.com/article/siberian-caves-reveal-permafrost-thaw/). The IPCC projects a rise of 6°C for Siberia, over preindustrial temperatures. That would amount to more than 4°C above the present temperature.

45 **The Maldives:** The average height of the Maldives is just over 1 meter above sea level; the highest point is 2.4 meters. The Bay of Bengal is, on average, about 1.5 meters above sea level. Estimates suggest that over a third of North Africa's urban population lives in low-elevation coastal zones (i.e., at elevations sufficiently low to pose a risk of flooding).

45 **60 million people worldwide:** Anil Ananthaswamy, "Sea Level Rise. It's Worse Than We Thought," *New Scientist*, July 2009. Also the *World Ocean Review,* "Living in Coastal Areas," http://worldoceanreview.com/en/wor-1/coasts/living-in-coastal-areas/. Another useful source is the report "Climate Extremes: Recent Trends with Implications for National Security," available at environment.harvard.edu.

46 **the Greenland ice sheet:** See Mann and Kump, *Dire Predictions,* 110–111.

46 **Temperatures in sub-Saharan Africa:** The IPCC report provides an excellent summary. See Chapter 22 on Africa, and Chapter 24 on Asia.

48 **"fat tail":** See Martin L. Weitzman, "On Modeling and Interpreting the Economics of Catastrophic Climate Change," *The Review of Economics and Statistics* 91 (2009), 1–19. See also Nassim Nicholas Taleb, *The Black Swan* (New York: Random House, 2007).

49 **Figure 2.1**: Figure 2.1a was obtained from http://www.hko.gov.hk/blog/en/archives/00000115.htm. (It comes originally from the IPCC 2007 report.) Figure 2.1b was drawn to parallel 2.1a, showing a fat-tailed distribution. The source for the fat-tailed curve was obtained from http://www.nap.edu/read/18373/chapter/6#151.

Figure 2.1b shows a normal distribution giving way to a skewed distribution with a fat tail as the climate warms. This may not be an accurate representation, since the original distribution might also be skewed. The important point is that *if* the initial distribution is skewed with a fat tail, the new distribution is *more* skewed with a *fatter* tail.

50 **a theoretical reason:** See Hansen, *Storms,* 252–58.

50 **extreme events:** Good sources are http://nca2014.globalchange.gov/highlights/report-findings/extreme-weather#intro-section-2 and the IPCC report. A distillation of the IPCC findings is given at http://www.wri.org/blog/2011/11/five-takeaways-ipcc-report-extreme-weather-and-climate-change. Joseph Romm provides an excellent concise summary in Chapter 2 of his *Climate Change.*

51 **smaller snowpack:** For data on changes in the snowpack in the western United States, see https://www3.epa.gov/climatechange/science/indicators/snow-ice/snowpack.html. For a cautious review of the situation in the Himalayas, see http://na.unep.net/geas/getUNEPPageWithArticleIDScript.php?article_id=91.

51 **trouble for shellfish:** An accessible review is provided in the report of the National Research Council, "Ocean Acidification. Starting with the Science."

52 **world tour:** Jo's account reviews major features of the 2014 IPCC report. The "Summary for Policymakers" provides an overview, and the chapters on the individual continents offer more detail.

52 **Africa and Asia:** The predictions in this paragraph are counted as almost certain in the 2014 IPCC report. See Chapters 22 and 24.

55 **"above the bugline":** For a careful study documenting mosquitoes bearing malaria at higher elevations in Ecuador, see https://malariajournal.biomedcentral.com/articles/10.1186/1475-2875-10-236.

56 **some new one:** For an analysis of the hurricane record for the East Coast of the United States, see http://nca2014.globalchange.gov/report/our-changing-climate/changes-hurricanes.

56 **periodic droughts:** A brief assessment of the situation for the American Southwest is given at https://www3.epa.gov/climatechange/impacts/southwest.html.

56 **incredible floods:** See https://www3.epa.gov/climatechange/impacts/northwest.html and https://www3.epa.gov/climatechange/impacts/midwest.html.

56 **Eastern Seaboard:** There are several good interactive maps, showing flooding risks for cities along the East Coast of the United States. See for example: http://www.climatecentral.org/news/the-human-fingerprints-on-coastal-floods-20050.

57 **we ought to try to prevent it:** Joe is criticizing what has been called the precautionary principle. Cass Sunstein gives a simple formulation: "Avoid steps that will create a risk of harm." See his "Beyond the Precautionary Principle" for a valuable discussion of the principle (http://papers.ssrn.com/sol3/papers.cfm?abstract_id=307098).

59 **it won't be like that:** As forcefully argued by Naomi Oreskes and Erik M. Conway, *The Collapse of Western Civilization* (New York: Columbia University Press, 2014).

59 **The migrants of the future:** Jo's more realistic characterization undermines the ideas of those (like Matt Ridley) who think climate change will bring some good things, and that we can manage the difficulties.

61 **cost–benefit analysis:** For a concise introduction to decision theory and cost-benefit analysis, see the early chapters of Michael D. Resnik, *Choices* (Minneapolis: University of Minnesota Press, 1987). A quick online approach to the basics is provided at http://www.siue.edu/~evailat/decision.htm.

62 **one with the highest expected value:** There may be a unique winner, or several options may be tied. In the latter case, choosing any of the alternatives with the highest expected value is a "rational" decision.

64 **the exact strength of your preferences:** The idea is that the strength of your wishes for a particular outcome can be elicited by a situation in which you are equally happy obtaining that outcome or receiving a particular amount of cash. The cash then serves as the equivalent of the strength of your desire. For a sub-

tle and rigorous development of the fundamental idea, see Richard C. Jeffrey, *The Logic of Decision* (Chicago: University of Chicago Press, 1989).

64 **an answer to this question:** Elizabeth Anderson, *Value in Ethics and Economics* (Cambridge, MA: Harvard University Press, 1993), provides an illuminating defense of the thesis that not all things we value have economic equivalents.

64 **Charles Darwin considered:** The text of Darwin's "memorandum" is available at the Darwin Online website: http://darwin-online.org.uk/content/frameset?pageseq=1&itemID=CUL-DAR210.8.2&viewtype=text.

65 **good judgment:** For a more systematic approach to judgment under situations of risk and uncertainty, see the many books and articles of Gerd Gigerenzer and his colleagues. Gigerenzer's *Risk Savvy: How to Make Good Decisions* (New York: Viking, 2014) provides a lucid, accessible, and entertaining introduction.

67 **two further questions:** These questions are taken up in the next two chapters.

CHAPTER 3: WHY CARE?

71 **more urgent things to fight for:** Once again, Joe echoes the views of Bjørn Lomborg, *The Skeptical Environmentalist.*

73 **the growth of the past century:** Angus Deaton, *The Great Escape* (Princeton, NJ: Princeton University Press, 2013).

73 **a new plateau:** Robert J. Gordon, *The Rise and Fall of American Growth* (Princeton, NJ: Princeton University Press, 2016).

75 **have a claim:** William James, "The Moral Philosopher and the Moral Life," in *William James: Writings 1878–1899* (New York: Library of America, 1992), 595–617.

75 **the most urgent demands:** T. M. Scanlon, "Preference and Urgency," *Journal of Philosophy* 72 (1975), 655–69.

77 **lots of kids:** Robert D. Putnam, *Our Kids* (New York: Simon & Schuster, 2015).

77 **It's transformed my life:** See L. A. Paul, *Transformative Experience* (New York: Oxford University Press, 2015).

78 **continuing indefinitely:** Jo seems to envisage an ambitious argument. If her life is to go well, her boys' lives must go well; if their lives are to go well, their children's lives must go well. So, as long as the chain of descendants extends, all will have to thrive if her life is to go well. Joe will point out that her assumptions are too strong. Commitment to the future is a matter of decreasing degree.

79 **an interesting book:** P. D. James, *The Children of Men* (New York: Vintage, 1992), also adapted as a film. Jo's interest in the book recapitulates an insightful analysis by Samuel Scheffler. See his *Death and the Afterlife* (New York: Oxford University Press, 2013).

79 **connect with the lives of others:** For an elaboration of Jo's point, see Chapter 4 of Philip Kitcher, *Life after Faith* (New Haven, CT: Yale University Press, 2014).

80 **die away as rapidly as you imagine:** The disagreement is the ethical analogue of debates among economists about how to discount the future. In the context of climate economics, see Stern, *Global Deal,* and Nordhaus, "A Review of the Stern Review on the Economics of Climate Change," *Journal of Economic Literature* 45 (2007), 686–702. Jo's attitude recapitulates ideas suggested in a classic article by F. P. Ramsey ("A Mathematical Theory of Saving," *Economic Journal* 38 [1928], 543–59).

82 **If you'd sent the money:** Peter Singer, "Famine, Affluence, and Morality," *Philosophy and Public Affairs* 1 (1972), 229–43; Peter Unger, *Living High and Letting Die* (New York: Oxford University Press, 1996).

83 **this other voice:** The tension in Jo's thinking is explored by Thomas Nagel in *Equality and Partiality* (New York: Oxford University Press, 1991).

83 **as much happiness:** For an accessible introduction to the kind of utilitarianism Jo considers here, see J. J. C. Smart and Bernard Williams, *Utilitarianism: For and Against* (Cambridge, UK: Cambridge University Press, 1973).

83 **the most fundamental human rights:** Ronald Dworkin, *Taking Rights Seriously* (Cambridge, MA: Harvard University Press, 1978).

83 **your closest . . . concerns:** John Rawls, *A Theory of Justice* (Cambridge, MA: Harvard University Press, 1971); Bernard Williams, "A Critique of Utilitarianism" (in Smart and Williams, *Utilitarianism: For and Against*); Peter Railton, "Alienation, Consequentialism, and the Demands of Morality," *Philosophy and Public Affairs* 13 (1984) 134–71.

84 **get together and talk:** Different versions of this approach are offered in T. M. Scanlon, *What We Owe to Each Other* (Cambridge, MA: Harvard University Press, 2000); Jürgen Habermas, *The Structural Transformation of the Public Sphere* (Cambridge, MA: MIT Press, 1989); Philip Kitcher, *The Ethical Project* (Cambridge, MA: Harvard University Press, 2011). PK's version figures in later discussions—and is the basis of "Jo, Conflicted."

84 **a balanced plan:** Kitcher, *Ethical Project,* Chapter 9.

85 **similar things they lack:** Amartya Sen, *The Idea of Justice* (Cambridge, MA: Harvard University Press, 2009).

88 **passages in the Gospels:** Matthew 19:16–22; Matthew 12:46–50; Mark 3:31–35.

88 **notion of stewardship:** *Laudato Si',* especially Chapter 4. As Susan Neiman points out in Chapter 8 of her *Moral Clarity,* rev. ed. (Princeton, NJ: Princeton University Press, 2009), people who have abandoned doctrinal religion can nonetheless honor an ideal of stewardship, based on reverence for a world *they* surely didn't create. Her example of Voltaire is particularly telling.

89 **Whichever of these frameworks:** Peter Singer, *One World* (New Haven, CT: Yale University Press, 2002), 26–43.

90 **what is most deeply human vanishes:** As argued by Bernard Williams and Peter Railton in the articles cited in a note to p. 83.

90 **ancient thinkers:** Aristotle's *Nicomachean Ethics* is a classic source.

91 **profess happiness with the roles:** Sometimes the coercion can penetrate very

deeply, so that people whose lives have been very tightly confined acquiesce in what has been done to them. The contentment of the slave who accepts daily humiliations is not something to celebrate.

CHAPTER 4: WHAT CAN BE DONE?

97 **the big fuss about ozone:** Oreskes and Conway, *Merchants,* Chapter 4.

98 **CCS:** Sometimes also referred to as "carbon sequestration." For a good introduction to the basic ideas see https://www3.epa.gov/climatechange/ccs/.

99 **Reforestation can help:** For a cautious estimate of the potential benefits, see http://www.ucsusa.org/publications/ask/2012/reforestation.html.

99 **before or after the fossil fuel is burned:** One process—gasification—converts the original fuel into a mixture of hydrogen and carbon dioxide. The hydrogen can then be used and the CO_2 is captured and stored. See http://www.ccsassociation.org/what-is-ccs/capture/pre-combustion-capture/.

100 **CCS can help:** The 2014 IPCC report envisages a role for CCS, while recognizing its limits in mitigating climate change. For a more pessimistic assessment, see Romm, *Climate Change,* 208–14.

100 **between 80 percent and 90 percent:** See http://www.c2es.org/technology/factsheet/CCS for a more optimistic assessment and http://ccs-info.org/climate-efficiency.html for a more pessimistic one. The IPCC has tended to use the 80 percent to 90 percent range.

101 **to "seed" the atmosphere:** See Mann and Kump, *Dire Predictions,* 193.

103 **very close to zero:** Jo's response allows the possibility that the costs of eliminating emissions increase rapidly as you approach the zero-carbon state.

105 **in a dark wood:** The scenario is akin to one considered by William James at the end of "The Will to Believe" (*Writings 1878–1899,* 457–79). Jo's conclusion from it concurs with the one James draws.

107 **agricultural reform:** Estimates of the contributions of agriculture to climate change vary. For a high value, see http://www.nature.com/news/one-third-of-our-greenhouse-gas-emissions-come-from-agriculture-1.11708.

108 **Lettuce is three times worse than bacon:** The claim was made in several British newspapers, including the *Daily Telegraph*: http://www.telegraph.co.uk/news/earth/environment/12052711/Lettuce-worse-than-bacon-for-the-environment-scientists-claim.html. For a sharp rebuttal along the lines of Jo's rejoinder, see http://www.vegan.com/debunking-claims-that-lettuce-is-3-times-worse-than-bacon/.

112 **solar-powered airplane:** There is more promise here than Joe allows, although the technology clearly needs further development. See http://www.solarimpulse.com/adventure.

112 **my real worry about replacement:** Joe's concerns about securing international cooperation have been discussed extensively in excellent books on climate change. In *Climate Casino,* Chapters 21–22, Nordhaus offers a careful economic

perspective. Chapter 3 of Gardiner's *Perfect Moral Storm* presents a lucid philosophical analysis.

113 **build some nuclear power plants:** Some climate activists have argued that using nuclear power is a helpful and tolerable intermediate step on the path to a world dependent only on renewable sources of energy. See Hansen, *Storms,* 194–204; and Mark Lynas, *Nuclear 2.0* (Cambridge, UK: UIT Cambridge, 2014). The data on the actual impact of previous nuclear accidents (Chernobyl, Fukushima, etc.) support Hansen's claims about relative risks; as Lynas points out, the survivors of Hiroshima and Nagasaki had an increased risk of 0.5% of dying from cancer between 1950 and 2000 (*Nuclear 2.0,* 51–52). On the other hand, it's evident that the consequences of the nuclear accidents could easily have been enormously worse. Worries about the effects of nuclear waste over the centuries to come are vividly captured in the film *Containment* (produced by Peter Galison and Robb Moss).

113 **costs of storage and distribution:** How to harness intermittent sources of energy to meet large and variable demands is a major topic of energy research. For reviews of the difficulties and assessments of potential solutions, see http://energystorage.org/energy-storage/technology-applications/bulk-wind-generation-distributed-storage and http://www.ucsusa.org/clean-energy/how-energy-storage-works.

115 **the temptations to cheat:** As many authors have explained, the structure of the interactions encourages defection from agreements. See Nordhaus, *Climate Casino,* Chapters 21–22, and Gardiner, *Perfect Moral Storm,* Chapter 3.

116 **"climate club":** William Nordhaus, "Climate Clubs: Overcoming Free Riding in International Climate Policy," *American Economic Review* 105 (2015), 1339–70. Nordhaus presents the central ideas more accessibly at http://issues.org/31-4/climate-clubs-to-overcome-free-riding/. He also concludes a review of Wagner and Waitzman's *Climate Shock* (http://www.nybooks.com/articles/2015/06/04/new-solution-climate-club/) with a concise discussion of climate clubs; the final paragraph of this review offers a candid evaluation of the relation between the theoretical analysis and practical policies.

118 **the right standard:** It is possible to play variations on Nordhaus's basic approach. For a rival attempt to solve the problem of international coordination, see Humberto Llavador, John E. Roemer, and Joaquim Silvestre, *Sustainability for a Warming Planet* (Cambridge, MA: Harvard University Press, 2015).

120 **none of this is new:** Economic models often ignore awkward facts about the displacement of workers, assuming that the flow of the unemployed to some new sector is frictionless. That assumption underlies Adam Smith's original discussion of the invisible hand (*Wealth of Nations,* Book IV, Chapter 2) and is inherited by many of his successors.

121 **Lots of solar collectors:** According to a *Fortune* report (January 2015), in 2014 there were more people in the United States installing solar collectors than

working as coal miners: 173,807 to 93,185. See http://fortune.com/2015/01/16/solar-jobs-report-2014/.

123 **reboot economies:** In a recent lecture (given at Harvard on May 2, 2016), Nicholas Stern used this phrase to make the point on which Jo relies here.

126 **costs of photo-voltaic cells:** http://www.seia.org/policy/solar-technology/photovoltaic-solar-electric and http://www.pv-magazine.com/news/details/beitrag/irena--pv-prices-have-declined-80-since-2008_100016383/

128 **the increase in costs:** For comparisons of the costs of renewable energy and fossil fuels, see http://www.renewable-energysources.com/, http://energyinnovation.org/2015/02/07/levelized-cost-of-energy/, and http://www.eia.gov/forecasts/aeo/electricity_generation.cfm.

129 **generate similar conclusions:** Stern, *Global Deal,* 48–49.

129 **Many people:** Stern, *Global Deal,* 54.

130 **More recent analyses:** The figures given are from the 2014 IPCC report. Stern (http://www.nature.com/news/economics-current-climate-models-are-grossly-misleading-1.19416) has criticized the figures on the grounds that they rest on ignoring the economic effects that climate change is likely to have.

CHAPTER 5: WHO PAYS?

137 **political leaders kept trying:** For the requests for aid, and reactions to them from leaders in prosperous countries, see https://www.theguardian.com/environment/2014/sep/20/us-climate-change-aid-poor-nations-un-summit and http://www.vox.com/2015/11/30/9818582/paris-cop21-climate-talks.

137 **Especially electricity:** Jeffrey Sachs, *The Age of Sustainable Development,* 155–57.

138 **our sphere of operation:** Joe represents the approach presented in the Climatescope Report 2014. The report can be obtained via http://about.bnef.com/white-papers/climatescope-2014-full-report/.

143 **and of justice:** For sophisticated recent discussions of global justice, see Thomas W. Pogge, *World Poverty and Human Rights*, 2nd ed. (Cambridge, UK: Polity Press, 2008) and Mathias Risse, *On Global Justice* (Princeton, NJ: Princeton University Press, 2012).

146 **a container of finite size:** This idea is presented by Peter Singer in *One World.* Jo's calculations address a slightly different issue than the one Singer considers.

147 **400 ppm as the appropriate target:** Estimates vary. James Hansen et al., "Target Atmospheric CO_2: Where Should Humanity Aim?" (https://arxiv.org/pdf/0804.1126), treats 350 ppm as the safe level. A report from the Union of Concerned Scientists, "How to Avoid Dangerous Climate Change: A Target for US Emissions," sets a figure of 450 ppm as the upper limit. (This report can be found at http://www.ucsusa.org/sites/default/files/legacy/assets/documents/global_warming/emissions-target-report.pdf.) In an article in *Slate* (http://www.slate.com/blogs/the_slatest/2015/07/20/sea_level_study_james_hansen

_issues_dire_climate_warning.html), Eric Holthaus, discussing Hansen's predictions about the imminent dangers to the world's coastal cities, remarked that Hansen "is known for being an alarmist, and also right."

152 **the actual emissions:** Data on annual emissions from any country can be obtained from http://www.globalcarbonatlas.org/?q=en/emissions. Jo's total is obtained by adding the amounts from the years between 1980 and 2010.

162 **a conversation:** Jo continues the ethical approach advanced by her counterpart in Chapter 3. For sources, see note to p. 84, especially Kitcher, *Ethical Project* (Chapter 9).

166 **to stick with an earlier decision:** See https://news.mongabay.com/2016/02/bangladesh-sticks-with-coal-power-plant-project-despite-major-backlash/ and https://www.theguardian.com/environment/2016/mar/02/thousands-to-march-protest-coal-plant-threat-bangladeshs-sundarbans-forest.

172 **ride roughshod over the demands of others:** Proposals to work out solutions through fully representative conversation are often greeted with the objection that prospects for any solution acceptable to all are very dim. Participants with different religious affiliations will be unwilling to abandon the maxims they draw from their favored sacred texts. If that were to occur, those discussants would fail to meet the conditions on proper democratic discussion. One straightforward way to recognize this point is to see it as a failure of mutual engagement: dedication to finding a solution all can accept requires only advancing reasons others can recognize. (This approach is offered by John Rawls, *Political Liberalism* [New York: Columbia University Press, 1993] and by Scanlon, *What We Owe to Each Other*.) Another is to see the insistence on the particular doctrines of a religion (or a secular ideology) as failing to assimilate the best available information: protracted disagreements among rival doctrines about the religious foundation of ethics are evidence for the unreliability of each. (See Philip Kitcher, *Life After Faith*, Chapter 1.) Hence the ideal of working out ethical problems through representative, democratic conversation is not impugned. The issue becomes one of practical politics. How can we encourage actual people to engage in the ideal democratic discussions? This section of the text, and the dialogues of the next chapter, are preliminary attempts to engage with this difficult question.

CHAPTER 6: A NEW POLITICS?

177 **We've read some of the things:** Presumably sources expressing the ideas and arguments voiced by Jo in Chapter 5.

178 **structures for global democracy:** For valuable discussions of global democracy, see the work of David Held and his collaborators: *Climate Governance in the Developing World* (Cambridge, UK: Polity Press, 2013) and *Gridlock: Why Global Cooperation Is Failing When We Need It Most* (Cambridge, UK: Polity Press, 2013).

181 **The US contributed:** For these figures see http://www.globalfirepower.com/defense-spending-budget.asp.

182 **Like the pope:** *Laudato Si'*.

186 **education of girls:** Amartya Sen, *Development as Freedom* (New York: Random House, 1999); Jean Drèze and Amartya Sen, *India: Development and Participation*, 2nd ed. (Oxford, UK: Oxford University Press, 2002).

187 **some theorists have seen:** This emphasis is prominent in works elaborating and defending deliberative democracy. See James Bohman and William Rehg (eds.), *Deliberative Democracy* (Cambridge, MA: MIT Press, 1997); Amy Gutmann and Dennis Thompson, *Democracy and Disagreement* (Princeton, NJ: Princeton University Press, 2002); Bruce Ackerman and James S. Fishkin, *Deliberation Day* (New Haven, CT: Yale University Press, 2005); and Fishkin, *When the People Speak*.

197 **provide all children:** Joseph E. Stiglitz, *The Price of Inequality* (New York: Norton, 2012).

197 **Social mobility in the US:** Documented in a report from the Russell Sage and Pew Foundations (http://www.russellsage.org/blog/new-rsfpew-report-shows-social-mobility-limited-us). For international comparisons, see the Brookings Institution Report on International Comparisons of Economic Mobility, and the similar conclusions drawn by the Economics Policy Institute, http://www.epi.org/publication/usa-lags-peer-countries-mobility/.

200 **demands certain abilities . . . capacities**: Jo is offering an account of freedom to achieve well-being as dependent on fundamental capabilities. For extensive development of this approach see Amartya Sen, "Capability and Well-being," in Martha C. Nussbaum and Sen (eds.), *The Quality of Life* (Oxford, UK: Oxford University Press, 1993), 30–53; Nussbaum, *Women and Human Development: The Capabilities Approach* (Cambridge, UK: Cambridge University Press, 2000); and Sen, *Development as Freedom* (New York: Knopf, 1999).

200 **why planned economies fail:** The classical source for this argument is Friedrich Hayek, "The Use of Knowledge in Society," *American Economic Review* 35 (1945), 519–30. (Available online at http://www.econlib.org/library/Essays/hykKnw1.html.)

201 **All economists know:** The point stems from Book V of Adam Smith's *Wealth of Nations*. For penetrating examinations of the limits of markets, see Karl Polanyi, *The Great Transformation* (New York: Farrar and Rinehart, 1944); Charles E. Lindblom, *The Market System* (New Haven, CT: Yale University Press, 2001); and George Akerlof, *An Economic Theorist's Book of Tales* (Cambridge, UK: Cambridge University Press, 1984).

205 **The shadow of the future:** Gardiner, *Moral Storm*, explains this in careful detail.

206 **building the right sort of market:** Joe may be inspired by the work of Alvin Roth. See Roth's Nobel Lecture, "The Theory and Practice of Market Design" (2012), available at http://www.nobelprize.org/nobel_prizes/economic-sciences/laureates/2012/roth-lecture.html.

206 **a radical program we don't need:** Jo's position has affinities with the views of Naomi Klein (*This Changes Everything*, New York: Simon & Schuster, 2014).

In an often sympathetic review (*New York Review of Books*, December 2014), Elizabeth Kolbert describes Klein's book as a "polemic" and sees it as offering a "fable"—although, as she points out in a subsequent exchange with Klein (*New York Review of Books*, January 2015), the environmental movement began with a fable. The movement Jo recommends is more open to modifications of capitalism than Klein seems to be. Nonetheless, we view the central argument offered by the various Jos as complementary to Klein's impressive marshalling of important facts. We have attempted to provide an argumentative structure in which the power of those facts will be amplified.

216 **grounding ethics in religion:** Plato's *Euthyphro* famously argues that religion cannot provide a grounding for ethics. Plato's challenge has inspired many attempts to meet it. The most prominent contemporary efforts are due to William Alston and Robert Adams.

219 **the core humanist position:** Jo is presenting an idea that is prominent in contemporary political liberalism. See John Rawls, "The Idea of an Overlapping Consensus," *Oxford Journal of Legal Studies* 7 (1987), 1–25; and *Political Liberalism*, 134–49.

219 **a farsighted politics:** *Laudato Si'* §197.

ACKNOWLEDGMENTS

About seven years ago, the two of us discovered our common interest in and shared concern about climate change. The discovery led to many conversations and e-mail exchanges, and, in 2013, to our teaching a course together at Columbia on philosophical issues about climate change. We are grateful to Pierre Force, then the Columbia Dean for Arts and Humanities, who provided the funds for the joint course. We also want to thank the students who enrolled, who contributed to lively discussions, and who offered appropriate resistance to some of our embryonic ideas. We—and they—were fortunate to hear from four distinguished visitors to the class: Deborah Coen, James Hansen, Michael Oppenheimer, and Jeffrey Sachs. We deeply appreciate the willingness of these eminent experts to take the time to contribute their insights.

Both before and after the class, we had talked about writing something together on this topic. We found that we also shared an ambivalent attitude towards doing so. On the one hand, the question was (and remains) indisputably urgent—few, if any, other contemporary problems demand as much attention. On the other hand, we were (and are) fully aware of the many talented people who have tried to increase public awareness about it. How could we hope to add anything more to what has already been written? So, for years, we have gone back and forth on what to do. Only in 2015, with the encouragement of our colleagues, did we make a firm decision to try to synthesize our ideas.

The final version of this book is very different from the proposal we originally submitted and the first draft that elaborated it. It was changed by three suggestions. Most important was an idea voiced by our editor, Phil Marino. Although he liked much of the content of the draft we sent him, he felt it would benefit from becoming more "dialogical." The second was EK's insistence that what the climate change issue needs is a grassroots movement—the kinds of focused discussions that once occurred in Vietnam Summer or in reaction to the AIDS epidemic. The third was PK's thought that the book might not only provide *material* for discussions, but actually *show* how such discussions might go—that being dialogical might mean writing dialogues. Together, these three ideas have led us to the (nonstandard) form in the accompanying pages.

We have benefited from the questions and comments of many outstanding scholars, people who know far more than we do about one or more aspect of our topic, and who have attended lectures we have given over the past few years. PK would like to thank those who provided valuable feedback at the annual meeting of the Society for the Philosophy of Science in Practice (held in 2011 in Exeter); at the University of Bielefeld (2011); the University of North Carolina at Chapel Hill (2012); the Universidad Autonoma de Barcelona (2012); Sabanci University in Istanbul (2012); the

University of Aachen (2012); Seton Hall University (2012); Wesleyan University (2013); the University of Durham (2013); Dalhousie University (2013); Erasmus University Rotterdam (2013); the College of the Holy Cross (2014); Ohio University (2014); the University of California at San Diego (2014); the University of San Francisco (2014); Dartmouth College (2014); the University of Antwerp (2014); the workshop on foreseeable catastrophes at the Wissenschaftskolleg zu Berlin (2014); and UNAM in Mexico City (2015). Among people who deserve special thanks are Amy Allen, Scott Barrett, Jack Bender, Martin Carrier, Hasok Chang, Jose Diaz, Jerry Doppelt, John Dupré, David Held, Gürol Irzik, Anne Kapuscinski, Marc Lange, Anna Leuschner, Bence Nanay, Wendy Parker, Laurie Paul, Joseph Rouse, Todd Sandler, David Stump, and Jack Vromen. PK would also like to thank Stephen Gardiner for valuable conversation at a moment when we were trying to redefine our book. EK would like to thank respondents to her talks at NYU (2010); University of Santiago, Chile (2010); University of Paris (2010); CUNY (2011); Stellenbosch University (2011); LSE (2012); SUNY Purchase (2012); Dalhousie University (2013); and KLI, Klosterneuburg (2014).

We are also profoundly grateful to the people who took time from their busy schedules to read earlier drafts and to offer us wise counsel. We want to thank Mark Cane, Michael Mann, Gavin Schmidt, and Loup Verlet for the significant and generous help they have given us in improving our presentation of climate science; Anuk Arudpragasam, Stephen Monsell, and Pranay Sanklecha, whose comments have helped us write better dialogues; Robin Einhorn and Susan Neiman for important organizational suggestions that have enhanced the accessibility of what we have written; Ron Findlay, Dan O'Flaherty, and Michael Rothschild for invaluable assistance in thinking through the economic issues; John Dupré for planting the seed for our prologue; Scott Barrett, Raine Daston, and Peter Galison for enabling us to see how to make important points more effectively; Robbie Kubala and Kyle Mahowald for encouraging us to contrast climate science with the social sciences; Michael Fuerstein, Jon Lawhead, Clement Loo, and Matt Slater for detailed advice about philosophical issues; David Helfand for some interesting challenges to some of our claims; Cynthia Rettig for offering the perspective of an avid reader; and, by no means least, Clark Glymour for a characteristically penetrating response to an earlier draft, one that has enabled us to see where positions needed to be clarified and arguments strengthened. We're also grateful to Peter Ohlin of Oxford University Press, who altruistically did not make publishing with OUP a condition of his good advice. As on so many previous occasions, Patricia Kitcher provided PK with wise counsel about the penultimate draft. Of course, none of these people should be held responsible for any errors that remain—but they have surely helped reduce the number of our mistakes and infelicities.

Philip Marino has been an outstanding editor. He has helped transform a pedestrian draft into something we've found much more exciting. We appreciate his insightful suggestions, and all his support.

During the course of working together we have talked our way through a very large number of questions, on some of which we originally disagreed. Conversation, we've found, can succeed. We have almost always reached a shared final opinion. But there is one large exception. Because the period in which the book was written was one during which EK was in ill health, PK undertook the task of writing. In light of this, EK maintained that she should not count as a full coauthor, proposing that the book be by "Philip Kitcher in collaboration with Evelyn Fox Keller." Philip believes that that formula would not do justice to Evelyn's role in the project—from his perspective, we designed and built the house together, and he merely took on the task of decorating it. Evelyn doesn't accept that metaphor. But even though she is now on the road to recovery, she's not yet vigorous enough to win the argument. We still disagree—but, taking unfair advantage, Philip declares victory.

A NAVIGATIONAL GUIDE

We hope the following "map" of the chapters will help readers find the discussions that particularly interest them.

temperature, 36–40; predicting local climates, 40–44; sea-level rise and elevated temperatures, 45–47; constant effects and episodic effects, 47–52; predictable impact for different continents, 52–56; the importance of scenarios with small or unassignable probabilities, 57–61.

Cost-benefit analysis and qualitative decision-making: *61–67.*

CHAPTER 3

Caring about the future, and weighing future demands against those of the present: *addressing known problems, 71–72; extrapolating from past economic growth, 73; advantages of prevention, 74–75; personal ties to the future, 76–78; the distant future, 78–79; sharing the burdens across generations, 80–83; partial and global perspectives, 83–87; an integrated ethical perspective, 88–93.*

CHAPTER 4

Addressing the threats posed by climate change: *geo-engineering, 98–102; potential costs of social experiments, 103; reducing and replacement, 104; limits of planning, 104–5; possibilities of reduction, 107–11; approaches to replacement, 111–12; effects of economic competition, 113–16; carbon taxes and climate clubs, 116–19; consequences for unemployment, 120–23; cost estimates for cutting emissions, 126–28; effects on global wealth, 128–34.*

CHAPTER 5

Global justice in distributing burdens: *climate aid for developing nations, 137–38; economic partnerships, 138–40; constraints on development, 141–43; the past emissions record, 144–49; fair emissions shares, 148–53; politics and morality, 153–59; political realism,*

159–62; recognizing four duties, 162–64; working out how to share the global burdens, 165–73.

CHAPTER 6

Changes in economic and political arrangements: *the need for global democracy, 176–78; an alliance against atmospheric carbon, 179–80; funding the alliance, 181–83; deliberative democracy, 183–85; population growth, 186; multilevel democracy, 187–92; nationalism, 192–96; transforming capitalism, 196–206; religious and secular perspectives, 203–4, 206–7.*

An alliance among different worldviews: *overlapping consensus, 212–17; religious humanism and secular humanism, 217–20.*

ABOUT THE AUTHORS

Philip Kitcher is the John Dewey Professor of Philosophy at Columbia University. Born in the UK, he earned his BA in mathematics/history and philosophy of science at Christ's College Cambridge and his PhD in history and philosophy of science at Princeton University. Prior to his arrival at Columbia, Kitcher taught at various universities including the University of Minnesota and the University of California, San Diego. A fellow of the American Academy of Arts and Sciences, Kitcher was the first recipient of the American Philosophical Association's Prometheus Prize for work in extending the boundaries of science and philosophy. He has served as president of the American Philosophical Association (Pacific Division) and as editor-in-chief of *Philosophy of Science*. He is the author of seventeen books, including *Deaths in Venice: The Cases of Gustav von Aschenbach* and, more recently, *Life After Faith: The Case for Secular Humanism*. Kitcher's articles have appeared in many scholarly journals, and he has contributed to the *Los Angeles Times*, *New Republic*, and the *New York Times*. He lives in New York City.

Evelyn Fox Keller is a professor emerita of history and philosophy of science at the Massachusetts Institute of Technology. She received her BA in physics from Brandeis University and her PhD in theoretical physics at Harvard University, and has taught at Northeastern University, Northwestern University, Cornell University, Princeton University, State University of New York at Purchase, New York University, University of Maryland, and University of California, Berkeley. In addition to her widely read essays, Keller has written many books including *The Century of the Gene*; *Secrets of Life, Secrets of Death: Essays on Science and Culture*; and, most recently, *The Mirage of a Space Between Nature and Nurture*. A recipient of the MacArthur Fellowship, Keller was inducted into the American Philosophical Society in 2006 and the American Academy of Arts and Sciences in 2007, and was awarded the John Desmond Bernal Prize from the Society for Social Study of Science in 2011. She lives in Massachusetts.